JFK, Nixon, Oliver Stone and Me

JFK, Nixon, Oliver Stone and Me

An Idealist's Journey

from Capitol Hill

to Hollywood Hell

Eric Hamburg

PublicAffairs   New York

*Book design and composition by Mark McGarry, Texas Type & Book Works.
Set in Sabon.*

Library of Congress Cataloging-in-Publication data
Hamburg, Eric.
JFK, Nixon, Oliver Stone and me: an idealist's journey from Capitol Hill
to Hollywood hell / Eric Hamburg
p. cm.
Includes index.
ISBN 1-58648-029-4
1. Stone, Oliver. 2. Motion picture industry—California—Los Angeles.
I. Title.
PN1998.3.S76 H36 2002
791.43'0233'092—dc21
2002068390

FIRST EDITION
10 9 8 7 6 5 4 3 2 1

To my parents

And to Jacqueline and our son David

Contents

Introduction

First, let me say what this book is not. It is not a Hollywood gossip column run amok. It is not a dirt-dishing, tell-all tome like Julia Phillips's classic *You'll Never Eat Lunch in This Town Again*. (I'm not big on Hollywood lunches anyway, but I hope that if the dire fate indicated in her title does befall me, I can at least still go to the Coffee Bean for an iced mocha every once in a while.)

Neither is this a "revenge" book. In early summer 2002, the *New York Times* ran a front-page story about a new genre of literature, which it called "Revenge of the Underlings," about books such as *The Nanny Diaries* written by young people who had worked for famous people or institutions. Though I did work for a senator, a congressman, and a famous movie director, it is not my intent to seek revenge on any of them, and I would like to think that I was slightly more than an underling. I learned a lot from John Kerry, Lee Hamilton, and Oliver Stone, even (or especially) when the going was rough. I drafted speeches for Senator Kerry, worked on legislation and hearings for Rep. Hamilton, and coproduced two major movies and a documentary with Stone. I am grateful for all those experiences.

This book also is not a biography of Oliver Stone (nor of Presidents Kennedy or Nixon). It does attempt to explore crucial episodes of the Kennedy and Nixon presidencies through the lens of Oliver Stone's films and my various involvements with them. As Nixon would say, let me make one thing perfectly clear. I believe that Oliver Stone is a great filmmaker and that *JFK* and *Nixon* were great films that have been unjustly criticized. I will go into these thoughts at greater length later in this book.

What, then, is this book? Well, for starters, it is a Hollywood book for political junkies, and a political book for Hollywood junkies. It is about the forces that increasingly rule us: the impact of political and celebrity power, combined with the myths spawned by scandal. Yes, it's all here—the stars, the conspiracies, the idealists and the cynics, the bluster, backstabbing, and intimidation. But most of all, this book is about power—who has it, who wants it, and why being in the movie business in today's world is like making history because movies are what people remember.

The point of this story is how important movies, media, politics and power are in our messy world today. We will march through the big events—the murder of John F. Kennedy, Watergate, Vietnam, scandals involving Noriega, the CIA, and drugs, and we'll see the pols and moguls in the strange synergy that is the Hollywood-Washington axis. The main players in this drama are the investigators of the assassination of JFK, the makers of the movie *Nixon*, the brilliant and mercurial Oliver Stone, and this author, who had the fortune or misfortune of ricocheting around these worlds for a decade or so and witnessing them at first hand. I am trying to understand them by relating and explaining my experience to the reader.

I hope this book has a deeper purpose than either vengeance or idolatry. What I found on my journey into and between Washington and Hollywood is that Hollywood style and purpose, a blending of facts and fantasies, have come increasingly to influence politics, and both to influence American culture. This is not an altogether new insight, but my experience, and my dismay, is perhaps more vivid than most. We live in a world in which politics too often becomes theater, and the lines between them become too easily blurred or even erased.

One recent example is the thirtieth anniversary of Watergate in June 2002, which became a media circus. John Dean, Nixon's White House counsel and a good friend of mine, had promised to reveal the identity of the infamous "Deep Throat" on June 17, 2002, the anniversary of the Watergate break-in. Dean had told me privately that after extensive research with new Nixon documents, he was convinced that he had nailed the identity of this elusive character. However, as the time grew nearer, the person adamantly denied it, and Dean became convinced that he was not "Throat" after all. He narrowed the list down to four names but could go no further.

What ensued was a media lunch in New York complete with characters from the past, ranging from Dean to George McGovern to Lucianne Goldberg, of Monica fame, to a former star of *Gilligan's Island*. The only person who wasn't there was Deep Throat.

But I have a scoop—a worldwide exclusive! I can now reveal for the first time the real identity of Deep Throat. He is ... Hal Holbrook, who played Deep Throat in the movie *All the President's Men*. It was that movie, not the book by Woodward and Bernstein, that made Deep Throat an enduring source of fascination and mystery. The veteran journalist Dan Schorr first pointed out a very interesting fact: In the movie, Deep Throat gives Bob Woodward (a.k.a. Robert Redford) an unforgettable piece of advice. He leans over to Woodward and portentously intones these words: "Follow the money."

Follow the money. Probably the most famous line in the movie and a watchword of every subsequent investigation since then. There's just one small catch. The real Deep Throat never said, "Follow the money." It's not in the book. It was never reported in the *Washington Post*. In fact, it never happened. Those words were written by William Goldman, a great Hollywood screenwriter who wrote the movie script. But they have become more than just Watergate lore. They have become part of American history.

This is the conflation and confluence of Hollywood and Washington in its quintessential form. It is movie fiction becoming fact. And the movie wasn't even made by Oliver Stone! But many great political films were made by Stone—*Salvador, Platoon, Wall Street, Born on the Fourth Of July, JFK,* and *Nixon,* to name a few. He has gone where others dared not go, and he has not just rewritten our history—he has written history, and he has made history. For all his flaws as a human being, I believe he will be remembered in the pantheon of artists such as Dickens, Zola, Picasso, and Hemingway—not as a mere filmmaker but as a chronicler of his times and one who defined them. What more can we ask from an artist?

I would also like to say a word about a lesser character who pops up in this drama—someone I like to call Danny the Weasel. He is real, he exists, but think of him not as a person but as an archetype. He represents the end product of decades of evolution in Hollywood. He is a twenty-first-century version of the immortal Sammy Glick, with a touch of Willy Loman thrown in. Like any animal in the Hollywood jungle, his philosophy is simple— kill or be killed. These are the harsh realities of life, just as they exist on the Serengeti plains of Africa. As an agent or a producer, he behaves no differently than a wild dog hunting its prey in the wild. Although his behavior may appear vicious at times, he should be neither hated nor pitied. If anything, he deserves sympathy, for he could not be other than what he is, or behave otherwise. There are many such creatures in Hollywood, some much bigger and far more deadly. Of course, the same archetypal characters appear in Washington.

When I came to Hollywood, I was naïve, just as I was when I first started working in Washington. As a result, I made many mistakes, but I hope I learned from them. Owing to my Washington training, I was an outsider, a sightseer in Hollywood—almost a visitor from another planet. I think that many of the problems I had with people like Danny was that we came from different worlds and had totally different mentalities. We were not speaking the same language and hence were not communicating. Oliver and I had more in common, although we were also very different people. He had an intellectual side, he was interested in history, he read books, and he liked to get to the truth behind the scenes. These interests we shared.

I believe Oliver also deserves sympathy, though for different reasons that I will explore in this book. I hope that if he reads this book it will hold up a mirror he can look into and see what he has become, as well as what he could be. At times I may describe him in humorous or sarcastic terms. Let me make clear, though, that when on occasion I use words such as "paranoid" or "psychotic," I am using them in a layman's sense, often facetiously, but never in their technical, medical, clinical sense. Rather, I use them with a sense of humor. I've often been called paranoid by Oliver—but I always took it as a compliment!

In the end, this book chronicles my own passage from innocence and idealism to a harder sense of realism. If nothing else, it was a cathartic experience to revisit these experiences in the course of writing about them. But I hope that this book is about something larger than myself and my particular set of experiences. I hope it will tell us something about where we are as a society today, when politics and showbiz mix freely, and film, fact, and fiction are intermingled and intertwined.

I also hope that this book, like the film *Nixon*, might inspire a new generation of readers and students to do further reading and studying and to learn more about our past as well as our present. I hope it will shine light into some dark corners, just as Stone's films have done. And I hope it will make us think about the nature of power in this country in the twenty-first century—who should have it, how it should be used, and what kind of country we want to become.

In the Beginning

· ·

This is the strange story of how I went from working as an aide to senators and congressmen on Capitol Hill to making movies in Hollywood with Oliver Stone. Over the past few years, many people have asked me how such a bizarre shift could have happened. I'm still not sure myself. The whole experience was so surreal, I sometimes wonder if it really happened at all.

I was born in Washington, D.C., and spent the first eight years of my life living in and around Washington. From an early age, I was fascinated with American history. I memorized the presidents, and loved to visit places like the Lincoln and Jefferson Memorials with my parents. I even remember the night when President Kennedy was elected, and the day he was inaugurated, although I was only seven at the time.

My mother likes to regale captive dinner guests with the story that when I was in the first grade, my teacher was explaining to the class why President Eisenhower was leaving office. "He's tired," she said. "He's been president for eight years and he wants to rest now." I chimed in, "Yes, and the twenty-second amendment to the Constitution says that a president can only serve two terms in office." I don't really remember this incident myself, but my mother has repeated the story so many times that it must be true.

I distinctly remember my parents' elation when John F. Kennedy was elected president. I also remember how upset they were when he was killed in 1963. I recall even more clearly how upset we were when Bobby Kennedy was killed in 1968. By then we lived in California, and RFK had just won the California primary that night and was on his way to the nomination and the White House. By the next morning, he was gone.

Shortly after John Kennedy took office in 1961, our family moved to California, where my father taught at Stanford University for many years. My mother also taught there after my sister and I were older. I loved to read, and at times probably dreamed of becoming a writer. I don't think I ever had any thoughts of producing films, though, or of getting involved in the movie industry in any way. As a teenager in high school, I liked to go to screenings of foreign films at Stanford by directors like Godard, Truffaut, Pasolini and Antonioni. These captured my imagination much more than the American movies being churned out by Hollywood in those days, like *The Sound of Music* or *Mary Poppins*.

When I went off to college at UC Santa Cruz, I hung around with artists, writers, musicians and people with similar proclivities. I wanted to be creative myself, but didn't think I had the ability or a means of expression to do so. The desire stayed with me, though. At that time, I didn't know exactly what I wanted to do, and didn't even have a real major until it was time to graduate. Then, for lack of a better alternative, I went to law school. Needless to say, it was boring.

Growing up in northern California near San Francisco in the late 1960s, with the hippies, the antiwar movement and the counterculture in general, exerted a powerful influence over me and my friends. Like almost everyone I knew in those days, I listened to bands like the Grateful Dead and Jefferson Airplane, and experimented with pot and other substances. If you grew up in the Bay Area in the late sixties and early seventies, and went to high school and college in Palo Alto and Santa Cruz as I did, this was considered normal and the thing to do—at least as I saw it then. Later, I realized that drugs were not fun anymore and had become a problem. I decided to stop, to get help and get into a recovery program. This was one of the best decisions I ever made. For this reason, I felt that I could give the same advice later to Oliver Stone. After all, it takes one to know one.

After Bobby Kennedy and Martin Luther King were killed, and Richard Nixon became president, there was little hope left in politics. I was only a teenager, but I knew even then that Nixon was bad news. My grandfather had been a delegate to the 1932 Democratic convention that nominated FDR, and my parents were avid liberal Democrats. It was in my blood. I did get involved in the McGovern campaign in 1972, but that was a lost cause. However, I became even more of a political junkie during the Watergate hearings in 1973. Home from college for the summer, I watched them on TV every night with my parents, and most days as well. My hero was John Dean, the young White House counsel who turned against Nixon, coolly testifying for days before the Senate Watergate Committee with devastating effect, and ultimately bringing about Nixon's downfall. I could not have imagined then that some two decades later we would work together on a movie about these events, and become good friends as well.

When I graduated from the University of San Francisco law school in 1979, I was offered a one-year internship as an attorney at the Department of Housing and Urban Development in Washington. I went, but found the bureaucracy extremely frustrating and deadening. The political atmosphere of Washington was depressing to me, as President Carter struggled through his last year in office and the Iranian hostage crisis. I liked Carter and supported him, and found it dismaying to see how the press, the Republicans and even his own party were ganging up against him and tearing him down. When my year at HUD was over, so was Carter's presidency. I left and went back to California to practice law. I worked at a mental health law center in San Jose, representing mentally ill clients whose disability payments had been cut off by the Reagan administration.

The work helped some people who needed it, but there was no sympathy for public interest lawyers in the early years of the Reagan administration, and no money in it either. And private law firms held no appeal for me. It turned out that I shared the fate of many a law school graduate—I really didn't like practicing law. I decided to return to Washington and look for a job working for a Democratic senator.

I found that it was not easy getting a job on Capitol Hill. It helps to have some connections, but in Washington you are competing with the best and the brightest, and someone always has better connections than you do. Besides, having been unemployed in Palo Alto just a year before, and in a twelve-step treatment center a year before that, I did not feel that I was the most qualified person. On the other hand, I felt that I had nothing to lose.

I discovered what I call the "name game" rule in my job search. Each person I went to see would give me three names of people to call. I would call each and make an appointment to see them. Each of them, in turn, would give me three more names. This process would go on ad infinitum, and I still wouldn't have a job.

At one point, I thought I had a pretty good shot at a job with newly elected Senator Paul Simon of Illinois. I had several good references and connections to people who were close to him, and eventually got a meeting with him, which I thought went well. I told him I was willing to do anything, even empty the trash if necessary. When I left his office, I was pretty sure I had the job. It ended up going to a member of the Kennedy clan.

But then one of my connections came through. My father, who

had been head of the Institute of Medicine in Washington, knew Senator Ted Kennedy through his work on health issues. I was able to get a short meeting with Kennedy in his office, and told him about my desire to work in the Senate for a "Kennedy Democrat." I also told him that during my brief legal career I had represented disabled people whose benefits had been cut off by the Reagan administration.

Kennedy appeared to be very ill with a bad cold, and I suggested that he should go home and rest; I wasn't sure he had been listening. He then introduced me to his son, who happened to be visiting the office that day. Ted Jr. had lost part of a leg to cancer, and has been active as an advocate for the disabled. Kennedy told him that I had also worked for disabled people as a lawyer. Senator Kennedy also introduced me to his chief of staff, Ranny Cooper, who gave me some helpful hints on job-seeking in Washington. She said, "Whenever you meet with someone, always write them a thank you note afterwards." It turned out to be good advice. She also put in a timely call to Senator John Kerry's office.

In the Senate

In law school, I had spent two summers as a summer clerk for Chief Judge David Bazelon on the United States Court of Appeals for the District of Columbia Circuit. Judge Bazelon was a very kind man as well as a very liberal and progressive judge. He was also a family friend and a grandfatherly figure who helped many people on a personal basis, including me. Bazelon and Warren Burger were arch rivals on the court, which is second in prestige and influence only to the Supreme Court itself. Bazelon was the ultraliberal, while Burger was the ultraconservative. Judge Bazelon told me that when he heard that President Nixon had nominated Burger to be Chief Justice of the Supreme Court, "I was sick to my stomach and stayed in bed for a week." No wonder I liked him so much.

When I came back to Washington in early 1985, he offered me a job in his chambers doing research for a book on justice and criminal law while I looked for a job on Capitol Hill. This arrangement worked out very well. The book was eventually published under the title *Questioning Authority*, and I was offered a job by Senator Kerry's chief of staff, Ron Rosenblith, who had been married by Judge Bazelon. Small world . . .

I was very excited to go to work for John Kerry, who was a dynamic young senator in the mold of his Massachusetts predecessor, John F. Kennedy. They even shared the same initials. John Kerry had been a leader of Vietnam Veterans Against the War in the early 1970s, after returning from a stint in Vietnam as captain of a swift boat in the Mekong Delta. He was later awarded the Silver Star and other medals for bravery in combat. He had been a prosecutor in Massachusetts, then lieutenant governor under Governor Michael Dukakis. When Paul Tsongas retired from the Senate in 1984, Kerry was elected to replace him. He was liberal, charismatic and a compelling speaker who had the ability to move people. It was easy to imagine him as a future presidential candidate in the mold of my political idols, JFK and Bobby Kennedy.

For a brief interlude before going to work for John Kerry, I spent a summer working for the Senate Committee on Aging. This was a step in the right direction, but not what I really wanted. First of all, the Senate in 1985 was still controlled by the Republicans, and consequently the committee was as well. The chairman was a very decent and progressive man, Senator John Heinz of Pennsylvania. Sadly, he was killed a few years later in a plane crash. I was happy to have the job, but the scope of my duties was rather limited. The only real issue I was responsible for was elderly housing, an area that received little attention during the Reagan years.

I remember sitting in on my first meeting with the Aging committee, a discussion of some financial issues. I took notes furiously, but I had absolutely no clue what was being discussed, or even what my notes meant. As they say in recovery, "fake it until you make it." I found this to be useful in Washington as well. Nevertheless, just being on the Hill, in the hallowed halls of the Senate, was a valuable learning experience. And when the opportunity came to work for Kerry, I jumped at it.

There is a palpable sense of excitement about working in the Senate. You feel that you are in the middle of the action, working on important issues, maybe even making history in your own small way. Senate staffers inevitably develop a sense of self-importance that is not really justified (as do many senators). But there is a stimulation, an energy level, an excitement about the meetings, the hearings, the press conferences, the speeches, that charges you when you are in the middle of it. In general, Senate staffers are young, and not very well paid, but they are not there for the money. They are there because they care about politics, about issues, about power, about feeling like they are somehow making a difference. It's an intoxicating atmosphere. Even seeing the lights on the Capitol Dome at night gave me a thrill, a sense of being part of something important.

I also began to learn more about how Washington really works. There are two things that everyone thinks they are an

expert on—movies and politics. Everyone is a critic. When I starting working on the Hill, I realized that there are many levels of
politics, far more than you see on the surface. Later I discovered
the same thing about Hollywood. In the beginning, I was quite
naive about these things. But I learned fast.

When I went to work for John Kerry, I became a legislative
assistant and also a speechwriter. Each legislative assistant, or LA,
is given a set of issues to cover. One of the areas I was assigned
was Vietnam veterans issues. Although Kerry did not serve on the
Senate Veterans Affairs Committee, and thus had no formal role in
this area, he was a Vietnam veteran himself and as such had great
influence on these issues. His stature as a decorated veteran was an
important part of his public image and personal history. For this
reason, handling these issues was a significant assignment for me.

I have to confess that before going to work for John Kerry, I
had very little sympathy for Vietnam veterans. I had been deeply
opposed to the war, and although I did register for the draft in
1971, I applied for and received conscientious objector status as
someone who was opposed not only to the Vietnam War but to all
wars as a matter of principle. It was hard to get a "C.O." defer-
ment, which exempted you from military duty but not necessarily
from "alternative service." I was given this status only after a
heartfelt discussion with Rabbi Sidney Akselrad, who had per-
formed my bar mitzvah and knew me well. He wrote a letter to my
draft board, which granted the exemption. I was proud of this status and frankly looked down on those who had served in Vietnam.

Of course I knew that most of the people who went to Vietnam
were drafted, and did not go there voluntarily. I knew that upper-
and middle-class college students were likely to get student defer-
ments, or else to be able to persuade some sympathetic doctor to
say that they had a "knee problem" or some other excuse to get

them out of the draft. I also knew that blacks, Hispanics and poor lower-class whites were much more likely to end up in Vietnam than people like me. Nevertheless, along with many other people, I had succumbed to some of the media stereotypes of Vietnam veterans as baby killers, war criminals, drug addicts and psychopaths.

This opinion changed drastically when I started working with John Kerry and with veterans groups, particularly with Vietnam Veterans of America. VVA was a very enlightened and progressive group of veterans who were struggling to achieve recognition against the opposition of establishment veterans groups like the American Legion, Disabled American Veterans and the Veterans of Foreign Wars. These groups, which represented the older, more conservative veterans of World War II and Korea, were derided as "hat people" by VVA, for the peaked soldier's caps that they affected. Despite their supposed status as champions of veterans, groups like the American Legion and others basically hated Vietnam veterans, who they regarded as hippies, dope smokers and anti-American upstarts.

As I got to know the men and women of VVA, I gained great respect for them. These were people who had been through a lot, fighting a war that in many cases they did not believe in but were forced to join, and facing rejection by society when they returned home. In addition, they were scorned by the "iron triangle"—the Veterans Administration, the Veterans Affairs Committees in the Congress, and the "hat people" organizations that received official government recognition, support and of course money. Nevertheless, the folks of VVA endured all of this with dignity, self-respect and a sense of perspective that helped them fight on for their rights.

One of the major battles we faced was just to get official recognition of VVA from the Congress as a veterans group, so that they could also receive the same benefits the other groups already enjoyed. We engaged in a tremendous battle with the forces arrayed against us, which included the American Legion, conservative Senate Republicans, the VA and, most dismaying of all, the Democratic leadership of the Senate Veterans Affairs Committee, led by Senator Alan Cranston and his vile chief of staff, Jonathan Steinberg. Steinberg resented Vietnam Veterans of America as upstarts—a new generation not part of the established "iron triangle" of veterans groups—and cared only about protecting his Senate turf. He regarded himself as lord and master of all veterans issues. He hated VVA and they hated him in return. He was often referred to as "Senator Cranberg," since he seemed to have more power over the issues than his nominal boss, Senator Cranston. To be fair to Cranston, he was preoccupied with what he considered to be more important issues, mainly nuclear arms control.

We had to fight Steinberg not only for recognition of Vietnam veterans, but also for their legal and judicial rights. Under an archaic law dating back to the Civil War, veterans could not go to federal court with their claims for benefits, unlike other American citizens. VVA and Kerry felt strongly that this was wrong and a symbol of the second-class treatment afforded to Vietnam veterans. But it was part of the iron triangle system, and they refused to budge. We fought them hard, and ultimately reached a compromise. "Cranberg" got a bill passed to establish a "Court of Veterans Appeals," a strange animal whose only purpose was to keep veterans out of the normal courts. He then got himself appointed to a fifteen-year term as a judge on this new court. It was a small price to pay to get rid of him. We also had to fight with him for several years to get benefits for victims of Agent Orange exposure. Ultimately we won these battles, but not without much blood on the floor and many hard feelings on all sides. It took a lot of guts for John Kerry to take on powerful interests like the old-line veterans groups that controlled many votes, especially as a freshman senator.

Kerry was the only true friend that Vietnam veterans had in the Senate, and they knew it. For this reason, and in recognition of all his battles on their behalf, VVA decided in 1987 to honor Senator Kerry with an award as Legislator of the Year. As his LA for veterans issues, and as the person assigned to write his speech, I went along with John for the occasion, which was held in the large ballroom of the Washington Hilton. As it so happened, another VVA honoree that day was Oliver Stone, who was being given yet another award for his film *Platoon*. That was how I happened to meet Oliver for the first time.

I had seen *Platoon* when it came out in 1986, and found it powerful and moving. I still think it's probably the best of Oliver's films, with the possible exception of *Nixon* (but of course I'm biased). It is a gritty, realistic and personal account of what it was like to be a "grunt," a Vietnam soldier on the front lines. It was based on Oliver's own experiences in Vietnam, although he enlarged and mythologized them in the film.

I recently saw an interview on C-SPAN with the man who had been the commander of Oliver's platoon in Vietnam, and later wrote a book about the experience. He said that Oliver had gotten it all wrong, that he had totally misrepresented that platoon and what it had done there. I don't doubt his word on that, but I think he missed the point of *Platoon*. It was not meant to be a documentary about one group of soldiers in Vietnam, but rather an allegory about all soldiers and all wars. As Oliver wrote later, it was meant in the spirit of a "Homeric epic." On that level, I think it succeeded.

The film became a sensation among Vietnam veterans. It was

regarded by them as the first honest depiction of their experience in the war, told by one of their own. While Oliver was a very atypical soldier, having come from a wealthy family on the Upper East Side of New York, and having volunteered to go to Vietnam rather than being drafted, he had in fact been there in the trenches with them, and it showed. I saw the movie in Washington when it was first released, and then again in New York with my father. I remember that when we came out of the theater he commented, "Every member of Congress should see this film." I felt the same way.

I've seen *Platoon* again since then, and some scenes still stick in my mind. One of the most poignant scenes shows a group of American soldiers out in the field, having a little party behind the lines, thousands of miles from home. The young, doomed GIs are smoking dope and dancing with each other to Smokey Robinson's "Tracks of My Tears," wearing their camouflage fatigues. I found this scene to be heartbreaking. Another that will always stay with me is an aerial view of all the young, dead bodies lying on the ground after a firefight, with Samuel Barber's mournful "Adagio" playing in the background. What a sad, sad waste of life....

At the very end of the film is a scene in which Chris, the young protagonist played by Charlie Sheen, is flying out of Vietnam. He is dictating a letter to his grandmother, saying words to the effect that those who have survived this war, who have lived through this experience, have an obligation to come back and do some good for the world, to make it a better place. That's the gist of it, anyway. I'd like to think that this represents Oliver as he once was, bruised but intent on making a difference.

That was certainly what I thought I was doing at the VVA convention in the ballroom of the Washington Hilton as I accompanied Senator Kerry on his rounds. Stone is a large man, and looks more like a fullback than an intellectual. I congratulated him on *Platoon*, and said I had heard that he was making a movie about Wall Street. "That's right," he replied, noticing that I was keeping one eye on John Kerry and the activity around him at the same time.

"You look like a Senate aide straight out of Central Casting," Oliver observed. He seemed to have an astute eye for sizing up people and types. I laughed. "Well, maybe you can put me in one of your movies," I responded. He laughed and we parted company. Years later, I almost got a very small part in one of his movies, playing an aide to (who else?) Senator John Kerry in a film Oliver wanted to make about General Manuel Noriega of Panama. Unfortunately, the project fell through at the last minute and the movie never got made, at least not by Oliver. Actually, that was lucky for me too, because he ended up making *Nixon* instead. But I'll come to that later.

At the time, I didn't give much more thought to Oliver Stone. I was happy working on Capitol Hill, and it never even occurred to me that I would end up in Hollywood. I did go see *Wall Street* when it came out and enjoyed it. I thought it was well written and well acted, and liked the idea of a movie about the greed of the Reagan 1980s.

I continued working for John Kerry on veterans issues and also on other issues like judicial nominations, civil rights and the South Africa sanctions bill. This entailed the nitty-gritty work of meeting with constituents, answering letters and trying to drum up support for legislation. When I started working in the Senate, I was very excited and felt that I had finally found my niche. But by the end of 1988, I was getting burnt out and felt I had reached a plateau. The work was no longer as exciting or novel to me, and had become more of a job and a routine in some ways. I had become much more interested in foreign policy, particularly in Mikhail Gorbachev's revolution in the Soviet Union, which to me was the

most exciting thing happening in the world at that time. I wanted
to learn more about the Soviet Union, about arms control and foreign policy, and have a chance to focus on these issues, which I
couldn't do in my present position.

At the same time, Governor Michael Dukakis of Massachusetts had just lost the presidential election of 1988, disappointing
many of us who had worked on his campaign. His son, John
Dukakis, had worked on our Senate staff. Had Dukakis won the
election, John Kerry would have been in a very strong position in
the Senate and in the new administration. But Dukakis lost.

While still working in Washington for Senator Kerry, I applied
for a fellowship at the Center for International Security and Arms
Control at Stanford, and had been accepted. Now I decided to
accept it. I was excited by the changes in the world brought about
by the end of the Cold War, and wanted to learn more about foreign policy. This was the place to do it.

Since I had almost grown up on the Stanford campus, I still
considered Palo Alto and Stanford to be home, and had a lot of
friends there, although my parents had moved to New York. I
always enjoyed going back to Stanford, although sometimes with
mixed feelings, since my family no longer lived there.

I returned to Stanford in January of 1989, and stayed at the
Center until August of that year. It was a great opportunity to
educate myself about foreign policy, arms control and the issues
that interested me at that time. I attended lots of seminars at the
Center by visiting experts, and did a lot of reading and research.
Sid Drell, the director of the Center, asked me to give a seminar on
legal issues in arms control, which I did after spending a lot of
time at the Stanford law library. I also wrote a monograph on the
subject that was published by the Center. I even had an op-ed
piece published in the *New York Times* at the end of 1989, enti-

tled "Constitution vs. Arms Control." I was well on my way to becoming a foreign policy wonk.

While I was studying and learning more about these issues, I was also indulging another long-standing interest of mine in my spare time. Before leaving Washington, I had seen a documentary on television in November 1988 on the twenty-fifth anniversary of the assassination of President Kennedy. Hosted by respected columnist Jack Anderson, it presented various conspiracy theories and facts, which I found fascinating. I had long been intrigued by the assassination and regarded it as an unsolved mystery. Like most Americans, I had never accepted the Warren Commission's conclusion of a lone assassin, but did not know enough to fully understand what had really happened.

Anderson's program presented the assassination as a conspiracy carried out by a combination of the CIA, the Mafia and the Cubans. Now at Stanford, away from the daily demands of my congressional job, I began to poke around again in assassination lore, drawn by the hope that one day a mystery that ate away at Americans' trust in our own government would be solved.

JFK 101

· · · · · · · · ·

In 1983 I saw a *Nightline* program about the assassination on the twentieth anniversary of the event. Congressman Louis Stokes, who had chaired the congressional committee that investigated the case, was Ted Koppel's guest that night.

Stokes mentioned that the committee had found a probable conspiracy in the killing of the president, three of the prime suspects being Teamster leader Jimmy Hoffa and Mafia figures Carlos Marcello and Santos Trafficante. I found it incredible that these facts had not been publicized by the American media, and that nothing had been done by the government to follow up on the congressional investigation, which took place in the late seventies. Most journalists simply accepted the "lone nut" version of the Warren Report and had done so since the beginning. And the Reagan administration had done nothing to follow up on the Stokes committee's findings.

Most Americans still don't realize that there are actually *two* official government findings with regard to the JFK assassination— that of the Warren Commission, which contended that Lee Harvey Oswald acted alone, and that of the House Select Committee on Assassination, which reinvestigated the case and found that there had been a conspiracy, probably involving members of the Mafia and possibly Cuban exiles. It also found that there had been two gunmen, one firing from behind the picket fence on the grassy knoll, although it could not identify him. These two official conclusions, of course, are completely contradictory and incompatible.

While browsing in the Stanford bookstore in early 1989, I found a recently published book called *Contract on America* by David Scheim. It laid out a theory that the Mafia had murdered President Kennedy, backed up by numerous facts and citations. I took it home and read it with fascination and horror. It shocked me that this crime, the murder of the president of the United States, had been so inadequately investigated and remained unsolved. This was an intolerable and shameful state of affairs in a country that is supposed to be a democracy.

At the same time, I did not find Scheim's book to be totally convincing or persuasive. While he laid out an overwhelming case that Jack Ruby, the killer of Lee Harvey Oswald, was a Mafia operative, I was less convinced by his efforts to tie Lee Harvey Oswald to the mob. Oswald, who had served in the Marines, defected to the Soviet Union and then returned to the United States, seemed to be an unlikely mobster. The Mafia theory was an important piece of the puzzle, but not the whole story.

Then I found a second book in another Palo Alto bookstore, which had also been published in early 1989, shortly after the twenty-fifth anniversary. This was *On the Trail of the Assassins* by Jim Garrison, the former district attorney of New Orleans. Garrison had investigated the case in the late 1960s, ultimately prosecuting Clay Shaw for the crime. Still later, of course, he became the subject and hero of Oliver Stone's film *JFK*.

I found the book fascinating but again not completely convincing. Garrison's approach was the opposite of Scheim's. Whereas Scheim focused exclusively on the Mafia, Garrison totally discounted and dismissed any Mafia role in the assassination. He explored many theories, but ultimately concluded that the CIA had planned the assassination. Like Oliver Stone years later, I think that Garrison was sincere but also in some ways misguided and even a little deluded. He was undoubtedly a publicity seeker, a self-promoter, and had a tendency to often trust the wrong people, as did Stone. I do think that Garrison's investigation developed some very important leads and information, although I personally doubt that Clay Shaw had much of anything to do with the assassination.

Reading Garrison's book, I felt that, like Scheim, he had an important piece of the puzzle, but not the full story. But putting the books together made a convincing case that both the Mafia and the CIA were involved in the plot. It is known that the two groups had earlier joined forces in an effort to kill Fidel Castro. In addition, lurking in the background of both books and both scenarios were various Cuban exile groups, supported by the CIA, sometimes linked to the Mafia, always violently opposed to Castro and often equally opposed to President Kennedy as well. The exiles, as well as many CIA men, felt that Kennedy had betrayed them at the Bay of Pigs, and then sold them out for good during the Cuban missile crisis. Even worse, Kennedy had then started back-channel efforts to reach a rapprochement with Castro. They felt that the only way to get Cuba back would be to assassinate both Kennedy and Castro.

It is a well-documented historical fact that the CIA and the Mafia worked together with these exile groups to try to assassinate Fidel Castro in the early 1960s. This was thoroughly investigated by the Senate's Church Committee in the 1970s (named for its chairman, Senator Frank Church of Idaho), and is no longer a matter of dispute. It seems logical and reasonable to surmise that some of these same forces, having failed to kill Castro, turned their attention to President Kennedy. Over the years, many books have been written about this subject, and more and more facts have emerged to support this thesis.

Over the past decade or so since 1989, I have learned a lot more, but this basic belief—that Kennedy was killed by a conspiracy of extremist Cuban exiles, Mafia gangsters and rogue CIA men—has only been confirmed and strengthened. I felt then that there were too many holes in the historical record, too much information that had been suppressed, and that more facts were needed if the full truth were ever to emerge about the forces behind the murder of the president. When I returned to Washington in late 1989, I was for the first time in a position to do something about it. Working in the Congress, I could help open up the files and reveal the facts.

Why It Matters

· ·

Recently, after patiently listening to one of my conspiracy theories, a friend of mine asked a simple question: "Why do you care who killed Kennedy? What difference does it make?" I was a little shocked at first. "Why does it matter?" I thought to myself. How could she even ask such a question? I began to explain my latest theory of the case, but she stopped me. "When I listen to this stuff, it's like reading the Talmud," she said. "It's like reading one rabbi's explanation of another rabbi's interpretation of another rabbi's commentary, when I haven't read the original Torah portion to begin with."

I began to see her point. What difference does it make, anyway? And why should anyone care? The man has been dead for almost forty years. Nothing is going to bring him back. There are so many theories and countertheories out there that it makes your head spin. And as people often say, "We'll never know what happened anyway."

But I find this latter statement maddening. Why shouldn't we know what really happened? I certainly don't think that everyone has to be obsessed with the Kennedy assassination, but neither do I think we should give up on trying to find out the truth.

Why does it matter? One on level, it's pretty simple. This was a human being, a man with a wife, children, parents, brothers and sisters, people who loved him, who was brutally gunned down in broad daylight for everyone to see. I was vividly reminded of this fact when I met his sister Jean in Cuba. For this reason alone, the crime should be solved and the true story told.

John Kennedy belonged not just to his own immediate family,

but to the American people. For all his flaws, he represented hope, idealism and a better future for America and for people all over the world. He was the president of the United States. Isn't that reason enough to want to find the murderers, the men who killed not only Kennedy, but all that he represented?

In the wake of the film Oliver Stone eventually made about the assassination mystery, *JFK,* many Washington pundits blamed him for falsifying history, for misleading a generation of young people and for spreading mistrust of government and paranoia throughout the land. I don't think that's quite fair to Oliver. One of the myths spread by these same pundits is that Stone's film caused the American people to believe in conspiracy theories, instead of accepting the "official" version of the Warren Commission. But this is not the case. In fact, polls have shown for decades that a large majority of the American people, anywhere from 70 to 80 percent or more, do not believe the Warren Report, and believe that there was a conspiracy behind the killing. These figures have remained fairly constant since the 1960s. America's suspicions were probably first aroused on November 24, 1963, when Jack Ruby gunned down Lee Harvey Oswald in the Dallas police station on live national television. If there ever was a "smoking gun" in a murder plot, surely it is the gun that killed Oswald.

Kennedy's death also matters because it changed the course of history. A few years ago, after he had left office, Mikhail Gorbachev happened to visit Dallas and gave a speech there. In it, he said that if Kennedy had lived, the Cold War might have ended twenty-five years sooner than it did. He added that perhaps this was the reason why Kennedy was killed. This could be just a fantasy, but it could also be correct. We don't know.

Some writers and amateur psychologists like to claim that JFK "buffs" have a psychological need to believe in conspiracy—that the assassination of a president must in their mind be caused by forces equal to the stature of the man who was killed. Supposedly, these conspiracy theorists find it unacceptable to believe that one man, for his own deranged reasons, might have killed a president.

In my view, the opposite is true. The majority of Americans are not that confused and misguided. It's not that we couldn't believe that a lunatic could kill a president; it's that, in this particular case, that explanation doesn't fit the facts. I have my own psychology theory: The anticonspiracy buffs have a psychological problem. It is called living in a state of denial. They simply refuse, despite all the evidence to the contrary, that a conspiracy could exist in the United States of America. They believe it had to be a lone gunman, a crazed nut. Otherwise, their entire worldview would suffer a shattering blow.

One such committed "lone-nutter," confronted with the evidence for conspiracy, said, "There is such a thing as coincidences. That's why they call them coincidences." True enough. There are also such things as conspiracies, and that's why we call them conspiracies. We have no trouble believing that they exist in other countries and other parts of the world. Obviously the murder of Julius Caesar was a conspiracy by his enemies. No one would dispute that. The Bolshevik revolution began with a conspiracy, and ended up murdering millions. That is obvious to anyone. The assassination of President Sadat of Egypt was a conspiracy carried out by Islamic fundamentalists. And we have no trouble believing that the many political murders in Mexico, some committed within a few miles of our own borders, are the result of conspiracies. But some believe that it can't happen here. After all, this is America. (Perhaps, after the events of September 11, 2001, some people will begin to believe that conspiracies can happen right here in the United States of America.)

When President Johnson appointed the Warren Commission, his explicit reason was to reassure the American public that there had been no conspiracy. He was afraid that any thought to the contrary might have brought about World War III if the assassination were blamed on the communists as the plotters had intended. Perhaps this is an understandable motivation. But even LBJ said later in life that he believed there had been a conspiracy. He said, "We were running a damned Murder Incorporated in the Caribbean." He believed that this operation, the CIA–Mafia plots against Castro, had led to the assassination of JFK. This instinct was undoubtedly correct. He even demanded a secret report from the CIA on all of the plots against Castro, which was delivered to him by CIA director Richard Helms in 1967. Some thirty years later, it was released to the American public. It showed that the CIA had joined forces with the Mafia to assassinate Castro, but had bungled the operation. Even Richard Nixon wrote in his memoirs that he could not get Helms and the CIA to give him all of the files relating to these events. "The CIA protects itself, even from Presidents. . . . The CIA was closed like a safe, and we could find no one who would give us the combination to open it," Nixon wrote.

But at the time of the Warren Commission, these facts about the CIA–Mafia–Cuban exile partnership were not known except to a very select few. Allen Dulles, a commission member and former head of the CIA in the Eisenhower administration, passed out a book to his fellow commissioners purporting to prove that American assassins throughout history have always been loners (which is patently false—the assassination of President Lincoln was certainly part of a conspiracy). But Dulles failed to inform the other members of the Warren Commission that the CIA had plotted with the Mafia to kill Fidel Castro—a fact that would likely have had some relevance to the proceedings. Dulles himself had first approved these plots in writing in December 1959. This is what is known as a cover-up. And where there's a cover-up, there's usually a conspiracy behind it.

Without going into a Talmudic explanation of my own theory, let me try to put it into simple terms. Imagine three overlapping circles drawn on a piece of paper. In the middle, there is a small area where all three circles overlap. If we use a pencil, we can color it gray. The three circles represent the CIA, the Mafia and anti-Castro Cubans. Where all three overlap in the gray area, we will find the assassins of President Kennedy.

Was JFK's death the end of innocence in America? I don't think so. Surely we lost our innocence much earlier—perhaps when the first American Indians were massacred, or when the first African slaves arrived on our shores. Perhaps we lost some innocence again when Lincoln was murdered. And we lost a bit more when we dropped the atomic bombs on Hiroshima and Nagasaki.

But surely something important was lost when Kennedy was killed. Not only a great man, but a great leader—a man who created the Peace Corps and the Alliance for Progress, and who signed the nuclear test ban treaty with the Russians. A man of peace as well as pragmatism. A man who represented hope not only to a generation of Americans, but to people around the world.

Would there have been a Vietnam War if Kennedy had lived? I think not. Would LBJ, and then Richard Nixon, have become presidents of the United States? Probably not. And would the country have been torn by racial discrimination, riots, protests and cynicism toward government in the 1960s as it was after he died? I don't think so.

I was only a child when Kennedy was elected, but I remember how overjoyed my parents were that night and the next morning.

And how crushed they were that November day several years later when he was killed. We all lost something the day that John Kennedy died. Maybe not our "innocence," but a sense of hope for the future. Instead, we were forced to endure Vietnam, Watergate, Iran–Contra and a host of other scandals. We lost faith in our government, and in the institutions of our society.

That's why I can't accept it when people shrug and say, "We'll never know what really happened." Americans have a right to know, no matter how long it takes to find out the truth. And sooner or later, we will know.

I have a fantasy that hidden away somewhere, deep in the bowels of the CIA in a locked safe, lies a report laying out all the details of the assassination plot—how it was planned, how it was carried out and exactly who was involved. Or maybe the report sits in a firebox deep underground in a secure nuclear bunker in West Virginia reserved for our government's highest officials. Or maybe, just maybe, it is buried in the backyard garden of a former CIA official.

When J. Edgar Hoover died in 1972, his faithful secretary Helen Gandy went to his home and burned all of his "Personal and Confidential" files—the most top-secret stuff—before the authorities could get there. When Richard Helms was fired by President Nixon in early 1973 and sent packing as ambassador to Iran, he conducted a small bonfire of secret documents before he left. Perhaps in those documents lay the secrets of the Kennedy assassination. But I have a feeling that those documents, and that report, will turn up sometime and see the light of day. After all, as the great Russian novelist Mikhail Bulgakov wrote, "Manuscripts don't burn." Neither does the truth.

Back to Congress

· ·

While still at Stanford, I had applied for and received another fellowship in arms control and national security, this one from the American Association for the Advancement of Science. The fellowship would pay my salary for a year to work in a congressional office on arms control and related issues. I applied and was accepted for a position in the office of Representative Lee Hamilton of Indiana, who was chairman of the subcommittee on Europe and the Middle East of the House Foreign Affairs Committee.

Lee Hamilton was a highly respected member of Congress. He was born and grew up in Evansville, Indiana, which also happens to be my father's hometown, although they were a few years apart and did not know each other then. Lee is a crewcut former high school basketball star, and a solid, no-nonsense Midwesterner. The politics of his district in southern Indiana are much more conservative than those of John Kerry's Massachusetts, but in practice the men's views on most issues were very similar. While I had gotten burnt out after several years in the Senate, I found I missed the Congress when I was away from it. And besides, now I could work on a new set of issues that interested me.

Hamilton had been co-chairman of the committee in Congress that investigated the Iran–Contra scandal, and in the past had also chaired the House Intelligence Committee. These experiences had led him to become very knowledgeable about intelligence-related issues, and to be deeply skeptical of the CIA and other intelligence agencies. It was and is Lee's firm belief that there is too much secrecy surrounding the work of America's intelligence agencies, and that far too many government documents are "classified," or kept from the public, on dubious grounds of "national security." I felt the same way.

Lee asked me to look into these issues, as well as working on arms control and U.S.–Soviet issues, and see if I could come up with any ideas or recommendations for how to cut down on secrecy and improper classification of government documents. This fit perfectly with my own growing interest in the mysteries surrounding the JFK assassination, and my conviction that the secrecy had to be stripped away and the documents of the Warren Commission and other agencies declassified if we were ever going to learn the full truth. However, the political realist in me also knew that this was considered a taboo subject that no one on the Hill or elsewhere in Washington would touch with a ten-foot pole.

In the meantime, I had discovered another book on the Kennedy assassination, *Conspiracy* by Anthony Summers, a British journalist who had worked for the BBC. The book had been cited as an authoritative source in other JFK-related books, but I had not been able to find it anywhere. When I got back to Washington, I was able to order it from the Library of Congress. The book was originally written in about 1980 and followed up on the congressional investigation. Summers is a dogged and thorough investigative reporter who uncovered a lot of new evidence in the case, and also followed up on many leads that were never properly pursued by the House committee, especially in the area of intelligence.

One part of the book that I found particularly interesting at the time was his discussion of the "French connection" to the JFK assassination. This section of the book was based on research done by Steve Rivele, an author and investigator who traveled to Marseilles and other places to look into the possibility that members of the Corsican Mafia, with ties to the American Mafia, were the actual killers of JFK. Rivele had written a book on the subject, which had never been published in the United States, and he and his theories had been the focus of a British TV documentary on the case (it has since been shown many times on the History Channel under the title *The Men Who Killed Kennedy*). The theory built on the work of the Church Committee, which found that the CIA had considered using members of the Corsican Mafia as hired assassins in places like the Congo.

The French connection was an exotic and cinematic theory, with overtones of the William Friedkin film of the same title starring Gene Hackman, as well as of *The Day of the Jackal*. As I have learned more about the JFK case, I have come to be less convinced that there were any French or Corsican killers in Dallas, and more convinced that there was instead a Cuban connection to the conspiracy. But at the time, I found the French connection to be an interesting and provocative theory. The Summers book also mentioned the name of Jim Lesar, an attorney who had helped Rivele with his investigation, and who ran the Assassination Archives and Research Center in Washington, D.C. I decided to call Lesar and meet with him.

Jim Lesar is a delightful, humorous, highly intelligent lawyer who is an expert on the Freedom of Information Act as well as the JFK case. He has mastered the obscure laws that govern the release of government documents under the Act, and has doggedly pursued many lawsuits against the CIA, FBI, Justice Department and other agencies over classified documents. He also oversees the largest collection of material on the JFK case and other assassination-related material anywhere in the country, and is an invaluable resource for serious researchers.

I called Jim and arranged to meet with him and his then partner, Bud Fensterwald, for lunch at the Kramer Books cafe near

Dupont Circle in Washington. I think they were very surprised to hear from me, as no congressional staffer had probably called them or expressed an interest in the JFK case since the end of the House investigation a decade earlier. Nevertheless, though they undoubtedly expected that nothing would come of it, they graciously agreed to meet and talk with me.

At the time, in early 1990, yet another dubious JFK-related story had cropped up in the press. A Texas man named Ricky White had held a press conference claiming that his father, a former Dallas police officer named Roscoe White, was the actual killer of JFK. Though there were some intriguing aspects to Ricky's story and to Roscoe White, there were also parts of it that seemed obviously untrue and likely to be a hoax. In the end, it turned out to be mostly fiction, with some factual elements blended in.

But when I met with Lesar and Fensterwald, I found Jim to be very credible and serious, and Bud to be a bit less so. The Ricky White story was in the news and Fensterwald was keen on it. He was an older man who had worked for a senate committee in the 1950s, investigating racketeering and the Mafia. Fensterwald was a lawyer from a wealthy Southern family who personally bankrolled many of the private investigations into various leads regarding the JFK assassination. He was an inveterate conspiracy theorist, yet liked to hint that he also had ties to the CIA. Whether he did or not, I don't know. Bud Fensterwald died about a year after I met him, before the case was reopened by Oliver Stone's film. He is missed by many researchers.

I found him to be a little nutty, at least in the one meeting I had with him. Lesar seemed like a much more solid and reliable person. However, he deferred to Bud to some extent, since Bud was the more senior of the two. Both of them felt, as I did, that a crucial step was to try and get the government's classified documents on the JFK case released and made public. Both Jim and Bud felt that this was an uphill and probably hopeless task, but that if it were to be accomplished, the place to start was with the documents of the House Select Committee on Assassinations. This was where I could make a difference.

The House committee, also known as the HSCA, had conducted an incomplete investigation, but one that was still a vast improvement over the Warren Commission. However, its chairman, Rep. Louis Stokes of Ohio, and his chief counsel, Robert Blakey, had arranged for all of the committee files to be locked up for the next fifty years, until the year 2029. The Warren Commission had adopted a similar provision, locking its records for seventy-five years for reasons of "security." When Chief Justice Warren was asked by reporters if all the facts would ever be made public, he replied, "Yes, there will come a time. But it might not be in your lifetime." I was hoping that it might be in *my* lifetime.

The main point that Jim and Bud made to me was that, because the HSCA's files had been generated by a House committee, they were still under the full control of the House of Representatives, where I worked. By a simple majority vote, the House could vote to release its own files. In this case, the classified files of the HSCA amounted to more than 800 boxes of material that were locked away—interviews, transcripts, tapes, depositions, CIA and FBI files acquired by the committee and a mountain of other material. It was criminal that this material had not been made public in the first place. An attempt had been made by Congressman Stewart McKinney of Connecticut in 1983 to introduce a bill in the House that would open up these files, but it had been blocked by Stokes and Blakey.

I don't know all of their motives, but I think a large part was simply to conceal what an incomplete investigation they had done. Blakey, who really ran things, was obsessed with the Mafia and equally determined to steer clear of any hint of CIA involvement. One CIA document showed that when he visited their headquarters, he did not even bother to look at their files on Lee Harvey Oswald. Why he was protecting them I don't know. But one of the committee's most dogged investigators, Gaeton Fonzi, became so disgusted with Blakey and the CIA that he later wrote a book, *The Last Investigation,* detailing this sorry record.

Lesar and Fensterwald suggested to me that if Lee Hamilton were to introduce such a bill, it might stand a better chance of passing owing to his great stature in the Congress. I saw their logic, but I did not think the time was right either politically or personally. George Bush, a former CIA director himself, was president, and I could not envision a groundswell of public support for such a bill at that time. On a personal level, I had just joined Hamilton's staff and did not want to make this my first issue. I was in the middle of a one-year fellowship with Lee Hamilton, and was also working on other issues such as the rapidly evolving situation in the Soviet Union and Eastern Europe. I did not want to jeopardize my position by proposing a bill on a subject that no one wanted to touch. I appreciated the suggestion, but decided to wait.

A year later, though, I felt a little bolder. By this time, my one-year fellowship had turned into a permanent full-time job working for Lee Hamilton on the staff of the House Foreign Affairs Committee. I had put together a series of hearings on U.S.–Soviet relations and arms control issues featuring testimony from both American and Russian experts—the first time this had ever been done in the Congress. I felt I had proven myself to Lee Hamilton and to his staff, and that I was now in a stronger, more secure position. And though I still thought it was a long shot to pass a bill opening the JFK files, I had come up with a new idea.

It occurred to me one day, while waiting for the subway on the underground platform of the Washington Metro system, that the best way to ease into this subject was by taking one small step to get started in the right direction. Rather than asking Lee to introduce a bill to open up the files of the House committee, which I felt he would be reluctant to do, it occurred to me that I could simply suggest that he send a letter to Congressman Stokes, who had chaired the committee, asking him to introduce such a bill.

This would be a private letter from Lee Hamilton to Louis Stokes, two men who knew each other well and had served together in Congress for years. It would not be made public or released to the press, but would serve to put Stokes on notice of our interest in this issue. It would also allow Lee Hamilton to get his feet wet on the issue, and would make it easier to take further steps later. If Stokes agreed to introduce such a bill, fine (although I doubted he would). If he didn't, at least it would clear the way for Hamilton to introduce a bill later if he should decide to do so.

I thought that to propose even this much would be a risky move on my part, but I decided to do it anyway. I felt that, as small and insignificant as my position was as a congressional staffer, I was still able to do something that others couldn't, perhaps to make a difference on what I considered a crucial issue in the history of this country. I summoned my nerve in March of 1991 and wrote a two-page memo to Lee Hamilton, outlining the history of the House investigation and the current state of affairs.

I decided that it would be wiser to avoid focusing exclusively on the JFK assassination, so I broadened my request to include the files of the HSCA pertaining to the assassination of Dr. Martin Luther King. The committee had reinvestigated the King killing and, as with JFK, found a likelihood of a conspiracy. But again, nothing had been done to follow up on these findings. At the end of the memo, I wrote, "I personally find it incredible that, almost thirty years after Dallas and Memphis, we still don't know what really happened." This was unusually emotional language for a congressional memo, but I thought it might have an impact.

Surprisingly, Lee agreed immediately to my suggestions. I don't know why for sure, but I think he had probably suspected for a long time that there had been a conspiracy. In a very matter-of-fact way, he instructed me in a staff meeting to go ahead and draft a letter to Stokes as I had outlined. I was quietly elated. This was the first real expression of interest in the JFK case by a powerful member of Congress in over a decade, if not longer. We were about to set the process in motion, and start the ball rolling toward opening the files and maybe, ultimately, learning the truth. I had no idea how far things would move in the next few years. I did not know what the files contained, but there was no way to find out except by opening them up.

A Film Called *JFK*

Through Jim Lesar, who was in touch with researchers all over the country and maintained a very good grapevine, I had heard a vague rumor that Oliver Stone was planning to make a movie about the JFK assassination.

The rumor was that Stone planned to focus his film on Jim

Garrison and his investigation. While I was pleased by the idea of a movie about the JFK case, the idea of making Garrison the hero seemed dubious to me. Garrison was a quixotic figure, who had tilted against all sorts of windmills in his quest, acquiring a mixed reputation at best and ultimately losing his case in court in a dubious prosecution of Clay Shaw. Having read Garrison's book, I thought that he had some good leads and a lot of courage, but also blind spots and holes in his investigation.

I decided to write a letter to Stone and offer to help him with his research and influence him in the right direction. I had no idea how to reach him or where to address a letter, though. But I did have one mutual friend who could get to him. This was Patti Davis, the daughter of Ronald and Nancy Reagan.

I had gotten to know Patti while I was working for Senator Kerry. Patti's first novel, *Home Front,* had been co-authored by a friend of mine, Maureen Foster, who was the wife of my old friend and college buddy Bruce Foster. Patti idolized John Kerry, and had even included a (true) scene of him testifying before the Senate Foreign Relations Committee in 1971 as a Vietnam veteran against the war. When she heard through Maureen and Bruce that they had a friend who worked for John Kerry in his Senate office, she got in touch with me.

Patti and I had a series of conversations on the phone, and eventually met in person in a Washington restaurant for lunch. She was researching her second novel, *Deadfall,* whose protagonist was a senator much like John Kerry who was leading a crusade against Reagan's illegal war in Nicaragua. I found Patti to be a very intelligent, engaging woman, surprisingly down to earth and unpretentious for a president's daughter. Like me, she was a product of California in the sixties—the music, the hippies, the protest movements and all the rest. I found it easy to talk to her. I sympathized with the difficult position she was in, feeling deeply opposed to many of the policies pursued by her own father, and feeling a need to use her position to do something about it if she could.

I had tried to help her with the novel as best I could, providing details about how a Senate office works and about government in general. Patti lived in Santa Monica and avoided Washington as much as possible while her father was president. I found her to be refreshingly innocent and even somewhat naive about the ways of Washington, although she had an intuitive understanding of how politics worked from having grown up with it. Patti was a very idealistic person, and I admired her for having retained that quality.

She was friendly with Oliver Stone and particularly with his wife Elizabeth. I called Patti and asked if she would be willing to personally forward a letter and a book from me to Oliver. She graciously agreed. I wrote a letter and attached my card to it with the official Senate seal, thinking this would make him take it a little more seriously. I also included a copy of Anthony Summers's book *Conspiracy*, which I regarded as the best book on the assassination at that time; it had just been reissued in paperback and updated. In the letter, I suggested that Oliver combine Garrison's approach with other investigations of the assassination, and that he look at the Mafia theory and other theories as well. I said that I thought the film could be very important and influential, and that I admired him for having the courage to do it.

Stone wrote back to me, thanking me for the letter and the book. He said that he remembered me from our previous encounter, and added, "I hope that you and others like you in government will stand up for me when the time comes." I guess he knew even then that the film would be controversial, but I don't think he had any idea just how controversial. He would soon find out.

My next contact with Stone came just before *JFK* was released in December 1991. Controversy over the film had already erupted while it was being shot in Dallas, with George Lardner of the *Washington Post* publishing a scathingly critical article based on a leaked copy of the script. Somehow the resourceful Jim Lesar had gotten hold of a bootleg script through a client of his who had some connections in Hollywood. He passed it on to me, and also to the late Harold Weisberg, a dean of the JFK research community who lived in Maryland. Weisberg had done some solid research and writing on the case, but was also a difficult and crotchety older man who, like many researchers, believed that he alone was privy to the truth, and that everyone else was misguided or just plain wrong. He took offense at Stone's approach, and leaked the script to George Lardner.

Lardner also had an ax to grind, having been the last known person to see David Ferrie alive. Ferrie was one of Garrison's key witnesses, who died suddenly and mysteriously just as he was about to be arrested by Garrison. Ferrie's death has been attributed variously to suicide, murder and natural causes. Whatever the true cause, he was likely a key figure in the plot, and his death was a serious blow to Garrison's case, from which it never recovered. It also prompted him to arrest Clay Shaw a week later, a panicky move by Garrison that was probably a mistake.

Lardner, while vociferously denouncing Stone's film-in-progress, admitted almost as an afterthought in his article that there probably had been a conspiracy, as the HSCA had found, and that there were probably two gunmen, one firing from the grassy knoll. He also mentioned in passing that the large majority of the American people had been shown in poll after poll to believe in a conspiracy. This is probably what accounts in large part for the film's success.

I had also read in the *Post* that Frank Mankiewicz, a former aide to Robert Kennedy and George McGovern in their presidential campaigns, was representing Oliver Stone as a lobbyist on behalf of his film. I knew Mankiewicz, who was vice chairman of the Washington PR firm Hill and Knowlton, through my father, and I made an appointment to go see him. I told Frank that I had been working with Lee Hamilton on a bill to open up the JFK files, and I hoped we could work together with him and with Oliver Stone, using the film to give new momentum to this effort. Frank was delighted to hear this, and immediately passed the message on to Stone.

Shortly thereafter, I received an invitation to the Washington premiere of the film at Union Station, and to a reception and luncheon afterward. By this time, Lee Hamilton and I had been thoroughly stonewalled by Louis Stokes, who as I had expected wanted nothing to do with this issue. When Lee asked me if I had any other ideas, I said yes. . . . As a matter of fact, there was this movie coming out by Oliver Stone. We could use it to generate publicity for the issue and to get a bill introduced in Congress.

When I saw the film for the first time, I was impressed by its power and its ambition. Others who saw it were similarly impressed. At the reception afterward, I talked with members of Congress such as Representative Pat Schroeder and Senator Tim Wirth, as did Oliver Stone. Their reaction was, "What can we do to help?" It was clear that many felt that there were too many unanswered questions, and that justice had not been done. It was only later, after the media firestorm erupted, that politicians started distancing themselves from the film. Stone was attacked by everyone from Dan Rather to Anthony Lewis for daring to suggest that there had been a conspiracy, something they had denied as professional journalists for thirty years. While I personally doubted some of the film's theories about the relationship of the assassination to the war in Vietnam, I thought its basic thesis of a conspiracy against the president was correct.

I had a chance to talk with Oliver after the reception was over. He told me he had heard what I was doing from Frank Mankie-wicz, and that he would like to set up a meeting with Lee Hamil-ton and me to discuss it further. I was delighted. Stone was flying to Dallas that night for another premiere and an appearance on *Nightline,* and would be back in Washington the next day. I rushed back to the office and proposed a meeting to Lee, who immediately agreed.

When Stone arrived at Lee's office the next afternoon, it was obvious that this was not your ordinary Washington lobbyist. He was accompanied by Mankiewicz, but also by an entourage of aides and hangers-on, including his young, blonde assistant Kristina Hare, who was wearing a black English riding hat and matching outfit. I had never seen this attire before in a congres-sional office (although I had seen a lot of strange things). Kristina and the others waited outside while Lee and I met with Stone and Mankiewicz.

Lee explained to Oliver what we were trying to do, and expressed admiration for his efforts, although he had not yet seen *JFK,* and as far as I know he never did. Lee's favorite film was *Hoosiers.* Stone smiled and looked bemused. I don't think he was used to being treated with such respect by an important govern-ment official. He told Lee that Warner Brothers was putting together a "Free the Files" campaign in support of the film, and that buttons with this inscription would be handed out in the the-aters where the film was showing.

Stone had also cleverly included a crawl at the end of the film stating that the House Select Committee on Assassinations had found evidence of a conspiracy, but that its files were sealed until the year 2029. This had been included at the suggestion of Jim Lesar and his associate Kevin Walsh, a private investigator who had worked for the HSCA. Lee asked me how many boxes of material from the committee were still classified. I replied that the total was over 800. Lee exclaimed, "That's outrageous!" This statement made a strong impression on Oliver, who later compared Lee Hamilton to Abraham Lincoln.

One of the strange and interesting coincidences surrounding the film was that a key adviser to Oliver on the movie, Col. Fletcher Prouty, was also a neighbor and friend of Lee Hamilton. Lee mentioned to Oliver that he knew and liked Prouty. This again made a favorable impression on Oliver. Prouty had written a book called *The Secret Team* about his experiences working in the national security apparatus of the United States. He had worked in the Pentagon as a liaison to the CIA during the Kennedy years, and had later become a major conspiracy theorist. Prouty was the model for the "Mr. X" character in *JFK,* a mysterious figure who meets with Garrison in Washington and reveals to him the true dimensions of the conspiracy. In reality, Garrison never met with Prouty during his investigation, but it made a dramatic scene in the film.

This Hamilton–Prouty–Stone link appeared to cement their relationship, at least in Oliver's mind. As I walked out with him and his group to their limousine parked outside the Rayburn House Office Building, Oliver seemed to be on a high. I think he realized for the first time that he might actually have some support and help for his crusade from an important and respected person in Washington. He was on his way to a press briefing about the film, and asked me if he could talk about the meeting with Hamilton. "Sure," I replied. It was good publicity for our cause. "What should I say?" Stone asked somewhat nervously. He was not yet used to these kinds of events. "Well, Lee used the word 'outrageous,'" I replied. "Just quote him."

And so began our beautiful relationship. I gave Stone my card and told him I would be in touch soon to follow up.

The JFK Bill

• • • • • • • • • • • • • • •

After *JFK* was released, there was a tremendous outpouring of publicity about the film. It was on the cover of *Newsweek* and many other magazines, and was debated endlessly in the press and on television. A week or so after the film was released, there was an article about the controversy in the *New York Times* news section. It quoted Louis Stokes as saying that there was no point in releasing any more files, because there was "nothing new" in them that could be learned. This had been his stance for years. Lee Hamilton was the only member of Congress who was quoted as calling for the release of the files.

Hamilton's office was immediately deluged with mail, as were other offices on the Hill. In my eight years on Capitol Hill, I never saw such an outpouring of emotion on any issue by ordinary members of the public. Congressional offices are used to getting organized mailings on many subjects by single-issue interest groups. These usually consist of hundreds or thousands of postcards and letters, all saying exactly the same thing. They are obviously orchestrated and are immediately discounted. This was different. The letters we were getting were handwritten and obviously sincere. They came not just from Lee's district in Indiana but from all over the country. Many of them praised Lee in highly emotional terms, practically canonizing him for having the courage to say that the truth needed to be told. It was clear that for many of these people, President Kennedy's death had been a traumatic event from which they had never fully recovered. They wanted to know the truth about what happened.

Evidently Stokes got the same kind of mail, because a few days later, he suddenly reversed his position and announced that he would introduce a bill to open up the JFK files. Lee called me into his office to tell me that Stokes had called him to let him know that he would be making this announcement. I was very pleased, even though I was surprised by Stokes's flip-flop. Finally, I thought, we are going to get this bill passed. I called Oliver's office and left a message to let him know what had happened.

But it wasn't quite that simple. First there had to be a series of hearings in the various interested committees of Congress (the HSCA had long since gone out of business). The House Government Operations Committee held a hearing at which both Lee Hamilton and Oliver Stone testified. Stone's presence was a big attraction for the media. As he prepared to testify, one of the congressmen commented, "This is the first time I've seen sixteen television cameras at a hearing of this committee." That got the members' attention. There's nothing a congressman loves more than a rolling television camera.

I sat behind Lee as he testified in support of the legislation, since I was handling the issue and had drafted his testimony. After he left for another hearing, I stayed and sat behind Oliver, acting as an unofficial staffer for him. I think he found it reassuring to have someone there who knew the Hill as well as the issues. At one point, after he had finished an emotional appeal for the truth about JFK's murder, I passed him a note. "Don't forget about RFK and MLK." Stone read it and immediately added, "I hope I won't have to make another movie about Robert Kennedy and Martin Luther King in order to get another bill passed."

As it turned out, we barely got the JFK bill passed. Stokes had a trick up his sleeve. He asked his trusty former counsel Robert Blakey, now a law professor at Notre Dame, to draft the bill for him. Blakey loaded up the bill with all kinds of provisions mandating the release of not just the congressional files from his own investigation, but also files from every agency of government past and present that had any relevance, including the Warren Commission, the Rockefeller Commission, the Church Committee, the CIA, the FBI, the Justice Department, the State Department, the Defense Department and others. At first glance, this appeared to be a laudable effort to open up all of the government's hidden files pertaining to the Kennedy assassination. In fact, it was a clever effort to kill the bill altogether. There was no other explanation for their 180-degree turn.

Blakey and Stokes reasoned correctly that all of these government entities would oppose the bill, and that their combined weight would bury it in Congress. They assumed that it was unthinkable that both houses of Congress would pass such a bill and that President Bush would actually sign it. In addition, the bill was drafted in such a way that at least six committees in Congress had jurisdiction over pieces of it, and all would want to hold hearings, amend the bill and control its fate. The turf battles alone would be enough to ensure that it never became law. They also knew that few people on the Hill, either members of Congress or staff, really cared about the bill or wanted it. The only people who did were the American public.

Their diabolical strategy almost succeeded. While endless hearings were held, the bill got bottled up in committees and tossed around in endless turf battles between powerful chairmen and staffers. While senators and congressmen like David Boren of Oklahoma, Jack Brooks of Texas, John Glenn of Ohio, John Conyers of Michigan and of course Louis Stokes paid lip service to the bill, no one was prepared to compromise or make a real effort to push it through. A stalemate developed between the House and Senate, neither of which was willing to accede to the other's version of the bill.

At the last moment, just as Congress was about to go out of session for the year, Lee Hamilton managed to work out a behind-the-scenes compromise whereby the House barons agreed to back off and accept the Senate version. As journalist Jeff Morley later wrote, "In response to the renewed interest in the JFK murder, open-government advocate Rep. Lee Hamilton, an Indiana Democrat, secured unanimous passage of the JFK Assassination Records Collection Act, intended to clarify public confusion about the Dealey Plaza tragedy." For this alone, Lee Hamilton deserves the Congressional Medal of Honor, in my opinion. He is living proof of the old adage that there is no limit to what you can get done in Washington if you don't care who gets the credit for it.

The bill then went to George Bush in the White House, who had thirty days to either sign it or veto it. Bush, indecisive as always, waited until the last minute to decide. As a former CIA director, and one who had served during the crucial period of the mid-1970s when CIA assassination plots were being revealed and the HSCA being formed, Bush had no interest in reopening the issue. Bush himself had written memos as CIA director asking for more information on Jack Ruby's activities in Cuba, his contacts with Mafia boss Santos Trafficante and related matters. He had even reportedly acted as a CIA informant on the Cuban exile community in the days after the assassination. The last thing he wanted was to remind the electorate of these kinds of things.

However, having waited until the last minute, he was now only one week away from Election Day of 1992. If he vetoed the bill, Bill Clinton would make an issue of it as one more example of a government cover-up. Bush's role in the Iran–Contra scandal was already an issue, one that would ultimately help cost him the election. Bush decided to sign the bill. He added an accompanying statement basically saying that if and when the bill became law, he would do everything in his power to weaken and undermine it. Fortunately by the time that happened, Bush was no longer president.

When Bill Clinton was elected president a week later, I rejoiced as did every other Democrat in Washington. I had helped out a little with Clinton's campaign from my position on the Hill. Michael Mandelbaum, a friend of mine and an old friend of Clinton's from his days in England, had asked me to help put together a memo for Clinton to prepare him for his first meeting with Boris Yeltsin during the 1992 campaign. I did so, and got a nice thank you note from then Governor Clinton. Like many other Democrats, I had almost given up hope of seeing another Democrat in the White House in the foreseeable future. Reagan had seemed invincible, and Bush even more so after the Gulf War. But Clinton had fought back and won.

I had harbored hopes that Lee Hamilton might be Clinton's running mate. In the end, the choice came down to Hamilton and Al Gore, and Clinton chose Gore. I can't fault him on the political wisdom of his choice, but I was disappointed. I was further disappointed when Lee was not chosen as secretary of state, a position that he was superbly qualified for. I had visions of myself at the State Department, but that was not to be.

That was the end of my hopes of joining the Clinton administration. But it became the beginning of a path that would lead me back to California to make movies with Oliver Stone.

Going to Hollywood

Lee Hamilton had ascended to the position of chairman of the House Foreign Affairs Committee, but I had already decided to leave Capitol Hill. After eight years there, with only a short break, I was burning out. I wanted to try something new and different.

A wild idea had been percolating in the back of my head, and I decided to act on it. At the end of the year, I wrote a letter to Oliver Stone. I said that I had been very impressed by the impact that *JFK* had made, and that we could never have passed the "JFK bill" without his film. This was very true. I also said that I felt that I might be able to have even more impact by working with a filmmaker like him than I could have as a congressional staffer. I wrote that I would be very interested in working with him, and that I would be happy to leave Washington and relocate to Los Angeles if that were possible.

I had no idea if Stone would even see the letter, let alone respond, but I figured I had nothing to lose. Amazingly, he did write back, inviting me to come to Los Angeles and have dinner with him and discuss the idea. I didn't know if he was serious, but I decided to take him up on it. I figured that, at a minimum, I would get a good story.

Through Stone's trusty assistant Azita Zendel, who had by

now replaced trusty assistant Kristina Hare, I set up a date for
dinner with Oliver in February of 1993. I flew to L.A. and at the
appointed time appeared at his home in a quiet, unpretentious
neighborhood in Santa Monica, where he lived with his wife and
two small children. It was a Spanish-style house with a front yard
and even a white picket fence with a gate. At least that's the way I
recall it. Everything seemed very ... normal.

When I got there at eight o'clock, Oliver was not home yet.
His wife Elizabeth welcomed me, and I sat down and watched the
end of a horror movie on video with her and their son Sean. When
Oliver got home a little while later, he said, "Welcome to the
glamorous Hollywood, where we work our asses off!" In fairness
to him, he was working pretty hard at the time, editing one film
and preparing to shoot another. I had brought him some newly
released JFK documents and pictures, which he was happy to see.

We had a pleasant, leisurely dinner, discussing the JFK case at
length as well as other topics. He told me he was interested in
doing movies on Hitler, Mao, Stalin and Martin Luther King,
among others. I said that I thought it could be dangerous to do a
movie on Hitler, since any attempt to understand him psychologically might be construed as some measure of sympathy. He
laughed at this idea and repeated it to Elizabeth. Obviously controversy and danger were not unfamiliar or unwelcome to him. He
knew a lot about the JFK assassination and seemed impressed by
my knowledge of some of the minutiae of the case. At one point,
we were discussing an obscure book called *Farewell America* that
had reputedly been written by an agent of French intelligence
under the pseudonym James Hepburn. I said, "That's right—his
real name was Herve Lamarr." Oliver was clearly impressed. I felt
right then and there that I had won him over.

He did seem to have a desire to be outrageous for its own sake.

At one point, when I expressed some standard liberal sentiments about gun control, he shook his head earnestly and contradicted me. "No—I think everyone in America should have the right to own a gun," he insisted. I wasn't sure if he was serious, and decided not to pursue it. He also vehemently denounced the Democratic Party, saying that they were only interested in raising taxes and were destroying individual opportunity in this country. I later learned that this was a recurring theme and an obsession of Oliver's. At the time, though, I just shrugged it off.

All in all, it was a very friendly dinner. I realized afterward that this had been my job interview. Though I was nervous beforehand, I relaxed when we started talking and actually found it very stimulating. Oliver Stone is a very intelligent person and has a strong interest in history. At times I felt my mind racing to keep up with his ideas, and I liked the idea of being challenged in a way that I hadn't been recently in Washington. He wasn't afraid to question the conventional wisdom, and I liked that. I decided that this was someone I wanted to work with if I could.

I went away with a good feeling, but nothing definite in terms of a job had been discussed. When I got back to Washington, I waited and wondered what would happen next, and what I should do to follow up. About a month later, I got a call from someone named Steve Pines in Los Angeles. He had a heavy Brooklyn accent, and turned out to be Stone's accountant and business manager. He told me that Oliver liked me and wanted to work something out. "Great," I responded. "So do I."

This left me more hopeful, but still a bit uncertain. I like to be 100 percent sure about things, not just 90 or 95 or even 99 percent. On the other hand, I didn't want to push too hard or overplay my hand. I decided to wait a little longer. After another month or so went by, I decided to make another trip out to California to see Oliver. I set it up through Azita, and met with Oliver at his office in Santa Monica on a Saturday afternoon. "I really want this to work out," he said. That was good enough for me. He told me that he wanted me to come work there, but that I should wait until he was finished shooting *Natural Born Killers* in August. That was fine with me.

I had brought a present for Oliver—a framed letter signed by Senator John F. Kennedy in 1960, just before he was elected president. This had been given to me as a boy by a friend of my grandparents. I had the idea that people in Hollywood like to give and receive exotic gifts, and thought this might make a good impression. It had the desired effect, although I wished later that I had it back. I also brought him a cartoon of Albert Einstein that I found in the Capitol Hill newspaper. The quote from Einstein was, "Great spirits have always encountered violent opposition from mediocre minds." Oliver loved it. He immediately called Azita into his office and said, "Have this framed. I want it in my office."

Oliver also told me that he was separated from his wife, and was living in a hotel. This surprised me, as they had seemed like a happy family when I saw them together only three months earlier. I did not realize then that this was the beginning of a prolonged midlife crisis that would result in Oliver breaking and destroying almost every meaningful relationship in his life over the next few years. I knew that Hollywood people got married and divorced all the time, so I figured that this was probably normal. At any rate, it was his personal business and didn't affect me.

As I left his office, I was silently celebrating. My wild idea was now on the verge of becoming a reality. From my small cubicle on Capitol Hill I had managed to get a bill passed to open up the JFK files, and had then persuaded one of the world's most important film directors to hire me to make political movies with him. It was a dream come true. But as the saying goes, be careful what you wish for....

Journey to Ixtlan

I started work at Oliver's film company Ixtlan on August 23, 1993. I believe the name Ixtlan was taken from Carlos Castaneda's 1972 book *Journey to Ixtlan,* about a mystical Mexican Indian healer who derived spiritual insights through ingestion of peyote and mescaline. Oliver had originally wanted to call his company "Quetzalcoatl," but had to abandon that idea because no one could spell or pronounce the word. His parking space in the underground garage below his office was adorned with a red sign reading "Reserved for Quetzalcoatl," though. Quetzalcoatl was the name of a Toltec and Aztec serpent-god with colorful plumage and large outspread wings. This seemed appropriate.

His offices occupied the top floor of a pleasant if nondescript six-story building overlooking the Pacific Ocean in Santa Monica. Oliver had the corner office, which had a clear view of the Pacific but was surprisingly small. I later realized that this didn't matter because he was rarely there anyway. Most of the time, he was off in far-flung corners of the globe. And when he did come in, it was rarely earlier than four or five in the afternoon. He had a small sofa in the corner, draped with a faux American flag with a picture of Jim Morrison on it. He also had some remnants of his previous movies, as well as a collection of various Oscars, Emmys, Golden

Globes and other awards scattered about. He seemed to like American Indian artifacts. The desk sat in the corner of the office, where he would talk on the phone and give orders to his staff. His actual meetings were usually held in a larger conference room.

The company was headed by Janet Yang, a film producer in her mid-thirties who had been with Stone for several years. Janet had an MBA from Columbia University and had been involved in importing Chinese films to the United States. She had also worked with Steven Spielberg as a translator on his movie *Empire of the Sun,* which was filmed in China, before persuading Oliver to hire her to run his newly formed company.

Ixtlan was a fairly small company, with a young staff. The other key people there were Lisa Moiselle, the director of development; Naomi Despres and George Linardos, the creative executives; and Azita Zendel, Stone's personal assistant. My own role at Ixtlan was unclear to me when I got there. I was not sure what my title was or what I was supposed to do. Oliver had the idea that, because I was a lawyer by training, I could handle legal and business affairs, thus saving him money on legal fees that he paid to his outside counsel, Bob Marshall, who was a partner in a big Century City entertainment law firm.

Needless to say, this idea did not appeal to Marshall, or to Stone's business manager, Steve Pines. Both felt threatened by my presence. Nor did it appeal to me, as I hated practicing law and knew nothing about the arcane business practices of the film industry. I wanted to help Stone make political movies, and to have creative input into his projects. Dealing with lawyers and agents on business deals did not interest me. Nevertheless, I was awarded the title of Vice President for Business Affairs at Ixtlan, and charged with these responsibilities.

While I hated attending to Ixtlan's business affairs, in retrospect it was useful for me to learn something about how business was done in Hollywood. One of the first things that struck me, and appalled me, was how much of the film industry revolved around money, business, lawyers and deals. I guess I was naive to have expected otherwise. I had never worked for a private company, other than a short stint in a law firm that I also hated. And I had spent the last eight years on Capitol Hill, where salaries are low and people are motivated by factors other than money. I had hoped that Hollywood would be a more creative, artistic environment. But it was all about money.

This was accentuated by Stone's own obsession with money. Again, I had naively thought that as an artist and as a committed social activist, he would be above such petty concerns. In fact, money came first, second and third with Oliver. I remember being with him at Skywalker Studios in Santa Monica shortly after I started working at Ixtlan. He was "looping" dialogue for *Natural Born Killers* with Juliette Lewis, who appeared to be pretty looped herself. In between takes, he was talking on the phone with Jeffrey Katzenberg, then a high honcho at Disney (he later left in a dispute over, what else, money).

Oliver was discussing with Katzenberg how much money he would have to give Yale University in exchange for an honorary degree, and what kind of degree he should hold out for. I jokingly said afterward that I thought he should get at least an honorary doctorate in fine arts, not just a bachelor's degree or a master's, if he was going to give them big bucks. Oliver had briefly attended Yale in his youth, but had dropped out to go to Vietnam. He eventually graduated from the New York University film school.

Oliver was vociferously complaining to Katzenberg, who was also known for his cheapness, about how Clinton was going to raise his taxes. "Next time I'm going to vote for Dole," he said. This was a theme I heard repeated many times, even after Dole denounced him for the violence in *Natural Born Killers,* and even after Clinton had welcomed him into the White House during his research for *Nixon.* Oliver continued to support Dole, and seemed to hate Clinton. On Election Day of 1996, Oliver called me from the set of *U-Turn* in Arizona to complain about Clinton's victory. In the beginning, though, I was naive and did not realize that he really took money so seriously. After all, he already had plenty of it.

Several things became clear very quickly after I arrived at Ixt-lan. One was that everyone is very insecure in Hollywood. Every-one around Stone, with the exception of Azita, seemed to feel threatened by me, even though I regarded myself as a mild-man-nered person who had no designs on anyone's job and no agenda other than to make meaningful films. Bob Marshall felt threatened that I wanted to take away his legal business. Janet Yang felt threatened by me as an intruder and interloper from Washington. Others felt the same way. This was probably not surprising, since Oliver had not told Janet and the others why I was coming or what I would be doing there. Azita had joked to the staff that Oliver might be thinking of running for president.

I decided that the best way for me to deal with this was to be myself—not to "go Hollywood" or compete with the others on their terms. I felt I could bring a unique set of skills that would add something without intruding on others' territory. To accentu-ate my un-Hollywood image, I decided to keep wearing the same drab, loose-fitting, comfortable clothes that I had always worn, so as not to look like a Hollywood agent or dealmaker. I was never much of a fashionable dresser anyway. My one concession to Hol-lywood was to stop wearing ties. I had always hated ties, and kept mine loosened most of the time on Capitol Hill. Now I could ditch them altogether. This made me feel better, but did not seem to make anyone else there feel more secure.

I think part of the reason why people are so insecure in Hollywood is that many people in high positions who are making a lot of money realize that they really don't have any particular qualifications for their jobs. Hollywood executives live in a revolving door world where they can be hired and fired on a regular basis, and usually are. Unlike Washington, there is no formal structure of power or seniority system in Hollywood. Anyone can rise to the top if they are aggressive and unscrupulous enough, and often do. But they can also be knocked off their perch by enemies they have made along the way. This breeds a constant sense of insecurity and paranoia among these people.

But I was surprised that Stone, who was known as Hollywood's leading political filmmaker, had no one around him with any kind of political background or even any knowledge of politics to speak of. Most of the people working for him seemed to have ended up there almost at random, just through wanting to be associated with a powerful film director who could advance their careers. For example, Stone's main producer on his films was Clayton Townsend, who had started working with Stone as a grip on his films at about age eighteen. He had worked his way up the ladder out of sheer loyalty to Stone, with no specialized training or other credentials in film.

"Loyalty" was the highest qualification to Oliver. In practice, though, this was a one-way street, with Oliver showing no loyalty in return, even to those who had been with him for many years. By the time I finished working with Stone, everyone significant who had been there when I started was gone—Bob Marshall, his lawyer of almost twenty years; Janet Yang, who had helped him start Ixtlan; Clayton Townsend, his longtime producer; and all of the staff at Ixtlan, including myself. Also on this sorry list were his wife Elizabeth, with whom he had two children, and his former business partners Alex Ho, Arnon Milchan, Andy Vajna and others. (Marshall would later be brought back, apparently in order to write a threatening letter to my publisher.)

When I started work at Ixtlan, I quickly became aware of tensions between members of Oliver's staff. Stone liked to foster friction and competition among people working for him. He was also very secretive, liking to compartmentalize information as if Ixtlan were a West Coast CIA, and operating on a "need to know" basis. In fact it was less than "need to know," since there were many things I needed to know as VP for Business Affairs that I simply was not privy to. Stone never fully trusted anyone, and always felt that if members of his staff were getting along too well, they were probably plotting against him.

After my first week there, I asked to meet with Oliver on a Saturday at Skywalker, a film facility where he was editing *Natural Born Killers* (which he called *NBK* for short). During a break, I sat with him in the lobby and outlined my concerns. He stared at me as I was talking, then gripped my arm dramatically and put his finger to his lips. "SHHH . . . People can hear you." I lowered my voice. I told him that Azita had given me a diatribe against Janet, and that I was concerned that I did not really know what was going on in the company.

Stone nodded knowingly. "Azita is a fucking paranoid Iranian," he pronounced. "She sees conspiracies everywhere. And Janet is a devious Chinese cunt. . . . Don't worry about it." With these reassuring words, I was left to fend for myself. My own policy, as it had been on Capitol Hill, was to try to get along with everybody. I try to find a niche that is not being occupied, so that I can have my own piece of turf without upsetting anybody else. I hate conflict, and try to work with people whenever I can on a friendly and cooperative basis. And I tend to trust people and be open in communicating with them.

These were precisely the wrong traits for succeeding in Hollywood.

By a strange coincidence, my first day of work at Ixtlan was also the first day that new documents were released by the government under the JFK bill. It was also the day that the book *Case Closed* by Gerald Posner was published. *Case Closed* was a tendentious and slanted effort to prove that there was no conspiracy in JFK's death, and that Oswald had acted alone. It was an updated version of the Warren Report, published with great fanfare and receiving lots of publicity in the media. For some reason, Random House had chosen to promote this book heavily, and the media picked up on it.

One of my first tasks for Oliver was to draft a statement for him welcoming the release of the new documents, and also a memo analyzing the flaws in Posner's book, in case he was asked about it by the media. This was the kind of work I was used to doing in Washington, and it was enjoyable.

This is not the place to detail all of the faults and mistakes in the Posner book. There is an entire book by Harold Weisberg, entitled *Case Open,* that was written specifically to point out all the things that Posner got wrong or distorted. To me, it was most revealing that he chose to publish the book and pronounce the case "closed" at the very moment that it was being reopened by the release of new documents and new evidence.

I don't have a problem with someone believing that Oswald acted alone, if they have looked into it and sincerely come to that conclusion. But Posner, like the Warren Commission before him, was not sincerely interested in seeking the truth wherever it might lead him. He was interested only in constructing a case for the prosecution—in slanting and construing every piece of evidence in favor of Oswald's guilt no matter how questionable, and in smearing and discrediting every JFK researcher and every piece of evidence pointing to conspiracy. If I were a conspiracy theorist, which I'm not, it would almost appear that Posner's book was timed precisely to divert attention from the new assassination files being opened. But I believe in facts, not theories.

Development Hell

One day soon after I started work at Ixtlan, Janet Yang took the entire staff to lunch at L.A. Farm, a trendy Hollywood restaurant, to go over a list of Oliver's projects that were "in development." This is a term of art in Hollywood, which basically means film projects that are listed on a sheet of paper but that probably will never get made. I didn't quite realize that then, although I got the idea pretty quickly. This state of affairs is known in the trade as "development hell."

Ixtlan's development list included a mixed bag of about twenty or twenty-five different projects, some of which had writers and scripts, some of which had actors and directors "attached" and some of which were just vague ideas. This, I learned, is typical in Hollywood. Out of twenty-five projects, you're lucky if one of them actually gets made. Just getting a film produced and on the screen is considered a great achievement in Hollywood. Whether it's any good or not doesn't really matter.

Ixtlan's list included some of Stone's pet projects like "In the Spirit of Crazy Horse," based on the Peter Mathiessen book about American Indian leader Leonard Peltier. Peltier had allegedly been framed by the FBI for a murder committed on an Indian reservation in the course of an uprising by the American Indian Movement in the early 1970s. The book had been controversial and had even been banned for a time because of legal action. The FBI later mounted a ferocious assault to prevent Peltier from receiving a pardon from President Clinton before he left office, and succeeded.

Oliver had an obsession with American Indians, and had wanted to make this film for a while, but could never get a script that he liked. He was also engaged in a battle with Robert Redford, who wanted to film Peltier's story himself. In the end, the film never got made, and Peltier remains in prison.

At the same time, Oliver also planned to make a film about George Washington, starring Redford as the late great president. The project was being developed jointly between Ixtlan and Redford's company Wildwood. David Franzoni, who later co-wrote *Amistad* and *Gladiator,* had written a very good script that made the characters of the American Revolution come to life. But Redford wanted to turn old George into a romantic hero, which was not exactly the point of the film. This movie too was never made.

It did create one funny incident, though. At one point during its development, Oliver swept through the office, stuck his head in Janet's office and commanded, "Come with me." Janet dutifully jumped up and followed Oliver, who was already on his way down the hall. The next thing she knew, she found herself following Oliver into the men's room. Oliver, never one to waste time, liked to talk to people while peeing, but this was a first for Janet. She blushed and felt ill at ease. Oliver unzipped and started to relieve himself.

"So how do you like watching?" he demanded.

Janet was flustered and at a loss for words. "Uh ... It's OK, I guess."

Oliver flashed her a dirty look. "What do you mean, OK? You don't like it?"

Janet was completely flummoxed and stammered, "Well, Oliver ... I mean ...," Oliver zipped up and zoomed out the door with Janet in his wake.

"So you don't like it. Maybe we should just forget the whole thing."

Janet had a sudden revelation. Oliver had said, "How do you like Washington?" — meaning how do you like the script — not what she thought he had said.

"No, I mean, I like it," she recovered. "I think it's really good. ... It just needs some more work." She exhaled and wiped the sweat from her forehead. With Oliver, anything was possible.

The development roster also included a couple of scripts by Oliver's buddy Richard Rutowski and Rutowski's partner Richard Wechsler. Rutowski has been described at length by Jane Hamsher, producer of *Natural Born Killers,* in her book *Killer Instinct.* Jane called him "Pimpowski" for his reputation for being Oliver's main supplier of women, tequila and other substances. She said he knew "where to find the best pot in America." The two Richards had written a script set in Brazil called "Surrender," full of voodoo and mysticism, and also a script about the Neville Brothers band. Neither one ever got made.

Another of Oliver's pet projects was called "Cancer Conspiracy." This was to be a film about the conspiracy by the FDA and the big drug companies to prevent cancer cures from reaching the

American public (!). Several drafts of a script were commissioned, and at one point Janet Yang, George Linardos and I actually met with Mike DeLuca, then head of production at New Line Cinema, to discuss the project. It was never made either. In fact, I don't think that any of the projects on that list were made, although a lot of money was spent on some of them.

Every Friday afternoon, Ixtlan would have a "development meeting" for the staff (Oliver never attended these meetings). Janet presided over them, and they were enjoyable in a strange way. In Washington, I was accustomed to weekly staff meetings in Lee Hamilton's office, with Lee Hamilton and his staff, starting promptly at nine A.M. They were very businesslike and each person would go over their action items for the week and update Lee on the legislative state of play on their issues. Lee had usually been in the office since six A.M., reading the newspapers and other briefing papers, and bringing himself up to speed politically. He was very methodical and thorough and was probably the best informed and most well respected member of Congress.

Ixtlan staff meetings were as unlike this as you could get. We would all gather in the conference room overlooking the ocean at about noon or so. The first part of the meeting was generally taken up with a lengthy discussion of which restaurant to order from for lunch, and what each person was having. This might take up half an hour or so. In due time, the lunch would be delivered and we would eat it while the meeting went on. Generally, we would go over a printed list of Ixtlan projects, which indicated their status and whether any "elements" (that is, writer, director, actor, etc.) were attached to the project. Very often none were. We would then go around the room and each person would give an update on their projects and activities. Usually there was very little movement even on the projects that had elements attached. We were often waiting for the writer on a given project to come in with his next draft, which could take from a month to forever.

This would be interspersed with discussion of any new Hollywood gossip, projects at other companies and even discussion of events in the news. The discussion was loose and freewheeling, which I enjoyed. It also gave me a chance to find out what was going on with each project (at least in theory), so that I could handle any business affairs that needed to be handled (that is, call so and so's agent and make him an offer). The only maddening thing about this process was that the discussion would be interrupted about every two minutes while Janet took another call. Evidently she had never learned the phrase "Hold my calls."

We would all sit around patiently while Janet chatted with her chums in Hollywood, or her real estate broker, or whoever it might be. This at least had the value of giving me some insight into what Janet was up to and what preoccupied her time and her thoughts. However, it was not conducive to holding a meeting or getting any work done. Janet's mantra was "Relationships are everything in Hollywood." I guess she thought that by not taking someone's call she might offend them or harm a relationship. On the other hand, she had a reputation of consistently being at least half an hour late for any meeting, which tended to alienate people and was not conducive to good relationships. Nevertheless, I enjoyed the development meetings, which could easily go on all afternoon. If this was hell, it was a benign form of hell.

Another strange feature of Oliver's operation was that alongside Ixtlan, there existed a parallel film company with its own set of projects in development. This was JD Productions, run by Jane Hamsher and her partner, Don Murphy. Don and Jane were upstart young film school graduates from the University of Southern California who had discovered an unknown writer named

Quentin Tarantino, obtained the rights to one of his scripts called "Natural Born Killers," and talked Oliver Stone into directing the movie and hiring them as the producers. This story is set out in detail in Jane's excellent book.

Don and Jane were likable characters, although sometimes brash and arrogant. Probably anyone who makes it very quickly in Hollywood lets success go to their head to some degree, and Don and Jane were no exception. While Jane was more withdrawn and hard to get to know, Don went out of his way to be friendly to me. He was often like a bull in a china shop from whom you could not escape. I realized quickly that he saw me as a valuable source of information and a potential ally, but I still appreciated his friendliness and warmth (most of the time) despite his agenda. He was too open and direct to be as devious as most Hollywood types. However, he detested Janet Yang, whom he regarded as a threat (the feeling was mutual). When I told Don that Oliver had described Janet as a "devious Chinese cunt," he started calling her "the DCC" from then on. This was Don's private nickname for her, like "Danny the Weasel" would become my private nickname to describe another producer.

To most people, it might seem strange for one film director to have two film companies operating side by side under the same roof. To Oliver Stone, though, it made perfect sense as an outgrowth of his divide and rule strategy. By fostering constant tension and conflict among his subordinates, he could maintain control over all of them. Azita shared a telling insight when she told me early on that "Oliver is a control freak." This was the essence of his character. He needed to be in control of everyone and everything around him, even though he often was not in control of himself.

Because I liked Don, and felt mistrusted and somewhat unwelcome among the Ixtlan staff, I took to confiding in him at times and sharing information about what Ixtlan was doing. He would likewise share information with me about what he and Jane were up to, some of which I would then pass on to people at Ixtlan. It made no sense to me that all of these film projects should be shrouded in secrecy, the only purpose of which seemed to be to generate more paranoia and mistrust. I thought that by creating greater openness, I could help foster a healthier atmosphere and decrease tensions.

However, I soon realized that I did not know a lot of what was going on in Oliver's little world. His own projects, those that he took a personal interest in and was considering as possible projects to direct, were shrouded in even greater mystery, worthy of the CIA or perhaps the National Security Agency. I discovered that in addition to the "official" list of Ixtlan projects in development, which was itself secret, there was an even more top secret list of Oliver's personal directing projects. I should explain that he would involve himself as a "producer" on certain projects, like *The Joy Luck Club* and others, that he himself did not direct. Usually his involvement in these kinds of projects was limited, basically making a few phone calls and allowing his name to be used. He did not take much interest in any projects except those that he planned to direct himself. Nevertheless, films like *The Joy Luck Club* might not have been made without his support as a producer.

The top secret list of Oliver's own projects as of late 1993 when I learned of it included four possible films: "Hoover," a biopic about the late FBI director; "A Bright Shining Lie," based on the Vietnam book by Neil Sheehan; "The Prostitute," a French-language script by Jean-Claude Carrière; and "Noriega," a script about the Panamanian dictator. None of these ever got made by Oliver. "Hoover," based on the book by Curt Gentry, was shelved after neither Oliver nor Francis Ford Coppola, who was also involved, decided to direct it. "Bright Shining Lie" was dropped after Oliver's third Vietnam movie, *Heaven and Earth,* was a flop at the box office. It was later made by HBO without Oliver's involvement. The prostitute movie drifted away after Oliver flirted with it briefly. Later there were other top secret projects, like "Project Y," which was based on a book about secret codes hidden in the Bible. Never got made. . . .

"Noriega" came the closest. It even went into preproduction and rehearsals, with Al Pacino set to star as the pockmarked Panamanian. But Stone and Pacino both decided that the script, with a sort of "black comedy" tone to it, really didn't work after they did read-throughs with the other actors. Stone dropped the project, which later got picked up and made by the Showtime cable network, with Bob Hoskins as Noriega. The main beneficiary of the Noriega period was Clayton Townsend, who divorced his wife and took up with the dictator's daughter Sandra. He later moved to Miami to live with her. Oliver, who actually hit it off with Manuel Noriega, kept a picture of himself and Noriega in a place of honor in his office. It was taken in the Miami jail. Next to it was a picture of Stone and Bill Clinton in the White House.

Pacino also benefited from the project. By the time it got to the preproduction stage, the "pay or play" clause of his contract had taken effect, meaning that he had to be paid $10 million as his fee regardless of whether the film was made or not. Oddly enough, he dressed in an old army jacket and looked like a homeless bum when he came to our office. Once the attendant in the parking garage, not recognizing Pacino, took pity on him and offered him a quarter.

Canceling the project put Oliver and the studio in a serious dilemma. Ultimately Pacino generously agreed to waive the $10 million in exchange for a promise to do another picture with Oliver later. This turned out to be *Any Given Sunday*—which probably did much better than "Noriega" would have.

The Joy Luck Club was released in late 1993. This had been Janet Yang's pet project. She had read part of the original manuscript of the book by Amy Tan before it was published, and had fallen in love with the book. Structured as a series of intertwined stories about generations of Chinese-American mothers and daughters, it was not exactly prime commercial fare by Hollywood standards, but it was something Janet could relate to on a personal level. Through her passion for the material, she managed to persuade Oliver to get involved, and then got one of the top screenwriters in Hollywood, Ron Bass, to write the script with Amy Tan. The film was directed by Wayne Wang and distributed by Hollywood Pictures, a division of the Disney empire. It did reasonably well at the box office, receiving generally good reviews.

My mother happened to be visiting at the time of the film's release, so we went to the premiere together with Janet. We drove to Janet's house in Brentwood, where we were picked up by a long black limousine. This was my first experience with the glamorous world of Hollywood premieres, and certainly made an impression on my mother.

After the screening of the film (at which they handed out boxes of Kleenex to the audience), there was a reception at the Armand Hammer Museum in Westwood. While relatively modest by Hollywood standards, it was still a lavish catered affair held under the stars in the museum's impressive courtyard. I introduced Oliver to my mother at the reception. He peered at her, then pronounced, "You look Chinese." This was a strange statement, as my mother is many things but is definitely not Chinese. I let it pass as just one more of Oliver's oddities. I was getting used to them.

Becoming a Hollywood Producer

I soon realized that the best way to get out of handling business affairs and into the creative side that interested me was to come up with some ideas for new film projects. When I first came to Hollywood, I didn't know exactly what a "producer" did (and still don't in a lot of cases), but I sensed that this was the direction to go in. Janet Yang was a producer. Don Murphy and Jane Hamsher were producers. Producers, at least the creative ones, came up with ideas, found writers to turn them into scripts, got directors and actors interested, and made movies. I had come to Hollywood to make political films, not business deals.

Since I knew no one in Hollywood and had no connections there, it was difficult to see where the material would come from. Normally, a producer uses his or her network of contacts in the Hollywood community to bring in new scripts, treatments, books or other fodder for movie projects. These would normally come from agents at the big agencies like CAA, ICM, William Morris and UTA, or smaller, more specialized agencies like Gersh, Endeavour, Paradigm and others. I knew nobody at any of these places.

I did know people in Washington, though, a lot of whom were very creative and fascinated with Hollywood and the movies. It has always been amazing to me that these two parallel worlds, Washington and Hollywood, hold such interest and mystique for each other. People in Hollywood are fascinated by the aura of power and importance that surrounds senators and presidents, while people in Washington seem to be entranced by the glamour and celebrity of Hollywood stars. Ever since President Kennedy was in office, there has been a commingling of Washington power and Hollywood celebrity that has only increased over time.

Kennedy mixed socially with Marilyn Monroe and Frank Sinatra. Ronald Reagan encompassed both worlds, as actor and president. And Bill Clinton loved nothing more than to host Barbra Streisand or Steven Spielberg at the White House. I also knew from my experience on Capitol Hill that the best way to call attention to an issue was to get a movie star to testify at a hearing.

Even before I left Washington, I had noticed this strange mutual attraction. I found that friends who I thought might be horrified by my decision to leave the respectable world of Capitol Hill to work with a odd character like Oliver Stone instead not only approved, but found it exciting and even thrilling. While I had always enjoyed political novels and films, I had never had a particular fascination for Hollywood stars and glamour, and had regarded it as frivolous and unserious. But I discovered that many otherwise sober Washington types dreamed of being involved in the movies in one way or another. Many had ideas for political films, some of which they had successfully sold to various Hollywood production companies. To my surprise, almost no one said to me, "Why are you doing this? You're out of your mind!" Although I sometimes thought that to myself.

Before I even left Lee Hamilton's office, I had gotten hold of a script about the Cuban missile crisis from my friend Bruce Allyn at Harvard. I had been with Bruce and his Harvard colleagues on trips to Moscow while I was working in the Senate and the House. Bruce worked with Graham Allison, then dean of the Kennedy School at Harvard, on arms control and U.S.–Soviet relations. He was a fluent Russian speaker who had lived in Moscow and knew his way around there. He had been involved in a series of conferences on the missile crisis in the United States, Moscow and Havana, bringing together American, Russian and Cuban participants in these events for the first time.

Several books had been published based on the new information that emerged out of these meetings. The Cuban missile crisis of 1962 was probably the single most dramatic event of the Cold War period, and much information about it had been shrouded in mystery for almost thirty years. The end of the Cold War offered an opportunity to bring together the opposing sides to see what lessons could be learned, and how future nuclear confrontations could be avoided. It also brought new revelations about how close we had actually come to nuclear war during those tense days in October of 1962.

At the final meeting in the series, held in Havana in January of 1992, Fidel Castro hosted the conference and took part in the entire four-day meeting. Bruce was there along with his Harvard colleagues. Also present was a veteran screenwriter, Ernest Kinoy. The idea was that Kinoy would write a script for a TV miniseries dramatizing the crisis from all three points of view—American, Soviet and Cuban. This had never been done before. A well-regarded TV movie had been made in the 1970s called *The Missiles of October,* but it was based on only partial information, and told only from the U.S. point of view.

The script that Kinoy wrote based on the Havana meeting was exciting and much more informative and balanced than the previous effort. NBC had paid for it and committed to broadcast the miniseries on the thirtieth anniversary of the crisis, in October 1992. However, there was a shake-up at NBC, and the person shepherding the project was ousted. The script was then put into "turnaround," meaning that NBC decided to get rid of it and to sell it to anyone who would pick up the expenses they had already incurred.

This had not happened by early 1993, when I got the script from Bruce. But I didn't know anything about the business side of Hollywood then. What I knew was that it was a great story, and would make a compelling film. It was also the only script I had in my possession, aside from the bootleg copy of *JFK*. I sent the script to Oliver Stone, who read it and liked it. When I got to Ixtlan, this became my first project.

Unfortunately, it proved difficult to persuade the right people that this was as great a project as I thought it was. Even with Oliver's name attached, it was a hard sell at the TV and cable networks. I met with some of the top people at a major cable network in Los Angeles, and their reaction was, "This is too political for us. The Cold War is over. And besides, it's already been done, hasn't it?" I got similar reactions from the other major TV networks. Nobody wanted to touch it.

Since the script was written as a four-hour miniseries, it had made sense to try television first. After I struck out there, I tried a few movie companies, but the reaction was more or less the same. Very few executives in Hollywood shared my taste for political films. The project never got off the ground. Later Kevin Costner starred in *13 Days*, a film about the missile crisis based on the memoirs of Kenny O'Donnell, an aide to JFK in the White House, with Costner starring as O'Donnell. It was an interesting and well-made film, but showed only the White House point of view. Ours would have been a more complex and multidimensional view of the crisis.

My next foray into political filmmaking also died an ignominious death. Before I left Washington, I had gone to see my old friend Jonathan Winer on Senator Kerry's staff. Jonathan is a wiry, intense intellectual with a great sense of humor, who had worked for John Kerry from the time he was lieutenant governor. He liked to croon Bob Dylan songs at the office in the style of Frank Sinatra. (He was until recently a high official in the Clinton State Department.) Jonathan was one of Kerry's closest political advisers, and had been a key player in one of Kerry's most dramatic political adventures: his investigation of the CIA–Contra–drug connection in Nicaragua, and his subsequent investigations into Manuel Noriega, the Colombian drug cartels and the Bank of Credit and Commerce International (BCCI) scandals.

Like a Zelig or a Forrest Gump, I seem to have the knack of happening into dramatic and even historic situations. This was one such example. Jonathan, together with Kerry staffers Ron Rosenblith and Dick McCall, had launched the Contra–drug investigation in early 1986, shortly after I arrived on Kerry's staff. Since I shared an office with Jonathan and Dick, it was hard not to know what was going on. We had a constant parade of dubious characters through our office, including mercenaries, gunrunners and what appeared to be Colombian drug dealers or at least their associates. It made for colorful and interesting days at the office. I used to half-jokingly say to Jonathan, "You're going to get us all killed." His response was to croon Bob Dylan, "Knock, knock, knockin' on heaven's door...." Very reassuring.

Jonathan had started to write a book about these experiences, entitled *The Inside Dope*. It occurred to me that this might make good movie material, and I had asked him for a copy of the manuscript, which I took with me to Hollywood. I passed it on to Oliver, who took it with him on a trip to Nepal and points east. One evening as I was about to leave the Ixtlan office, I got a call from Oliver in Nepal. "I like this Oliver North thing. How much is it?"

I was a little confused by this, and didn't know what he was talking about at first. "Oliver North? How much? Ah, I don't know...." Oliver was annoyed by my obtuseness. "The John Kerry thing ... Oliver North ... the drug connection ... How much for a treatment?" A light went on in my head. He meant Jonathan's book. To Oliver, the first question was always the money. How much would it cost? And who could he get to pay for it? I had not given this any thought.

"Uh . . . I don't know. But I'm sure it would be cheap. I'll ask him." Oliver grunted in response. "I want it cheap. Not more than five thousand. . . . Get back to me." He hung up the phone.

I called Jonathan in Washington to tell him the good news. Unfortunately, he was already asleep, having two small children at home. When I woke him up, he was too groggy to fully comprehend what I was saying. "Call me back in the morning and we'll talk."

The next morning, I received a fax from Jonathan when I came in to the office. "I had a strange dream last night, in which you called me and said that Oliver Stone had called you from Nepal about my book. . . ." I called him back and assured him it was true. He said he would be happy to write a treatment based on the book for $5000, as long as it could be done within government ethics guidelines for outside income. We worked out an agreement and he went to work.

Jonathan, who works fast, quickly wrote up a treatment of fifteen pages or so, providing a fictionalized account of the investigation. I gave it to Oliver, who didn't like it. "Why are you paying this guy so much money?" I tried to explain that we were only paying $5000, a pittance by Hollywood standards, and that Oliver himself had suggested the figure. He wasn't buying it. "I don't want to pay for this . . . I don't like it." He did not grasp the concept that once you had entered into a contract with someone and they delivered, you had to pay them.

"Well . . . I'll ask him to do another draft," I stammered. Oliver reluctantly and churlishly agreed to this. Jonathan wrote another draft, but it still didn't satisfy Oliver. In a last-ditch effort to salvage the project, as well as the near dead missile crisis project, I arranged to accompany Oliver on a trip to New York, and to have both Bruce Allyn and Jonathan Winer meet with him at a hotel. Unfortunately, the meetings were set for ten in the morning, and Oliver had been up till three or four the night before, drinking and partying. When they arrived, he was hung over, tired and in no mood to talk to anyone. The meetings did not go well. That was the end of "The Inside Dope."

Steve, Chris and the Beast

My next idea for a movie project proved to be a little more fruitful, though I did not anticipate it at the time. Since coming to Los Angeles, I had wanted to meet Steve Rivele, the intrepid JFK investigator and author of the book that had posited a "French connection" to the Kennedy assassination. I had obtained a copy of the unpublished manuscript in Washington from Mark Allen, a government lawyer who was a close friend and associate of both Rivele and Jim Lesar, head of the Assassination Archives.

My appreciation of Rivele's work was amplified when I saw him featured in the TV documentary series *The Men Who Killed Kennedy*. This series, originally made for British TV, was shown in the United States on the A&E cable network in the fall of 1991, shortly before the *JFK* film was released. Rivele was interviewed about his trips to Marseilles and his efforts to track down the alleged Corsican killers of the president.

It had been reported that threats were made against Rivele's life after the series was broadcast in England, and that he had gone into hiding. In any event, he seemed to be reclusive and hard to find. A visit by Mark Allen to Los Angeles presented an opportunity to meet Steve and have lunch with him and Mark. We arranged to meet at Trilussa, an Italian restaurant on the Santa Monica Third Street Promenade near Oliver's offices.

Mark was in Los Angeles to meet with Judith Campbell Exner, the former close personal friend of President Kennedy with whom he had an affair while in the White House. Mark had been in touch with Judith for years, and was working with her on a book project. Unfortunately, she did not join us for lunch, which would have been fascinating, as she is a very private person. I did, however, have the pleasure of finally meeting Steve Rivele in person.

Steve is a gruff, burly man with a beard, who can make a somewhat forbidding first impression. While he outwardly resembles a grizzly bear, the warm heart of a teddy bear beats inside his imposing frame—at least most of the time. We chatted about his work on the JFK case, Miss Exner and various other conspiracy-related topics. It turned out that Steve was not in hiding, but was in fact living quietly in Pasadena with his son Eli. He had become burnt out on JFK and the French connection, but was busy writing books and other things. Steve had written a series of unproduced screenplays with his partner Chris Wilkinson for the late Beatle George Harrison's film company, Dark Horse. I expressed interest in reading them.

I had given Oliver a series of articles that Steve had written on a mysterious pair of CIA agents, code-named QJ/WIN and WI/ROGUE, who had been recruited by the agency in the early 1960s to provide an assassination capability. Steve had researched their backgrounds and possible identities, as well as their connections to CIA assassination plots against Patrice Lumumba of the Congo, Fidel Castro and perhaps JFK as well. The articles were intriguing and dramatic, although not definitive in their conclusions. Oliver found them interesting but did not bite on them as movie material.

It had crossed my mind after my first dinner with Oliver that given his interest in figures like Hitler, Stalin and Mao, it might be interesting to explore the idea of a film about Richard Nixon. I would certainly not equate Nixon with the level of evil represented by those figures, but he seemed to me to be the darkest and most intriguing figure on the American landscape in the twentieth century. Since I had always been fascinated by Nixon myself, I thought it would be wonderful if I could interest Oliver in making a film about him.

I floated this idea past Steve at lunch, and he responded immediately. My original idea was to do a film that would be a sort of "The Worst of Nixon," incorporating all of his known misdeeds and some that we could only speculate about. For example, I thought it quite possible that Nixon had been behind the shooting of George Wallace in 1972. Wallace had almost cost Nixon the election in 1968, and might very well have done so in the 1972 election had he not been shot and eliminated from the race. Steve agreed with my analysis.

The Nixon agent Howard Hunt had been sent by Charles Colson to plant McGovern literature in assassin Arthur Bremer's apartment immediately after the shooting, but was unable to do so. While he was stalking Wallace, Bremer had apparently traveled around the United States and Canada, staying in luxury hotels although he had no visible means of support. According to some reports, he had been seen with Nixon operatives on a ferry in Michigan. Governor Wallace himself later expressed the view that it had been a conspiracy, and his son called for an investigation.

Still later, while we were making the film *Nixon*, John Dean told me that he believed Colson might have been behind the shooting. While Dean and Colson were in federal detention on an army base, Colson had confided to him that there was one thing he had done that he "still felt guilty about." Colson was a hard man who had famously said, "I would run over my grandmother to reelect Richard Nixon." Given the magnitude of his other crimes and misdeeds, for which he spent time in jail, what evil deed stood out so much that even Colson still felt guilty about it? Dean thought it might have been the Wallace shooting. He was quick to add that this was just speculation.

"Look at Colson," he told me. "He's effectively put himself in prison for life." Colson had become a born-again Christian after his conviction, and had started a "prison ministry" to preach to other convicts. As Dean jokingly put it, "Now he would run over his grandmother for Christ." In the end, though, we didn't use this scenario in the film. Since it was only speculative and we couldn't prove that Nixon and Colson were involved, it would have been unfair to put it in the movie.

I did not know all of this information when I first spoke with Steve Rivele. But we both intuitively felt that there was more to Nixon than met the eye, and that his story would make a great film. It turned out that Steve had previously thought about writing a play with the same theme. I encouraged him to write a film treatment instead. "Let me talk to my partner," he replied, referring to Chris Wilkinson. "It's an interesting idea."

Steve and Chris soon went to work on a treatment. A "treatment," in Hollywood parlance, is normally a short outline of a film in story form, running anywhere from three to five pages or longer, and usually laid out in three acts. Chris and Steve, however, produced something different and more original. On November 22, 1993 (the thirtieth anniversary of JFK's death), they faxed me their original treatment for *Nixon*.

The treatment was more a series of thoughts and ideas than a conventional story. At the center of it was their concept of "The Beast"—the shadowy, unseen political and economic forces that control the government from behind the scenes. As Chris later wrote, "We conjured up a most chilling truth about The Beast. Not that it exists—but that it does not know it exists." The Beast had created Richard Nixon, and then destroyed him. And The Beast also represented the dark side of Nixon himself.

It was this concept that grabbed Oliver. After reading their three-page treatment, he called me. "Let's hire these guys. Cheap.... I like this idea." That was all I needed to hear. I picked up the phone and called Steve Rivele. Steve is someone who can find the cloud in any silver lining, and is suspicious at the best of times. But even he had to admit he was pleased. "That's the best news I've heard all day," he told me. "Let's do it." That was the beginning of *Nixon*.

Larry Flynt, Maureen Dowd and Other Projects

I asked Steve and Chris to come in and meet with me and Janet Yang to discuss the project. I thought Janet should be there, since she was president of the company and nominally in charge of all its projects in development. Chris Wilkinson turned out to be a tall, thin man with prematurely white hair, with a quick wit and an infectious, almost manic sense of humor. Steve and Chris were both from Philadelphia and about the same age (late forties or so),

75 / JFK, Nixon, Oliver Stone and Me

but otherwise were complete polar opposites in personality. Perhaps this is why they made a good team as writers—a yin and yang combination that worked together to create magic.

They outlined their concept for the film, and Janet listened politely. I could tell she was skeptical, though. The Nixon film was a direct threat to one of Janet's cherished projects, a biopic of Martha Mitchell, the late wife of Nixon's attorney general John Mitchell. The Martha Mitchell project had been brought to Janet and Oliver by the actress Diane Ladd, who yearned to play Martha. Both women were from Arkansas, and both were loud, colorful personalities. Martha Mitchell was a heavy drinker and compulsive talker who made good copy during the Watergate scandal. I couldn't see her as the subject of a feature film, though. She was more of a bit player in the Nixon saga than a leading lady. And the relationship between Martha and her dour, pipe-smoking husband John hardly seemed to be the stuff of screen romance.

In the end, the Martha Mitchell film never got made. I'm sure Diane Ladd never forgave me for that, and Janet probably didn't either. As a consolation prize, Oliver offered Ladd the part of Martha Mitchell in *Nixon,* but she declined in a huff, feeling the role was too small. Madeline Kahn played Martha in the movie and did a superb job.

I was also partly responsible for the demise of another of Janet's favorite projects, called "Marita." This was to be a biopic of Marita Lorenz, a German woman who supposedly had an affair with Fidel Castro shortly after he took power. Lorenz was recruited by the CIA to murder Castro during their affair, but couldn't bring herself to do it. She later claimed to have been involved in the plot to assassinate JFK, along with Frank Sturgis and others. Sturgis, who had a close but strange relationship with Lorenz, later became famous as one of the Watergate burglars.

Lorenz's story had been investigated by the HSCA and also by independent JFK researchers. Though some were inclined to believe her, the consensus was that while the Castro part of her story was largely true, it was unlikely that she had anything to do with the JFK plot. She seemed to have picked up bits and pieces of information from Sturgis and others, and then woven herself into the story. Most serious researchers did not regard her as a credible witness.

In addition, Lorenz was a difficult personality, constantly in need of money and prone to hire and fire lawyers and collaborators at will. Several people had tried to work with her on a book, which was years in the making and finally got written. She had been represented by a reputable entertainment lawyer in Hollywood, but had fired him in favor of a Mafia type in New York. When I alerted Oliver to this and other aspects of her dubious background, he elected to drop the project. Marita later threatened to sue us over *Nixon*, but never did. (Her story was later made into a movie for Lifetime, the women's TV channel, in a watered-down version that did not include her JFK allegations.)

I had not intended to undermine Oliver and Janet's pet projects, but I felt that these two were particularly weak. In any case, Janet had plenty more where those came from. One of the most dubious in my view actually ended up getting made. This was a treatment brought to Ixtlan by two young writers about porn king Larry Flynt. The treatment was short but entertaining, sort of a rags-to-riches American story beginning with Larry's birth in a log cabin, and following his rise to celebrity through his creation of *Hustler* magazine, his shooting by a crazed zealot, his battles with drugs, the death of his wife from AIDS and his ultimate Supreme Court victory over Rev. Jerry Falwell in a First Amendment case.

The Flynt story was definitely unusual, but I hardly thought that he was a heroic figure worthy of canonization in a major motion picture. However, mine was the minority view at Ixtlan. Janet loved it, as did Oliver. The fact that Oliver could identify with someone like Larry Flynt was not that surprising to me by then. I thought it would be a disaster for his reputation, though, to direct a movie about this man. Janet pitched the idea to her friend Lisa Henson, then head of Columbia Pictures, who also liked the idea. The project was quickly set up at Columbia and put on the fast track. It was called *The People vs. Larry Flynt*—a title that proved to be prescient when it was released in 1996.

I found it hard to believe that Janet, who had produced the sensitive drama *The Joy Luck Club,* and Lisa Henson, who had made *Little Women* at Columbia, would want to make a movie about the leading purveyor of gross and disgusting pornography in America. I never did fully grasp their thinking, other than that it could be crudely comic and a successful film at the box office. In the end, it wasn't. Janet had wanted Oliver to direct the film, but he opted for *Nixon* instead. Mike Medavoy, the head of Phoenix Pictures, which was financing the film, suggested Czech director Milos Forman, and managed to convince him to direct it. Woody Harrelson starred as Larry, and rock star Courtney Love played his wife Althea. The movie was not bad, with convincing performances by Harrelson and Love, but it bombed at the box office. Sometimes sex doesn't sell, even in Hollywood.

The film caused something of a furor, with feminists taking offense. Gloria Steinem took out a full-page ad in *Variety* to denounce the film. The National Organization for Women also opposed the film, and a conservative group called Media Action Alliance started a campaign against it. They vowed to boycott all future films produced by Oliver Stone or Janet Yang. I was glad I had nothing to do with the film.

Another of Oliver's favorite pet projects went through several incarnations, but never quite made it to the screen. This was the "Media Project." It had been his own idea, and was meant to be a critique of the press and the media industry, à la *Wall Street*. The *New York Times* was a particular target. He felt that the *Times* had been grossly unfair to him during the whole *JFK* controversy, and he was determined to get even.

The first draft of the script was called "Press" and was written by Jay Cocks, a former film critic for *Time* magazine. Cocks had become a successful screenwriter, with credits including *The Age of Innocence* for Martin Scorsese. "Press" was supposed to be about the media coverage of a presidential race. Unfortunately, the script did not work very well and was dropped.

Oliver then hired Zach Sklar, his co-screenwriter on *JFK*, to pen a new script called "Power." This was about a takeover of the fictional *New York Record*, a paper much like the *Times*, by an evil media mogul patterned after Rupert Murdoch. A key character in the script was a conniving and bitchy columnist for the paper named Ashley Whittaker. She was modeled after columnist Maureen Dowd, a particular unfavorite of Oliver's. In the script, the character's nickname was "Ash the Slash," and she was prone to making comments like "Ashley's the name, sarcasm's my game." She also seduced the hero, a young, idealistic investigative reporter, wrecking his marriage and corrupting his morals.

Still not satisfied, Oliver later hired Stanley Weiser, co-writer with him of *Wall Street*, to do a rewrite of the Sklar script. The new version, entitled "Media," focused on the same characters and basic plot, but sharpened the knives and the satire. Oliver even asked me to pull up a collection of Maureen Dowd columns from the Internet for Stanley to use as background material. His script was very funny and insightful, but was eventually abandoned by Oliver in favor of his disastrous film *U-Turn*.

Later, after *Any Given Sunday* came out at the end of 1999, I got a call from Zach Sklar. He had seen my name on the screen and wondered if I could help him. He had written a new draft of the "Media Project," now called "Mediocracy," a year earlier at Oliver's request. "Oliver still hasn't read it," he said incredulously. "What can I do to get him to read my script?" I expressed sympathy for Zach, but there wasn't much I could do. Zach later told me that Oliver had called him and said he was keeping the script "in his back pocket."

It's clear that Oliver's hatred of Ms. Dowd continues unabated. In a speech given in New Orleans in July 2001, Oliver blasted the media, and singled out the *New York Times* for special criticism, saying "What do you want from a newspaper that considers Maureen Dowd to be an intellect?" This could mean that Oliver still has the project on his mind, so maybe Dowd will still make it to the silver screen one of these days. . . . At least in fictional form.

The Bay of Pigs Thing

In the spring of 1994, Oliver received a request from *Harper's* magazine to contribute a piece for a special issue commemorating the twentieth anniversary of Nixon's resignation. The issue appeared shortly after Nixon's death in April of that year. We had started the Nixon project while he was still alive, but his passing gave it greater urgency.

Oliver asked me to draft something for *Harper's* to appear under his name. What they wanted was a speculation of what was on the famous 18 1/2-minute gap on the Watergate tapes, a kind of fictional dialogue between Nixon and his chief of staff, H. R. (Bob) Haldeman. I jumped on this with relish. The conversation had taken place on June 20, 1972, three days after the Watergate break-in. In other tapes recorded during the same period, Nixon had carried on obsessively about what he called "the Bay of Pigs thing."

This mysterious reference seemed to be a code word for something else, something that Nixon did not want to discuss openly, even with Haldeman.

In his memoir *The Ends of Power,* Haldeman later speculated on what this might have meant. He wrote, "It seems that in all of those Nixon references to the Bay of Pigs, he was actually referring to the Kennedy assassination. . . . After Kennedy was killed, the CIA launched a fantastic cover-up. . . . In a chilling parallel to their cover-up at Watergate, the CIA literally erased any connection between Kennedy's assassination and the CIA. . . . And when Nixon said, 'It's likely to blow the whole Bay of Pigs,' he might have been reminding [CIA Director] Helms, not so gently, of the cover-up of the CIA assassination attempts on the hero of the Bay of Pigs, Fidel Castro—a CIA operation that may have triggered the Kennedy tragedy and which Helms wanted desperately to hide."

These were Haldeman's own words, from his own memoir. To me, this seemed to be the key to understanding Watergate. Obviously, the conspiracy and cover-up had a deeper meaning than met the eye. I decided to make this the focus of the imagined conversation. I also thought this would be a good opportunity for me to show Oliver that I could write dialogue, as a prelude to perhaps being given the opportunity to write a script for him later, which was one of my goals.

I started the piece by using some of Nixon's actual quotes to Haldeman from the famous "smoking gun" conversation, which took place three days later on June 23, 1972. Nixon said, "When you get in there with Helms, say, Look the problem here is that this will open the whole Bay of Pigs thing.... It would be very bad to have this fellow [E. Howard] Hunt, he knows too damned much.... It would make the CIA look bad, it's going to make Hunt look bad, and it's likely to blow the whole Bay of Pigs thing, which we think would be most unfortunate—both for the CIA and for the country...."

This was suggestive, to say the least. Our theory was that Helms, Hunt and the Cubans involved in the Watergate burglary were linked not only to the Bay of Pigs, but perhaps to the JFK assassination plot as well. This would explain why the tape had been erased. It would also explain Nixon's threats to Helms and the CIA, and his other references on the smoking gun tape, the release of which led to his resignation. And it provided a crucial theme for our film. The basic thesis of *Nixon* was that the CIA–Mafia plots against Castro that started in 1959–1960, the disastrous Bay of Pigs invasion in 1961, the Cuban missile crisis of 1962, the assassination of JFK in 1963 and the Watergate break-in in 1972 were all related. The thread running through all of them was Cuba.

Meanwhile, Chris Wilkinson and Steve Rivele had been researching Nixon and working on an expanded version of their treatment, while the lawyers worked out their contract to write the film. Neither Chris nor Steve had an agent, and only Chris had a lawyer representing him. For this and other reasons, it took several months to work out a deal, even though the money involved was not that great, and everyone wanted the deal to work. When this was finally resolved, they came to meet with Oliver and me.

Oddly enough, their treatment involved the same central thesis that we had independently developed for the *Harper's* piece—that

there was a link between Dallas and Watergate, and that the
18 1/2-minute gap provided that missing link. As Steve expressed
it, "What could have been so incredibly damaging on that particular tape that it had to be erased, when there was enough other
material left over to get him impeached? It had to be something
qualitatively worse, something that could never be revealed publicly, no matter what."

This was the only logical explanation. With this meeting of the
minds, it was clear that we were all on the same page, and that it
was time for them to start writing the script. While they were writing, Oliver asked me to make a trip to Cuba to investigate further.

Research in Cuba

I had been fascinated by Cuba for many years and had always
wanted to go there, but never had the opportunity. While in high
school in the late 1960s, I took a romantic view of the Cuban revolution as many others did. I even tried to learn Spanish, with limited success. Over the years, my view of the Cuban regime became
more skeptical, but I still sympathized with the original goals and
ideas of the revolutionaries, and even more so with the long-suf-
fering Cuban people. Cuba also had a whiff of the forbidden, as it
was off-limits to most Americans. This only increased my desire to
go there.

Shortly after going to work for Oliver Stone, I had read about
a Cuban television documentary produced for the thirtieth

anniversary of JFK's death. Based on a Cuban investigation, it boldly named two Cuban exiles and three Chicago Mafia members as being the actual gunmen in Dallas. I was intrigued by this and wanted to learn more.

I called the Cuban diplomatic mission in Washington, who suggested that I write to a Cuban film and television agency in Havana. I did so, not expecting to hear back from them. After a few weeks passed, I received a videotape of the program in the mail. It came not from Cuba, but from Brazil. It turned out that the program had been produced by Claudia Furiati, a Brazilian journalist with connections in Cuba. She had also written a book called *ZR Rifle,* about the plots against Kennedy and Castro, with the cooperation of Cuban intelligence sources. Her primary source was General Fabian Escalante, a high-ranking Cuban intelligence officer who had been in charge of Castro's personal security and counterintelligence efforts for many years.

Furiati's book had been published by Ocean Press, an Australian publishing house specializing in books on Cuba, with offices in Melbourne and Havana. After further inquiries, I was contacted by David Deutschmann, head of Ocean Press and a frequent traveler between Australia and Cuba. I arranged to meet with him in Los Angeles on his way to Cuba.

David was a lean, lanky and friendly man, with a vast knowledge of Cuba and a wealth of contacts there. I expressed my interest in the Cuban research on JFK, and also in making a film about the Cuban missile crisis. David immediately offered to arrange for me to visit Cuba, and to accompany me on a guided tour there. I quickly took him up on his offer.

I was a little nervous about going to this unknown place with someone I had just met, no matter how legitimate he seemed. I decided to ask my friend Rick English to join me on the trip. Rick is an old friend from high school, college and beyond, and someone with whom I have shared many adventures. He is a professional photographer, and also streetwise. We had traveled to Moscow a few years earlier, and I thought I would feel safer if he was with me in Cuba. Rick jumped at the chance to go, seeing it as an adventure and photo opportunity if nothing else.

Through his connections in Havana, Deutschmann had set up a series of meetings for us with a wide array of Cuban officials, filmmakers, journalists and other interesting people. The main purpose of the visit, at least for me, was the meetings with General Escalante. They proved to be both fascinating and fruitful. I later testified about these meetings before the Assassination Records Review Board, which had been created by our JFK bill.

Rick and I traveled through Mexico, and were met at the Havana airport by David and a large group of Cuban officials. This was the first surprise. Evidently we were being treated as VIP visitors. We were even provided with two cars and drivers. "My" car was a black Mercedes, which I was later told belonged to Castro's personal fleet of cars. Rick was driven around in a Soviet-made Lada car that was rather less comfortable. David and his Cuban colleague Mirta Muñiz acted as our guides and translators. Mirta was a very kind, grandmotherly woman who was the Ocean Press representative in Cuba. Her benevolent appearance notwithstanding, Mirta was and is a dedicated revolutionary who had been with Fidel since the early days.

On our first evening in Havana, we were taken to a dinner in our honor at a "guest house" of the Cuban Interior Ministry. There we were greeted by General Escalante and his colleagues. Escalante resembled a Cuban version of Clint Eastwood, with chiseled features and military bearing. I presented him with some documents I had brought that had been newly released under the

JFK bill. We then launched into a long discussion not only of the JFK case, but of Cuba, America, foreign policy and many other matters. I wanted to establish at the outset that while we were friendly visitors, we were not Communist sympathizers or fellow travelers, and that we would provide an independent and skeptical perspective in any film that we might eventually make.

At one point during dinner, I said to Escalante, "Stalin was in power for thirty years. But Castro has already been in power for thirty-five years. Isn't that too long for any leader? Isn't he really a dinosaur out of another era? Why can't Cuba find a younger leader to replace him?" There was shocked silence around the table. Comments like this were considered heresy in Cuba, especially when expressed openly in a guest house of the Interior Ministry! Escalante ably defended his leader, but his colleagues maintained a discreet silence. One of them later told me he could not sleep all night after hearing our discussion.

Rick and I spent a week in Cuba, much of it with Escalante. Our discussions were often vigorous and spirited, but we developed a mutual respect and personal friendship that made even the disagreements enjoyable. I wanted to build a basis of trust so that we could share ideas openly and develop an ongoing dialogue and exchange of information. I felt that Cuba was the key to understanding the JFK assassination. If we could put together the information held by the Cubans, which had never been made public, with the information now being made public in the United States, we might actually be able to solve the mystery. In the end, I think we came pretty close to doing just that.

We were given a sort of "assassination tour" of Havana, complete with a visit to the coffee shop of the Havana Libre Hotel, where

Castro was almost poisoned with a milkshake, and even a visit to the hotel suite where the femme fatale Marita Lorenz had dallied with Castro, but failed to kill him. We went on a boat ride with Escalante, and he showed us the spot where one of JFK's alleged assassins was captured and killed while trying to infiltrate Cuba in 1966. We also visited a Cuban resort at Varadero, where we spent a very pleasant afternoon on the beach. All in all, Cuba was a surreal experience—fascinating, exhilarating and depressing all at once.

We also visited the international film school outside of Havana, where I gave a talk and met young filmmakers. Rick and I returned to Cuba in December to follow up on these meetings, and also to attend the Havana Film Festival. On the final night of the festival, we accompanied Claudia Furiati and American film-maker Estela Bravo to a reception at the Palace of the Revolution. Claudia, a dark Brazilian beauty as well as a fine journalist, was friendly with Castro and immediately caught his eye at the reception. She introduced me to Fidel, saying that I worked with Oliver Stone and had helped him with *JFK*.

Summoning up my high school Spanish, I asked him, "Te gusta la pelica Jota Efe Ka?" ("Do you like the movie *JFK*?") I later realized that this was probably rude and impolite, as I was addressing him in the familiar form "Te" rather than the respectful "Usted," but Castro didn't seem to mind. Luckily, his translator was by his side, so I could understand his reply. He said that he had seen the movie and liked it, but wanted to see it again because he had seen a bad copy from Mexico. He asked if we put anything on the film to make it hard to copy. I said, "No, I don't think so . . . but I'll get you a better copy of the film." I sent him one through Ocean Press, and it was later shown on Cuban television.

Claudia jokingly complained to Fidel that his security people had taken away Rick's camera. Rick explained that he was a professional photographer and wanted to shoot pictures at the palace reception. Castro looked at him as if he were crazy. "Can you imagine if I let photographers come in here with their cameras?" he exclaimed. "Each camera could have a bomb in it. It's impossible!" Then, in his charismatic manner, he summoned his personal photographer to take a picture of us with him. After the picture, he motioned to Rick. "Give him your camera! He's a photographer. Let him take a picture!" The photographer handed over his camera to Rick, who took a great shot of Claudia, Estela and me with Fidel. Our trip was complete.

The First Draft

Back in California, Chris and Steve delivered the first draft of "Nixon" on June 17, 1994—the anniversary of the Watergate break-in. I took it home over the weekend and read it on a Saturday night, straight through in one sitting. When I had finished, my immediate reaction was that this could be a brilliant film, another *JFK*, and that Oliver had to make it. Luckily, Oliver had the same reaction.

He called me at the office the following Monday and said, "Where are these guys? I want to meet with them right away." I informed him that they were right here in L.A., where they lived. We set up a meeting. While Oliver loved the script, he of course wanted further revisions. He felt that the ending didn't quite come together, and that the "third act" needed more work. Chris and

Steve agreed, and went to work on another draft. This was delivered on August 9, the twentieth anniversary of Nixon's resignation (I was beginning to see a pattern here).

By this time it was becoming increasingly clear that Oliver was planning to make this movie. Characteristically, he never actually told me this. I had to figure it out through a series of signs and tea leaf readings, such as the fact that he had begun to read *The Haldeman Diaries,* which had just been published. Also, his Noriega film with Al Pacino had fallen through. Oliver then attempted briefly to revive another pet project of his, "Evita." He had written a script for it years before, and at one time had talked with Madonna about starring in it. They didn't get along, and the project had been shelved.

Oliver now revived the Evita idea, and wanted to do it with Michelle Pfeiffer. I was dubious about the idea of Oliver Stone making a musical with anyone, particularly about the wife of a quasi-fascist dictator from Argentina. He went so far as to travel to Argentina and meet with its president, but the project fell through. It was eventually made by Alan Parker, with whom Oliver had started his career by writing the Oscar-winning script for *Midnight Express* in 1978. Stone and Parker had a falling out over *Evita,* with each claiming credit for the "screenplay" (which was actually a collection of Andrew Lloyd Webber and Tim Rice songs). Eventually, after a legal dispute and an arbitration by the Writers Guild, Parker and Stone ended up sharing a writing credit.

The demise of the Evita project, from Oliver's point of view, made "Nixon" pretty much inevitable as his next film. When I realized this, I decided to start keeping a journal of events relating to the project. I had been urged by my friends Anne and Michael Mandelbaum to keep a journal from the time I first moved to Hollywood, but I had originally shrugged off the idea. However, when "Nixon" started to become a reality, I changed my mind.

I felt that this was a unique adventure, an experience unlikely to be repeated at least by me, and that I should keep a record of it. I also felt that the "inside story" of how a film like *Nixon* actually gets made might be of interest to others, at least those with interest in the overlapping worlds of film and politics. I have drawn upon those journals in writing the following account. When I went back and read them five years later, I realized how much you can forget if you don't write it down.

A Big Deal

Anytime Oliver Stone decides to direct a film, it's a big deal. It's a big deal to him, to the people around him and to Hollywood in general. It's also a big secret—or at least it's supposed to be.

By the time I had been working with Oliver for a few months, I realized that he was not the person I had thought he was. I had assumed that he was sort of a statesman figure of the film world— misunderstood at times, but trying to do the right thing and make the world a better place. I had compared him in my mind with my former boss John Kerry, also a Vietnam veteran and of the same generation. I thought that working for Stone would be something like working for a senator like Kerry—frustrating at times, but ultimately challenging and satisfying in knowing that you were on the right side and fighting the good fight for a good man.

My mistake . . . Oliver's modus operandi was more akin to that of a one-man, top secret CIA field operation, operating on a strictly need-to-know basis. Kerry trusted his people. Oliver didn't. He called the people around him his "satellites"—which of course placed him at the center of his imagined universe. The more interested he was in a project, the more secretive he would become. It began to dawn on me that he was really going to make *Nixon* when he ordered me to remove all copies of the script from the office and keep them at my home. Then, one day he wanted the script right away. He called me into his office.

"Where is it?" he complained in his plaintive, childlike way. This could be charming or annoying, depending on the circumstances. The wrong answer could incur his wrath, unleash a torrent of abuse, or worse.

"I have it at home," I told him as cheerfully as I could. "Remember . . . you told me not to keep it in the office."

He ignored this. "Well, go get it. Now!"

I dutifully left the office and drove home in the middle of the afternoon to get the script. Luckily my apartment in Brentwood was only about a fifteen-minute drive from our office in Santa Monica. As I was driving along San Vicente Boulevard, I had a light-headed feeling, almost a natural high. "He's actually going to make this movie," I said to myself. "He's really going to do it."

It was unbelievable but true. Out of the hundreds of scripts that were submitted to him, out of the thousands of ideas that could have turned into films, my project was going to be the chosen one. To use a Hollywood term, the movie gods had smiled on me. The sun was shining. I felt great. This was what I had come to Hollywood for. This was why I had left Washington. We were actually going to make *Nixon*.

I picked up the script and quickly drove back to the office. When I delivered it to Oliver in his private office, he was sitting behind his desk.

I summoned my nerve. "Are you really going to make this?" I dared ask. He gave me a strange look.

"I might. . . . I'm thinking about it," he replied. That was all I needed to hear.

I went back to my own office and sat staring out the window toward the ocean, with my feet up on the desk. I felt dazed. Naomi Despres stuck her head in and saw me staring off into space.

"You're working hard," she said playfully. Naomi was one of my favorite people in the office. A Princeton graduate, she was smart and had good taste in films. Her parents had worked on the Hill for Bill Bradley, and her grandmother taught art at Stanford, so I felt a certain kinship with her. I beckoned with my finger for her to come in.

"You know what Oliver's next film is gonna be?" I said jauntily.

"What?" Her eyes widened. She was intrigued.

I motioned for her to move closer. I leaned over and whispered dramatically.

"Nixon."

Her eyebrows shot up in amazement.

"Wow! That's awesome!"

I appreciated her response. She knew how hard it was to get any project made, let alone one that Oliver himself would direct. She knew that this had been an idea I brought to him, and had seen it develop from an embryonic stage to this point. By comparison, Oliver had never personally directed any of Janet Yang's projects. I saw this thought flash through her mind, and then she looked suspicious for a moment.

"What happened to 'Evita'?"

I smiled and gave her a wink.

"She's dead. . . . But don't tell anyone."

Lawyers and *Natural Born Killers*

Once I realized that *Nixon* was really going to happen, I figured it was time for me to get a lawyer. I wanted to get a producer credit on the film (as well as a fee), and I knew I would need a lawyer to protect my interests in this shark tank.

I had made the mistake of going to work for Oliver without any conditions or negotiations, and without any representation. I felt I could trust him, and when I met with his business manager Steve Pines to discuss my salary and other details, I accepted his initial offer. It seemed like good money to me at the time, since it was about twice what I had made on Capitol Hill, but I knew it was peanuts by Hollywood standards. However, I did not want to seem mercenary, nor was money in fact my motive for wanting to work with Oliver. I also hated to discuss money or deal with money matters in general. On the Hill, it was never a problem, because there was never any room for negotiation. You were told what your salary would be, and that was it. If you didn't like it, there were plenty of other people who would be happy to have your job. Of course, this was often true in Hollywood also, but at least the money was better.

I hadn't known when I went to work for Oliver what my title would be, or for that matter what my duties would be either. Eventually it was decided that my title would be Vice President for Business Affairs, and that I would handle legal and business matters for Ixtlan.

As on Capitol Hill, in Hollywood I had to start at the bottom of the learning curve. I thought I understood politics when I went to work on the Hill, but I quickly realized that I did not. There were layers and depths and complexities to the political process that I had never imagined. Nevertheless, I had managed to grasp the lay of the land and get up to speed by the end of my first year there. The same process more or less was repeated when I went to Ixtlan. I thought I knew something about what made a good movie, but I knew nothing about the movie business. In that respect, being forced to handle business affairs was good training and an essential part of my Hollywood education, although not one that I would have chosen myself.

By the end of a year, though, I had had enough of business affairs. I now knew (sort of) what a producer was, at least the kind that I wanted to be: the person who came up with the ideas for projects, found the writers, worked with them, researched and developed a script, and then helped make the film. That was what Janet Yang had done on *The Joy Luck Club,* and what Don Murphy and Jane Hamsher had done on *Natural Born Killers.* I figured I could do the same thing on *Nixon.*

The only problem was, I didn't know how to approach Oliver about this. Or rather, I didn't want to. Oliver was moody and unpredictable, often irrational, and absolutely insane when it came to money. This was a very dangerous subject with him. To go to him and ask for money would be a pointless and potentially suicidal move. To ask him directly for a producer credit would be only slightly less so. What if he said no? Then where would I be? What recourse would I have if he happened to be in a foul mood that day, or at that moment? I didn't want to take that chance.

I decided the best thing to do was to ask the advice of Don Murphy. After all, he and Jane had been upstart young punks straight out of film school, who had managed to persuade Oliver to make their movie, to not only give them each a producer credit but allow them to act as producers on the film, and to pay them a handsome fee in the process. I felt theirs was a good example to follow. I knew that they had a lawyer who negotiated their deal for them, just as Janet had her own lawyer, separate from Oliver's lawyers. I thought I better have one, too.

I wandered down the hall to Don's office and plopped myself down for a chat. Don was friendly and liked to talk, partly to see what information he could get out of me, but also because that was just his nature. Jane was a bit more reserved and standoffish. She also affected black leather jackets sprayed with silver paint, and combat boots to match, which was a bit off-putting. Janet Yang, on the other hand, wore flowing and exotic clothes much of the time, but had a cool air that conveyed the clear sense that she did not appreciate my presence at Ixtlan. I decided that Don was my best bet for advice. He warmed to the subject of negotiating with Oliver, and agreed wholeheartedly that of course I should get a producer credit on *Nixon*. He asked if he could have one too.

"Only if you give me one on *Natural Born Killers*," I joked. *NBK* was scheduled to be released very soon, and it would obviously have been impossible to give me such a credit—not that I deserved it or even wanted it. I had heard that veteran producer Thom Mount had received an executive producer credit on *NBK* and a fee of $250,000 simply for arranging one meeting between Oliver and Don and Jane. But I was not in his league in Hollywood.

Don recommended that I use his lawyer, Craig Emanuel.

"He's a very smart guy, very aggressive," Don told me. "He'll get you a good deal."

"Do you trust him?" I asked.

"Absolutely. I'll call him myself and set it up." I thanked Don profusely, although I later had cause to regret it. But that was later.

I met with Craig for lunch at a restaurant in Westwood. He was a youngish, hip Australian with an air of self-confidence. I explained to him that I would be producing Oliver's next movie, *Nixon,* and needed a lawyer to represent me. He agreed on the spot.

I was glad I had a lawyer when I saw what happened next. *Natural Born Killers* was released in late August 1994, just about a year since I had started working for Oliver. Late August is generally considered a slow time in the movie industry, but Oliver regarded it as auspicious for him, and it turned out to be. The movie was number one at the box office on its opening weekend, earning over $11 million. While this is not a huge amount by Hollywood standards (a real blockbuster would earn at least two or three times as much on its first weekend, if not more), it was good by Oliver's recent standards. *Heaven and Earth,* his previous film, had grossed only $5–6 million in toto, just half what *NBK* made in its first three days. Warner Brothers took out ads in the trades to celebrate.

When I went down to Don's office to congratulate him, I expected to find him in a good mood. Instead, he was almost in tears.

"Oliver is kicking us out," he said sadly, shaking his head in disbelief.

"Why?" I was astonished and perplexed by this turn of events, and felt sympathy for Don and Jane.

"Pines just called us. Our contract is up and Oliver wants us out."

I couldn't believe this. Oliver's career was on the skids, and they had just revived it. Why kick them out now?

"Why don't you fly to Hong Kong and confront him directly?" I asked Don. "Just talk to the guy ... try to reason with him. It can't hurt."

Don shook his head.

"It's too late ... it's over."

He proved to be right. Oliver had brought in Don and Jane as producers of *Natural Born Killers,* and given them a chance straight out of film school. This was almost unheard of in Hollywood. He had wanted them to bring in a blast of fresh air and punk energy, and generate new projects that would make him seem young and hip again. They had done all that for him. But he had also had a clause written into their contract that allowed him to kick them out of his office as soon as *NBK* was released. Now he was exercising that power.

I realized then that Oliver was loyal to no one but himself. Don and Jane's honeymoon with him was over. From his point of view, they were too aggressive, confrontational, demanding and generally a pain in the neck to deal with. I could see his point. Though Don and Jane had discovered Quentin Tarantino, who had written the original *NBK* screenplay, they had alienated him to the point where he took his name off the writing credits of the film. Now they had alienated Oliver as well. Oliver had to be the one in control at all times, and anyone who challenged his authority had to be removed. It was their turn to get the ax. I realized that the same thing could happen to me at any time.

Don and Jane were smart and resourceful, and landed on their feet. They got a producing deal and offices on the Sony lot for their company JD Productions. They went on to produce several more films without Oliver, before eventually splitting up. Don then formed his own company, appropriately called Angry Films, and stayed on at Sony. Jane left and wrote a very insightful book about the making of *NBK* called *Killer Instinct.* For anyone who is a fan of the movie, or wants greater insight into the psychotic side of Oliver Stone, the book is must reading.

Natural Born Killers became a highly controversial film, as well as a mild success for Oliver. It grossed about $50 million domestically, which made it a profitable movie, although not a major hit in Hollywood terms (which are defined solely by the box office). Ironically, *Natural Born Killers* was eclipsed later that year by *Pulp Fiction*, written and directed by Quentin Tarantino, which grossed over $100 million on a budget of about $10 million, and put both Tarantino and Miramax on the map. Oliver was deeply resentful of Tarantino, whom he saw as a threat. Oliver's main fear was that he would no longer be seen as the nation's cutting-edge director—which was why he made *NBK* to begin with. He felt his position had been usurped by this upstart Tarantino, who had only recently been working as a clerk in a video store. Tarantino had been accused of stealing his ideas and plots from obscure Hong Kong action movies, and Oliver once complained to me that "The only reason Quentin Tarantino is famous is that he has a great name." I suppose the same could have been said about Oliver, whose given name was William Stone.

Personally, I did not like *Pulp Fiction*, which seemed to be an attempt at sensationalism, shock value, cleverness and coolness for its own sake, with no redeeming social value. I thought *Natural Born Killers* was a more interesting film, although very confused about its messages. Perhaps this was to be expected, given the drug-addled conditions under which it was made (according to Jane's book and other accounts I heard). I should emphasize that I was not on the set of *NBK*, was not involved in its making in any way and was not a producer on the film, despite my joke to Don.

To me, *NBK* was basically the Bonnie and Clyde story as updated for the MTV generation. Its style was new and flashy for a big-budget movie, although it borrowed heavily from the genre of music videos. Jane described it as the world's most expensive experimental film (its budget was about $35 million). *NBK* tried to satirize the media and criticize it for glorifying killers, but was guilty of the same sins itself. The fact that its protagonists, Mickey and Mallory, became stars and heroes through the media, and then literally got away with murder, made the film's message reprehensible. I do believe that *NBK* was responsible for several copycat killings, although the people who committed them were obviously demented to begin with. Nevertheless, I would not want the murder of another human being on my conscience as a filmmaker or producer.

In a bizarre turn of events, one of the people killed in a copycat case was a friend of author John Grisham. Grisham and the family mounted a fierce campaign against *NBK,* and actually sued Oliver in court for causing the death. The case went all the way to the Supreme Court on First Amendment grounds, and the Court decided the trial could go forward. Ultimately Stone was acquitted of wrongful death charges, but I'm glad that he was called to account for at least one of the killings, and had to face trial in a courtroom, where the measure of his responsibility could be sorted out. He won in court, but not in my eyes.

Following the earlier tumultuous aftermath of *JFK,* the new controversy over *Natural Born Killers* made Oliver something of a pariah in the media. Perhaps this worked to my advantage, as it made him more eager to redeem himself by making a serious film like *Nixon.* Oliver always wanted to have it both ways—to be a provocateur and stir up controversy, and to enjoy critical and commercial success at the same time. He was always very envious of Steven Spielberg, who was and is regarded as the top filmmaker in Hollywood, and whose films made far more money than Stone's ever did. (I once made the mistake of suggesting to Oliver that we take a project to Spielberg's company Dreamworks. He looked at me as if I were insane. He said, "That's the stupidest idea I've ever heard." End of discussion.)

The only blockbuster Stone had made was *Platoon,* which was a phenomenon both critically and at the box office (it grossed over

$150 million domestically on a budget of about $5 million). More importantly, it was recognized by Vietnam veterans as the gritty and faithful depiction of their experience. But by the time Oliver made *Natural Born Killers,* less than a decade later, *Platoon* had been forgotten. The Oscars and honors he had received for that film and its "sequel," *Born on the Fourth of July,* had been eclipsed by Oliver's newfound reputation as a paranoid conspiracy theorist and irresponsible, self-indulgent auteur.

After *JFK,* Stone's name had become something of a national joke—a code word for a nut and a kook. After *Natural Born Killers,* he became a punching bag for politicians and moralists of all stripes who were itching to take on Hollywood. Much of the criticism was justified, but in my opinion some was not. There were far more violent films made in Hollywood on a regular basis, most of which did not even attempt to make any kind of social commentary. But it was Oliver Stone and *NBK* that became a symbol of Hollywood's excesses. He has not lived it down, and probably never will.

The *Nixon* Team, Starring Danny the Weasel

Having dispatched Don and Jane, Oliver now began assembling his team for *Nixon.* At this point, I should explain a little more about some of the characters involved in this enterprise.

Bob Scheer was and is a liberal columnist for the *Los Angeles*

Times. I usually agreed with his views on most political issues, and liked his columns. Bob had been one of the founders of the radical *Ramparts* magazine in the late 1960s, and had later become a fixture of the Los Angeles left wing political scene, writing newspaper columns and doing a radio show with Ariana Huffington. Bob could be maddening at times, but I had to admire him. He had written a groundbreaking book in the early 1980s, *With Enough Shovels,* which was one of the first critiques of the Reagan–Bush nuclear policies like Star Wars (now revived by Bush Jr.).

Bob had been hired by Oliver as a consultant on the Nixon film, and was working on a script with his son Chris, an aspiring screenwriter who lived in the San Francisco Bay Area. This was an arrangement normally prohibited by the Writers Guild of America rules and regulations, which forbade having two teams of writers working on the same project at the same time. Nevertheless, Oliver (who had been honored by the WGA with a lifetime achievement award) had no qualms over breaking or at least bending the union rules. He also frequently hired writers at less that the WGA required minimums, out of his own cheapness.

Oliver kept Bob's script top secret, of course, so I was never allowed to see it. I got one brief glimpse for a few minutes in secret (it was called "Nixon Redux"), but that was it. I don't know all of what was in it, but I know Oliver respected Bob's opinion and listened to him. Bob and Chris Scheer were ultimately credited as "Creative Consultants" on the film. Bob felt he should have gotten a writing credit, but Oliver grabbed it for himself instead.

Steve Pines was Oliver's business manager, a CPA from New York with a heavy Brooklyn accent. Pines was short and stocky with a bristly, stubbly beard that made him resemble Yasir Arafat. He wisely kept his offices separate from Oliver's, which shielded him from some of Oliver's wrathful moods. Steve claimed to have been a student protester in the 1960s, but seemed to be totally apolitical in the 1990s, concerned only with money and the making of it. He was notorious for being incredibly cheap and doling out Ixtlan's funds extremely grudgingly to everyone except Oliver. I eventually had to bring my personal computer from home and keep it in my office, because I could not get him to put out a thousand dollars or so for a decent machine at work.

I always had the feeling that Steve was involved in things he wasn't telling me, but I didn't know what. Pines had a manner of speaking that was very garbled, confusing and inarticulate, to the point that I could rarely understand what he was talking about. I realized after a while that this was probably intentional, a self-protective mechanism so that he could not be pinned down or blamed for anything that went wrong.

Stone's lawyer, Bob Marshall, was similarly murky and confusing in his speech, though in more mellifluous tones. Marshall was a slick, arrogant entertainment lawyer with a big firm, reminiscent of the slimy corporate insurance lawyer played by Jon Voight in Coppola's film *The Rainmaker*. He had been with Oliver for many years and had made most of his deals. (He was eventually dropped after the disaster of *U-Turn* in 1997.) Like Pines and others around Oliver, he seemed to share none of Oliver's politics, and was concerned only with money, deals and fees. Oliver periodically complained that Marshall was costing him too much money, but generally did nothing about it. However, he did cast Marshall in a cameo role in *Nixon* as the ignominious Spiro Agnew. I sometimes thought of Pines and Marshall as Oliver's Haldeman and Ehrlichman. Oliver, of course, was Nixon.

Arnon Milchan was Stone's business partner and financier as head of New Regency, a production company based at that time on the Warner lot. Milchan was a shadowy, mysterious Israeli wheeler-dealer who had been involved in the international arms trade before coming to Hollywood. He had reputedly sold nuclear triggers to the racist white regime in South Africa, and was also involved in the Iran–Contra scandal.

Clayton Townsend was basically a "line producer" for Oliver—someone who handled the nuts and bolts of moviemaking, supervising the scouting of locations, hiring of drivers and crews, drawing up budgets and payrolls, and generally catering to Oliver's whims. At one point during the preparations for *Nixon,* Oliver barked at Clayton, "Get me an anteater!" Clayton scurried off to hunt down the obscure animal, before Oliver informed him it was just a joke. Like all those who lived off of Oliver and depended on his largess, Clayton was very insecure about his position. (He was later dismissed by Oliver after finishing *Any Given Sunday.*)

Clayton physically resembled the actor Tom Sizemore, who played a thuggish cop in *Natural Born Killers* who tries to rape the Juliette Lewis character in the film. He had clashed repeatedly with Don and Jane on *NBK,* and avoided the Ixtlan crowd as much as possible. Around the time *Nixon* shooting was starting, he was in the middle of a messy divorce, and was in the process of moving in with Sandra Noriega, daughter of the pineapple from Panama.

My favorite person in the Ixtlan office was Azita Zendel, Oliver's personal assistant. She had worked for Oliver for four years, starting as an intern in college, and was on call twenty-four hours a day. Azita was a very smart, attractive and energetic graduate of UCLA, from a Persian family who had fled to the United States after the Islamic revolution. She had long dark curly hair and a quick mind. Despite her hardships, Azita was very friendly, positive and outgoing, putting up with Oliver's moods and frequent bouts of insanity with good humor. How she managed to last four years in that environment, working closely with Oliver on a daily basis, always on call, I can't imagine. But somehow she did—although it took its toll.

I also began to hear a bizarre rumor that Oliver was planning to bring in a Disney executive named Danny Halsted to run a new company, now that Don and Jane were gone. This was disturbing news, so absurd that I did not believe it at first. Danny "the Weasel" Halsted was known as one of the shallowest empty suits in town—the Dan Quayle of Hollywood. His nickname derived from Oliver's habit of referring to him as a "spineless weasel"— usually to his face. Danny the Weasel was best known for promoting the career of Pauly Shore, the airheaded MTV beach boy who makes Kato Kaelin look like a thoughtful intellectual. Danny the Weasel was responsible for the Pauly Shore vehicle *Encino Man,* about a caveman who awakens in the late twentieth century in the San Fernando Valley and becomes a surfer dude. He had also made several other Shore movies as a studio executive at Disney's Hollywood Pictures.

If you've ever seen Robert Altman's brilliant film *The Player,* then you know Danny the Weasel. He is Griffin Mill, the sleazy studio executive played by Tim Robbins, who will lie, cheat, steal and literally kill to promote himself and his career. In the film, Mill murders a writer, gets away with it and ends up as head of the studio. This roughly parallels the career of Danny the Weasel, except that Danny never actually killed anyone. He had started off as an agent at Bauer-Benedek, which later became the United Talent Agency. The story goes that Danny the Weasel confronted one of the partners and said, "I think my name should be on the door, too." The partner turned to him and replied, "The only way you'll get your name on that door is if you change it to Agency."

In fact, Danny the Weasel did change his name. His real name was Cohen, but he had changed it to Halsted, which sounded less Jewish. Chris Wilkinson once met Danny's sister at a party and told her that he was working with him on a film project. The sister told Chris, "Don't hold him against me—he's only my brother. I can't help it." Screenwriter Lou Holtz, who wrote *The Cable Guy*, had gone to Beverly Hills High with Danny the Weasel, and had been on the golf team with him. He told me that, even then, Danny the Weasel was renowned for cheating at golf.

Yet the Weasel was consistent in his phoniness. Although prematurely balding, he affected what he thought of as a hip look. Once, while visiting Disney with him on a project, we ran into an old colleague of his. The man took a look at him, shook his head and said, "From *Encino Man* to *Nixon*—that's amazing!" Danny the Weasel beamed and said, "How do I look?" His friend replied, "You look like a Jewish surfer—like a thirty-five-year-old guy trying to look twenty-five." Other times, of course, Danny would don the standard Armani suit uniform of most Hollywood agents.

After leaving UTA, Danny the Weasel landed at Hollywood Pictures as an executive. He met Oliver during the abortive effort to make "Evita," which was set up at that studio. Somehow, Halsted got it into his head that he should work for Oliver—in fact, that he should run Oliver's company. He managed to sweet-talk Azita into letting him ride on the Warner jet with Oliver to Colorado, where Oliver had a vacation home in Telluride. During the course of the plane ride, Danny the Weasel made his pitch.

His idea was that Stone should be a brand name, like megadirector Steven Spielberg. He should have his own hit factory, like Dreamworks, cranking out one blockbuster after another, raking in millions and millions just for putting his name on a film. This appealed to Oliver's greed, and to his jealousy of Spielberg. Danny the Weasel, being a combination of Sammy Glick and Willy Loman, was nothing if not a good talker and a better hustler. He sold Oliver on this idea, notwithstanding the fact that he already had a production company, Ixtlan. Thus was born Illusion Entertainment (or as I called it, Delu$ion Entertainment).

I subsequently spent many sessions with Steve, Chris and Azita trying to figure out how he had snowed Oliver. I think it basically came down to greed. Oliver wanted to be as big as Spielberg, and Danny the Weasel convinced him that he could do it—that he could turn Oliver into a "brand" whose name on a project would automatically rake in the dollars. It was a seductive vision for Oliver, who always complained, "I have no money!" Unfortunately, it didn't work out that way.

Danny the Weasel later confided to me that he had no interest in Oliver's politics and did not want to make political films. The reason he decided to hook up with Oliver was that he was "the only A-list director that didn't have a major production company wrapped around him." Halsted envisioned Illusion as a creator of product that would make him rich, and that he could sell off in a few years for hundreds of millions, like Rob Reiner's Castle Rock or other successful film companies.

The idea behind Illusion was that it would make big-budget mainstream movies that would gross huge amounts, like *Titanic* or *Star Wars,* generating sequels, spin-offs and all kinds of cash flow from now until time immemorial. The only flaw in this scheme was that Danny the Weasel had terrible taste in movies, and the ones he produced for Oliver were absolute bombs. After a string of fiascoes with titles like *Freeway, Cold Around the Heart, The Corruptor,* and *U-Turn,* Oliver eventually axed him. But not before the Weasel had destroyed Ixtlan and nearly wrecked Oliver's career as well.

Danny the Weasel quickly showed his true colors at Ixtlan. Steve and Chris were immediately turned off by him, and formed a permanent revulsion to him after a short exposure. Halsted had insisted that I introduce him to them, since they were obviously key figures in the "Nixon" project. He took us all to lunch at a trendy restaurant, The Palm, populated by Hollywood agents and other well-dressed vermin. After showing them off and accepting congratulations for *Nixon* (which he had nothing to do with developing), he spent much of lunch trying to pitch the writers on the agency that handled Oliver, CAA. Steve and Chris listened and politely declined, having already made their decision to go with UTA. After lunch, the Weasel started making calls from his car (a Range Rover, like Griffin Mill had in *The Player*). Brandishing his cell phone, he proclaimed to me, "The telephone is my weapon." He then brazenly called his former boss at UTA and tried to take credit for Steve and Chris signing with that agency, even though he had just tried to talk them out of it. That was the moment when he truly earned his nickname in my mind....

The Return of Sammy Glick

I never could understand why Oliver had hired Danny the Weasel—a character notorious throughout Hollywood for his dishonesty, lack of brains and creativity, and proclivity for malfeasance. On the other hand, maybe that's just why he hired him. Chris Wilkinson guessed that "Oliver feels like he's been kicked around by Hollywood weasels for so long, he wants to have one of his own to kick around."

But a bigger mystery to me was how someone like Danny the Weasel came to exist in the first place. How did someone still relatively young develop the traits of a compulsive, pathological, sociopathic liar and backstabber? Was it genetic? Was this something like autism or Down's syndrome that he was born with? Was it caused by some pernicious chemical contamination in Hollywood bottled water that manifested itself only upon entering the movie business? If so, I might have mustered a certain amount of sympathy for him (while holding on to my wallet). Or were these acquired traits—perhaps developed during a warped and twisted childhood, or a stint in prison or in Vietnam? In other words, was it nature or nurture?

As far as I know, Danny the Weasel never served any time in prison or in Vietnam (the same could not be said for Oliver, who at least had an excuse for his psychotic behavior). And I don't know anything about Danny's childhood, other than that he had a seemingly normal sister from what I had heard. Perhaps it was a telling indicator that he had changed his name from Cohen to Halsted. This would seem to indicate a rejection of his past—especially his Jewishness—and a certain shame over his origins. This Gatsby-esque move might explain something. On the other hand, my understanding was that he had grown up in Beverly Hills and gone to Beverly Hills High School, one of the most status conscious schools in the country—not exactly an underprivileged start. As Chris said, "He's the only guy stupid enough to change his name in the most Jewish industry in the country!"

The whole thing was a puzzle to me. But ironically, it became much clearer after I left Oliver's office and cut off all contact with Danny the Weasel. I happened to read an insightful article by Rick Lyman in the *New York Times* Arts and Leisure section, dated May 7, 2000. This article, entitled "The Long Run of Sammy Glick," is worth quoting at some length. Lyman had probably never met Danny the Weasel, who was a relatively minor player in the Hollywood scheme of things, but the article nailed his character.

For those not familiar with ancient history, Budd Schulberg wrote a classic novel in the 1930s called *What Makes Sammy Run?* about a character named Sammy Glick, who was an aspiring Hollywood mogul. He described him as "a little ferret of a kid, sharp and quick ... in the midst of a war that was selfish, ruthless and cruel, Sammy was proving himself the fittest, the fiercest, and the cruelest." It was meant to be a cautionary tale. As Lyman wrote, "Back then, Sammy Glick was the villain of the piece, the awful example of what might happen if you let individualism and free enterprise run away with you."

But then something happened in the collective American psyche. In the 1970s, Schulberg noted a "180 degree turn in our national attitude towards Sammy." In a 1989 edition of the book, Schulberg added an afterword: "The book I had written as an angry exposé of Sammy Glick became a character reference." One student told him of his admiration for Glick: "He put out his hand, the hand that would soon be knifing friends and colleagues in the back," Schulberg wrote. "As I took it hesitantly, I asked myself, what have I done?"

It is tempting to imagine that this ambitious student was Danny the Weasel himself, but I don't think he had ever actually read a book, so it is probably unlikely. He had, however, absorbed the core cultural values of that student and others like him. Interviewed in 2000 by Lyman, Budd Schulberg said, "This new generation has absolutely no consideration of any such matters. It's another world. They appear to feel that any kind of moral brakes on what you do seem old-fashioned or out of date or even nonexistent. I don't think they even worry about it. I think, in a sense, they see themselves as super Sammys."

That was Danny the Weasel—a super Sammy, an über-Sammy who had discarded his moral values along with his Jewish name. In the book, Sammy had made his way to the top in part by stealing a script. Ironically, Danny the Weasel had done almost exactly the same thing with *Any Given Sunday*—stealing the idea and having a script written to match it. I had noticed this trait of his on other occasions as well.

For example, I had noticed that Oliver for some reason had a fondness for Rodney Dangerfield and Don Rickles. Perhaps he identified with them because, like Dangerfield, he felt he got "no respect" and, like Rickles, he enjoyed insulting people just for the hell of it. In any case, he wanted to make a "buddy picture" starring Dangerfield and Rickles. They were not exactly the most bankable stars in Hollywood, but Oliver didn't care about that.

I thought about it, and came up with the idea of a pair of comedians like Dean Martin and Jerry Lewis, who were the epitome of comedic camaraderie on stage, but offstage hated each other. Yet they were chained together by their success, and by the public's perception of them and love of their act. I thought that perhaps one of them might decide to hire a hit man in Las Vegas to have the other one killed. This would rid him of his hated partner, and engender even more public sympathy and popularity at the same time. This premise had comic possibilities and would be a perfect vehicle for these two aging Vegas comedians.

I wrote up a memo to Oliver suggesting this idea. It was my standard practice to write a memo first before discussing any idea with him. I had developed this practice on Capitol Hill, where it was standard procedure in most offices, but had refined it with Oliver. This way you could lay out your idea in the words of your choice (preferably limited to one page, by Oliver's insistence). He could read it at his leisure and think about it. Then if he liked the idea, or even if he didn't, you could at least have an informed discussion whenever the whim happened to strike him. To go into his office cold and try to discuss a new idea would have been a disaster. You never knew what kind of mood he might be in, what time pressures he might be under or what drugs he might be on. Something totally irrelevant to your project might have put him in a foul mood, which would be taken out on you and your stupid idea. This could easily kill a project, and was not a smart way to deal with Oliver, who actually liked to read memos if they were to the point and not too long-winded.

On this occasion, I had written up such a memo, and left it with Oliver's assistant Annie in her in-box to give to Oliver. I heard nothing further from him about it, which was not that unusual. Then one day, while in Annie's office, I happened to notice a memo from Danny the Weasel to Oliver (which of course I had not been copied on). It concerned a meeting that Danny the Weasel had had with a writer about a project. The idea was that Rodney Dangerfield and Don Rickles would play these two comedians who hated each other....

This was a perfect example of the modus operandi of Danny the Weasel. Since he had no original ideas of his own, he had to steal them from other people. Since he seemed to have a pathological need to lie, he could not tell the truth about where the idea had come from. And if Oliver liked the idea, he could take the credit for it, and try to set up the project somewhere. Hopefully the originator of the idea, such as myself, would not find out until it was too late.

In this case, I happened by chance to discover what he had done (the project never got made anyway for commercial reasons). But how many times had he gotten away with this kind of treachery? The answer was unknowable, and probably uncountable. As Rick Lyman perceptively wrote, "this feral Hollywood character keeps popping up through the decades, wearing different hats to reflect different moral attitudes but always recognizably the same: ruthless, power-hungry, egomaniacal and hedonistic.... Sammy Glick's education was founded on even less than this; his gift was for bluff and betrayal. He fashioned himself a screenwriter but could hardly write his name. He stole other people's ideas, without a backward glance."

The only difference between Sammy and Danny was that Danny the Weasel fashioned himself as a "producer," not a screenwriter. Like Sammy, Danny the Weasel could barely scrawl his own name on a memo. When it came time to write "notes" on a script, meaning comments and ideas that would improve the next draft, Danny the Weasel relied on a sidekick, a mini-Sammy who actually could read and write. Danny the Weasel would then submit these notes to Oliver under his own name or that of his company Illusion, with no indication that he had not in fact written them himself.

The other side of the coin was that if Oliver liked a project that had not come from Danny, the Weasel would find a way to kill it. One amusing instance of this was what came to be known as the "PLO Project." A New Jersey-based journalist named Morgan Strong had written to Oliver with an idea for a film about the Middle East struggle told from the Palestinian point of view. It pulled no punches about the corruption and terrorism of the PLO, but at the same time showed a certain sympathy for the struggles and suffering of the Palestinian people. Oliver liked the idea, and I had to admire his guts for being willing to consider taking it on. He saw it as a Palestinian version of *Exodus,* the Paul Newman film of 1960, and gave it to me to work on.

Danny the Weasel immediately went to work, enlisting Steve Pines and anyone else he could convince to oppose the project and try to kill it. Even though Strong was a respected journalist who had served in Vietnam and had good connections throughout the Middle East, he was an unknown quantity in Hollywood. For this reason, he had agreed to write the screenplay for less than WGA scale at Oliver's insistence (even though this was illegal). His lack of status in Hollywood was one point of attack for Danny the Weasel.

But he managed to find an even better one. With incredible chutzpah, Danny "the Weasel" Halsted (né Cohen) said that as a "good Jew" he simply could not morally support a film about the PLO. Never mind that this "good Jew" had become a devotee of Eastern religion in order to ingratiate himself with Oliver, who proclaimed himself to be a Tibetan Buddhist. Danny the Weasel, being ignorant of such distinctions, had become a follower of an Indian guru who was actually Hindu. He set up a small altar in his office, similar to the one in Oliver's home, and on each day's schedule card had the words printed "Om Guru Om." I'm not sure what this meant, but a rough translation might be "Please let the movie gods shine on my projects, and destroy everyone else's." This was a manifestation of another famous Hollywood truism: It's not enough that your projects succeed, but that everyone else's must fail. Danny the Weasel was like the Russian peasant who was granted one wish from heaven. He thought about it, then said, "I wish that my neighbor's cow would die."

The culmination of the PLO affair was that we flew Morgan out to meet with Oliver and Bassam Abu Sharif, a top adviser to Yasir Arafat and a good friend of Morgan's. Bassam was considered a moderate among Palestinians, and had even co-authored a book with an Israeli dove about the peace process, despite the fact that part of his hand and face had been blown off by an Israeli letter bomb. He had been sent a package in Beirut that contained a book about Che Guevara. When Bassam opened the book, it exploded, almost killing him and causing him to lose several fingers and one eye and to become almost deaf. Remarkably, his attitude toward peace with Israel had mellowed over the years.

I went out to lunch with Morgan and Bassam on the Santa Monica Promenade and talked about ideas for the project. Bassam thought he could help us find financing in the Middle East, as well as providing access to Arafat and other leaders. The idea seemed intriguing, and we went back to the office to meet with Oliver. Unfortunately, Oliver was running late as always, and asked Danny the Weasel to sit in for him until he got back.

The Weasel took this opportunity to pretend that he was Oliver himself. I did not realize what was going on at first, as Bassam could not hear the questions and comments directed to him. Each comment had to be repeated by Morgan, who sat next to him and shouted into his good ear. Finally, I realized that Danny the Weasel was playing games with this man, and trying to kill the project before Oliver got there. When Stone finally arrived, we had to start the meeting all over again. Bassam was naturally offended by Danny the Weasel's behavior, and things did not go well. In the end, the project did not get made. Morgan Strong rewrote his original treatment and published it as a profile of Arafat in *Icon* magazine, though, so it was not a total loss.

Strangely, after scorning and dismissing the PLO project, Oliver returned to the idea several years later. In March 2002, at the height of violence in the West Bank, Oliver traveled to Arafat's headquarters in Ramallah and interviewed him with a film crew for a documentary. He said it would be a story of "David and Goliath." This came shortly after a similar visit with Fidel Castro in Havana.

Another inexplicable aspect was that while Oliver had a mania for secrecy, Danny the Weasel had a mania for publicity and self-promotion. Oliver would go ballistic if you even mentioned one of his projects to an outsider. During the *Nixon* period, I used to jokingly say, "Don't tell anyone that Nixon resigns—or Oliver will kill you." On the other hand, the Weasel was constantly leaking items to the press—either *Daily Variety* or the *Hollywood Reporter*—about Oliver's "next project," with his own name prominently included. I witnessed this often myself. This was how you knew he was the source of the leak. His modus operandi was to call some studio executive or agent and tell them that some crummy script was going to be Oliver's next movie (which of course it wasn't). He could then set it up at the studio and collect a fee. But Oliver never seemed to notice, which was puzzling in light of his obsession with secrecy and control. But the Weasel was a pure product of Hollywood; he had no other frame of reference.

Naturally, a big shot like Danny the Weasel had to have a big office—in fact, twice as big as anybody else's. This was also standard practice in Hollywood. The bigger the office, the smaller the mind. So Danny the Weasel had the wall torn down between Don and Jane's offices, and took over both—making it bigger than Oliver's. With his own campy sense of interior decorating, he filled the place with kitschy knickknacks and bookshelves lined with books he had never read and didn't intend to. But they looked good in a meeting. His acute sense of insecurity and paranoia had given him a peculiar ability to notice immediately if the smallest object had been moved or if a book was missing from his shelf. Because of this strange quality, his own secretary called him an "idiot savant." She was right about the first part. . . .

In many ways, Danny the Weasel was like an overgrown adolescent, striving to make it into the "in crowd" of Hollywood.

One of his many annoying habits was to use the latest Hollywood expressions, in or out of context, such as "At the end of the day..." or "Don't dress for it." He also liked to gather his staff in his office, get a writer on the phone and put the speakerphone on with his end on mute. He would then make fun of the writer in front of his assembled audience, often saying things like "He sounds gay. I bet he's getting it right now."

In her posthumous book *Washington,* Meg Greenfield compared the culture of Washington, D.C., to high school—with its in-groups and out-groups and general level of immaturity. I found this particularly interesting, since Hollywood was often described by insiders as "high school with money." A better description might have been "junior high school with money." The difference was that the level of maturity in Washington was slightly higher, and most people were not in it for the money, but rather for the power, prestige and even the ideals and the chance to make a difference and advance the causes they believed in.

The only cause that a character like Danny the Weasel believed in was himself. In this, he followed suit in a long Hollywood lineage. In 1941, Budd Schulberg had written, "Hollywood is a jungle, and the smaller animals have to run for their lives." In 2000, Rick Lyman added a comment: "Many of the Hollywood hustlers trying to break into the movie game would puff with pride at such a description.... After all, if I'm surviving, I must be a big animal.... Nebbishes from any walk of life ... are free to fantasize about playing out their own Sammy Glick melodrama. All they have to do is brush up on the local lingo, buy a lot of black clothes and jettison their moral compass, just for the time being.... That's the message of the Hollywood wheeler-dealer stereotype. The only difference between the moguls and you is that they are willing to do what it takes."

Danny the Weasel's "moral compass," if he ever had one, had been lost long ago in the jungles of Hollywood. But he was not yet a "big animal"—just a small "ferret" as Schulberg would have said. A "big animal" in the world of Hollywood producers was someone like Don Simpson, the partner of Jerry Bruckheimer (who later made the cinematic disaster called *Pearl Harbor*). Together, Simpson and Bruckheimer had made such super blockbusters as *Top Gun* and *Days of Thunder*. Their specialty was loud, fast, superviolent action movies with big stars like Tom Cruise—the kind of summer popcorn movies that had no subtlety, quality or taste, but appealed to a mass teenage audience of bored kids.

Simpson had turned himself into a big animal in the Hollywood jungle, but had become a drug addict in the process. This did not stop his rise as long as his films made money, which they did in quantity. But eventually his appetites exceeded him. He would drink and take drugs endlessly, and no one could stop him. Simpson had been in and out of rehab several times, but it hadn't helped. Finally, he brought a doctor to live with him to help get him off drugs, primarily cocaine. Unfortunately, the doctor died of a drug overdose himself before he could help Simpson.

As Elvis Presley had proved before, it was not necessarily a good thing to have one's private doctor prescribing for you (although this did not stop Oliver from doing the same). One night, inevitably, Simpson was found dead—like Elvis, sitting in his bathroom. But Don Simpson had been reading a book when he died. It was a biography of Oliver Stone.

Finding Nixon

While this chaos and upheaval was taking place in the office, we were still moving forward with the "Nixon" project. Oliver, Steve, Chris and I were the true believers. Everyone else thought we were crazy.

There was also the small matter of finding an actor to play Richard Nixon. This was not easy. Tom Hanks was Oliver's original choice to play Nixon. Hanks had been "attached" to another script called "The Passion of Richard Nixon," which had been set up at Disney. The script covered the early years of Nixon's career and ended before he became president. I got hold of it and read it after we started making our film, but was not very impressed. Obviously, Hanks decided not to play Nixon in our movie. I don't know what his reasons were, but I think he probably was reluctant to be associated with such a negative character. Nixon, that is—or maybe Oliver Stone....

After Hanks passed on the project, Oliver started searching for other candidates. He tried Dustin Hoffman, who also passed. He tried Jack Nicholson, who passed. Gene Hackman was also briefly considered. Probably Oliver's most bizarre idea was Robin Williams, who is a brilliant comedian, but was hard to see as Richard Nixon. Chris, Steve and I all thought this notion was insane, but there was nothing we could do about it. Luckily, Williams decided to pass after he read the script. He didn't like the "conspiracy" aspect of the film and did not want to taint his lovable image with it.

Oliver then tried his old favorite Tommy Lee Jones, who had done his last three movies (*JFK, Heaven and Earth* and *Natural*

Born Killers). I thought Jones would actually make a very good Nixon (despite having been Al Gore's roommate in college). I even showed Oliver pictures of Jones from a previous film where he looked just like Nixon, without even trying! Oliver spent a drunken evening at the office with Jones, trying to persuade him to take the part. Jones insisted that Oliver give him a painting on the wall of a woman masturbating, which had been done by Oliver's good friend Sergio Premoli. Oliver gave him the painting, but Jones turned down the role anyway.

Warren Beatty then became the leading candidate. When I saw Beatty in the office, I was impressed by how much he actually resembled Nixon in person. I also thought he might be a good choice since he was a politically conscious and informed person, having starred in and directed *Reds* among other films. I did not get much of a chance to talk to Beatty, other than to offer him some pasta off my plate, which he was eyeing hungrily. But it turned out that he wanted too many changes in the script for Oliver's liking. He wanted to expand Pat's character and her relationship with her husband.

Oliver decided that he did not want to make the changes that Beatty wanted, and also did not want to fight for control of the film with a big star like Beatty who was also a producer and director in his own right. A few years later, I encountered Beatty and his wife Annette Bening at a fundraiser for Senator Paul Wellstone. I reminded Beatty of our earlier encounter, and told him that I had produced a second movie with Oliver, *Any Given Sunday*. Bening looked amazed. "You worked with Oliver Stone *twice*? You deserve a medal!" She gave me a pat on the back. Beatty chimed in, "That's like being married to Madonna twice!" I wasn't sure how his wife would take this, but she laughed and obviously thought it was funny.

Warren Beatty did make one important contribution to *Nixon*. He insisted on doing a reading of the script with an actress. Joan Allen was flown in from New York for this purpose. When the reading was over, Beatty turned to Oliver and said, "You've got your Pat." Oliver had been thinking of Jessica Lange to play Pat Nixon (and I had jokingly suggested Jane Fonda), but Allen got the part. She is a wonderful actress who humanized Pat Nixon and brought her to life on the screen. Joan was nominated for an Oscar for her performance, which she richly deserved. She was also a very nice, modest and down to earth person. She had spent much of her career in the theater in Chicago and New York and was very un-Hollywood, which I liked.

However, this still left Oliver without a Nixon. He came up with a brilliant solution.

I have to admit that I did not have the vision or foresight to think of Anthony Hopkins for Nixon. I had automatically assumed that he would have to be an American actor. All of the Americans who were approached turned out to be afraid of the role. Hopkins was a natural for the outsized figure of Nixon—a Shakespearean actor to play a tragic Shakespearean figure. We were fortunate that he had the courage to take on the role. I believe he is the greatest living actor today. He is also a very humble and unassuming person, with a wicked sense of humor. Tony Hopkins would amuse everyone by doing impressions of actors he had worked with in the past. His impression of Oliver Stone had me on the floor laughing.

But as always with Oliver, nothing was simple. He had met with Hopkins in London and offered him the part (Oliver's globe-trotting was incessant). After some initial hesitation, Hopkins accepted. Oliver then flew off to France to meet with John Malkovich, who he was also considering. Somehow Malkovich got the impression that Oliver had offered *him* the role of Richard Nixon, which he promptly accepted.

When he found out that Hopkins was getting the part (after Oliver had already gone home), he was naturally very upset. To make matters worse, both actors were represented at the time by different agents at the same agency, ICM. Malkovich's agent was afraid he would fire her over the incident, and came to the office to confront Oliver. Of course, Oliver refused to back down or admit that he had made a mistake, which was impossible for him under any circumstances.

He made the right decision, though. I could not see John Malkovich as Richard Nixon then, and still can't, although I loved him in *Being John Malkovich*. As one critic said, it was the role he was born to play....

Lost in the O Zone

Meanwhile, events were conspiring to make Oliver even more suspiciously than he already was. When he finally got back to the office, he discovered that he had received a letter from Fletcher Prouty threatening him with legal action. This caused Oliver to completely freak out and lose his cool.

Oliver had previously asked me to send a copy of the *Nixon* script, which was still being rewritten, to Prouty and to ask for his comments. I thought this was a bad idea, but I had no choice but to comply. My instinct proved to be right. Despite being a friend and neighbor of Lee Hamilton, Prouty was a controversial and somewhat flaky character. He had been the liaison between the Pentagon and the CIA at the time of the Kennedy assassination (according to Prouty), and had immediately suspected a conspiracy. He resigned from the military soon thereafter, and later wrote a book about the CIA's covert operations called *The Secret Team*.

Prouty had been a consultant on *JFK*, and had been depicted in the film as the "Mr. X" character—a shadowy figure who meets with Jim Garrison on the Mall in Washington to warn of the true dimensions of the conspiracy. In fact, no such meeting had taken place, but Oliver considered this to be acceptable dramatic license as a means of getting his point across in the film. Shortly after *JFK* was released, Prouty had appeared with Stone at a press conference at the National Press Club in Washington, which I attended. There, Oliver dramatically announced that the real Mr. X was sitting right in this room, and his name was Fletcher Prouty. Prouty proceeded to support Stone and his contentions, and later wrote a second book called *JFK: The CIA, Vietnam and the Plot to Assassinate John F. Kennedy,* to which Oliver contributed an introduction.

As the book's title suggests, Prouty believed that Kennedy's assassination was connected to a plot to escalate the war in Vietnam. I have already explained why I don't believe this, although I do think the war would never have taken on the dimension it did if Kennedy had lived. Prouty had gotten into something of a dogfight during the making of *JFK* with historian John Newman, a professor at the University of Maryland and author of the book *JFK and Vietnam.* Although their ideas were similar, there was just enough difference to cause a fracas between them, which was disruptive to the film. I was not working for Oliver at that time, but learned about it after the fact.

While working on the Hill, I had made it a point to meet with

Newman and get to know him. He was an unusual figure in that
he was an active member of the military, stationed at Fort Meade
in Maryland and working with military intelligence and the
National Security Agency, yet also a "conspiracy theorist" of sorts
spreading subversive ideas through his writing and by working on
JFK as a consultant to Stone. Although he was suspected by some
JFK buffs to be a spy, I found him to be an honest, straightfor-
ward, patriotic individual who was exactly what he said he was—
someone whose sole interest was in searching for the truth about
these historic events. John subsequently retired from the military
and wrote a second book called *Oswald and the CIA,* which was
one of the first to examine in detail the files released under our
JFK bill.

John had come to visit Oliver and me during the summer of
1994, bringing new information from the files about connections
between the Watergate burglars, the CIA and the Bay of Pigs invasion. This was one factor in Oliver's decision to make the *Nixon*
film. He believed in serendipity. He subsequently hired Newman
as a consultant on the film.

Prouty, on the other hand, had not been hired to help with
Nixon, although he had read the script and sent us comments on it,
some of which were incorporated into subsequent drafts. Prouty
was controversial in part because he had at times been associated
with the Liberty Lobby, a far right group. Oliver, however,
respected him as a former military man who had "been there,"
who had personally known the likes of Allen Dulles and other such
figures, and who agreed with his own views on the assassination,
which were heavily skewed toward a Vietnam connection.

Oliver was shocked and upset, then, when he received a letter
from Prouty complaining that he was not being compensated for
his work on *Nixon,* and that furthermore Oliver had appropriated

his persona in the film *JFK* without giving him proper compensation. Prouty said that he had consulted with legal counsel and had been advised that he had a good case against Stone.

Oliver went ballistic. Any threat of a lawsuit triggered an uncontrollable outpouring of fear, rage and hatred in Oliver. He also felt that people were constantly trying to "hold him up" for money. He cited former CIA analyst John Stockwell, who had his own JFK theories, as someone who had allegedly "held him up" for money with the threat of a lawsuit over the film. Oliver felt especially betrayed by Prouty, whom he had trusted and regarded as a friend.

Bob Marshall prepared a legalistic response to Prouty's letter, denying everything. Oliver also wrote a personal letter to Prouty, saying that "this is not the man I thought I knew" and expressing his sense of personal betrayal. Faced with this, Prouty backed down. He sent back a letter that was softer in tone and withdrew his threat of a lawsuit. While this appeared to settle the matter, it left Oliver in a state of heightened suspicion that lingered and affected those around him, such as me.

At the same time, Oliver was afflicted with another "betrayal." His producing partner and financier, Arnon Milchan, was balking at financing *Nixon*. Milchan evidently considered it to be an uncommercial subject and a losing proposition financially (he may have been correct). Oliver's deal with Milchan, though, gave him the right to make any picture he wanted up to a budget of $42.5 million, with Oliver receiving a director's fee of $7 million. These were called "put pictures." If Oliver wanted to make a film out of the Los Angeles phone book, he could do it under his contract with Milchan.

Yet Milchan was refusing to honor the agreement. He told Oliver that he would put up no more than $35 million to make

Nixon, an amount that Oliver considered insufficient. The only way he could do it for that price would be by waiving his own up-front fee and taking a chance on getting a percentage of the back-end profits, if any. But this was not an option in Oliver's mind to say the least. He was enraged, but he was also caught in a bind. He could sue Milchan, but the lawsuit would take at least a year, which would effectively kill his chance to make *Nixon* when he wanted to make it. By the time the lawsuit was finished, even if it went Oliver's way, Hopkins and many of the other actors might be unavailable. It had to be now or never.

Oliver claimed that Milchan was "holding him up" for $1 million. I'm not sure how he arrived at this figure, but he said that Milchan was demanding a million dollars in exchange for giving Oliver the right to break his contract and take the project to another studio. This was tantamount to treason. "He's not an honest man!" Oliver fumed to me. "I can't do business with him anymore. He's not honest." These were strange words, considering the source, but I let it pass. Reportedly Oliver and Arnon had almost gotten into a fistfight in a meeting over this issue. I was not about to defend Arnon, or even suggest that he try to reach a compromise. It was hard to defend someone who had sold nuclear triggers to South Africa's white regime (although Milchan claimed they were devices for Orthodox Jews to cook pot roasts on the Sabbath!).

"I'm finished with him," Oliver announced. "I'm going to take the movie to another studio." This is in fact what happened, although Oliver claimed that he had to pay Arnon a million out of his own pocket to get out of the deal. The bad blood between them has lasted to this day.

While the dispute was going on, though, I decided to have a little fun with it. One morning, I wrote up a short treatment for a film about an Israeli arms dealer who makes shady deals all over the world, starts wars so he can profit from them, and then moves to Hollywood and becomes a respected movie producer. I based it on a profile of Arnon that I had read in a magazine. I gave the treatment to Oliver with a note saying, "Why don't you send this to Arnon and tell him it's your next put picture under your deal?"

Oliver told me he thought the treatment was "hilarious"—a rare compliment—but he never sent it to Arnon as far as I know. Much later, after *Nixon* had been released and I was getting bored, I expanded the treatment into a satirical script called "The Uzi Factor." Oliver read it and in his inimitable fashion told me it was junk and worse than a Rodney Dangerfield movie—a curious comment since he liked Dangerfield and had cast him in *NBK*. Oliver then proceeded to have about thirty copies of the script made, and sent them to thirty of his closest friends and associates in Hollywood with a note saying, "This will be my next film. I want Tom Cruise to play Uzi Falafel" (the lead character). He obviously intended for a copy of the script to get back to Arnon, which I'm sure it did. I wrote the script under the pseudonym of "Maurice Bishop," so that I would not be killed by Mossad hit men if and when Arnon found out about it.

I think most people realized that Oliver was joking, but Danny the Weasel took it seriously. He came up to me after seeing Oliver's letter and said, "I'm so happy for you" (which meant, I wish you were dead).

"Are you going to get an agent now?" he inquired, trying to figure out an angle for himself in the situation.

"I don't know," I replied innocently. "Do you think I should?"

Unfortunately, the film never got made, despite my best efforts. But the script is still available, if anyone wants to make it....

Oliver did not like to deal with responsible and reputable businessmen like Bob Daly and Terry Semel of Warner Brothers, regarding them as "suits" and "straight people." He preferred to deal with rogue operators like Milchan, who operated outside the rules and the law. Andy Vajna fit perfectly into this category. A Hungarian moneyman and wheeler-dealer who had been around the movie business for many years, Vajna was Oliver's kind of guy. After trashing his deal with Milchan, Vajna seemed like the next best thing to Oliver. His company, Cinergi, had a similar co-financing deal with Disney, and could provide overhead and development funds for Oliver's companies, Ixtlan and Illusion. Vajna put up the money for *Nixon,* grabbing a producer credit in the process and hoping to win respectability and even an Oscar (he won neither). In the end, he lost money not only on *Nixon,* but also on *Evita, The Scarlet Letter, Judge Dredd* and several other fiascoes. Vajna was investigated by the IRS for tax fraud, and Cinergi went out of business. But at least they made *Nixon. . . .*

Oliver's anger and suspicion ultimately got directed not only at Prouty and Milchan, but at me as well in the early stages of the project. I had written him a memo commenting on the first draft of the *Nixon* script. In it, I mentioned in passing that Clayton Townsend had said to me that he thought the script was a little long at 160 pages, and I agreed with him (a normal script is 120 pages, which equals two hours of screen time). For some reason, the reference to Clayton sent Oliver over the edge. He called up Clayton and screamed at him, reading him the riot act and apparently telling him that even speaking to me about the script was close to treason. Oliver, as some astute observers have noted, is quick to suspect conspiracies, real or imagined. He seemed to think that Clayton and I were somehow conspiring against him.

In fact, I barely had any contact with Clayton, and had no intention of conspiring with him. The matter had only come up because I had bumped into him at Remi, a restaurant near our office, where I was having dinner with Chris and Steve. Since Clayton was a longtime associate of Oliver's, I felt it only proper to introduce him to the writers of Oliver's next film. Clayton said he had read the script, but added, "Cut it down, guys." He later compared it to a telephone book.

After being reamed by Oliver, and denying everything, Clayton called me and screamed at me for about half an hour. At first, I did not even understand what the fuss was about, since the reference to Clayton had been only part of one sentence in a memo of two pages. Furthermore, I had said that I agreed with his opinion and did not criticize him in any way. But after a while, I realized that this made no difference. Clayton was profoundly insecure, and his whole career depended on staying in Oliver's good graces. As a dropout with limited skills, he was dependent on Oliver's whims for his livelihood. His doglike loyalty to Oliver had earned him rich rewards, and he made hundreds of thousands of dollars as a producer on Oliver's films. Anything that upset Oliver, no matter how trivial, was a very serious matter to Clayton.

I realized that this was Oliver's way of creating an atmosphere of fear and mistrust around him, which was the miasma in which he preferred to operate. Like the CIA's legendary counterspy James Angleton, he was constantly searching for moles and plots against him, and often found them, even when they did not exist. His diatribe had ensured that I would never talk to Clayton about any matter of substance, and vice versa. It was also his way of asserting his authority and undermining those around him. He had done the same thing to me with Danny the Weasel to create mistrust and conflict.

I concluded that in the future it would be best not to mention anyone else's name in a memo, and simply express my own opinions. I realized that Oliver was surrounded by yes-men like Clayton, Bob Marshall, and Steven Pines (as well as yes-women like Janet Yang), and I considered it my duty to be a voice of truth that would not otherwise be heard. While Oliver realized this and respected it, it also caused my position in his circle to gradually erode, as I told him one unpleasant truth too many, and as his tolerance for any form of independent opinion fell lower and lower.

Oliver even had a fit when he discovered that I had given the first draft of the *Nixon* script to Janet Yang without his knowledge. I had naively assumed that, as president of the company, she was entitled to read it.

But the full force of his fury hit me a little bit later, in November of 1994. By this time, we had already been through several drafts of the script, and my lawyer had been through several rounds of fruitless discussions with Pines and Marshall about a contract and a producing credit for me on *Nixon*. It became obvious that they were jerking him around, and that neither wanted any contract that would keep me there, since they also viewed me as a threat. Although I despised dealing with business matters and wanted to get out of the position I was in as Vice President for Business Affairs at Ixtlan, both Pines and Marshall felt threatened by me as long as I held that title. Like Clayton, they were parasites who lived off Oliver, and the presence of someone like me threatened to upset that cozy arrangement.

After weeks of getting nowhere, I finally asked Craig Emanuel to draw up a letter setting out my requests in writing, and to send it to Bob Marshall. I knew this would get back to Oliver, but I didn't care. In fact I wanted it to, since only he could overrule Marshall and resolve the matter. I had gone to work for Oliver without any written contract, or any lawyer representing me, because I wanted him to feel that I trusted him and that I was not coming to Hollywood for the money (which I wasn't).

Of course I knew by now about Oliver's obsession with money. This was accentuated by the fact that he was going through a divorce from his wife Elizabeth, which was going to be very costly. But it was not just the divorce that was on his mind. I had slowly come to realize that Hollywood was all about money and deals, and that Oliver, as a successful Hollywood director, had adopted its values and priorities with a vengeance. Yet I still had not realized the depth of his greed and his conviction that everyone was out to rob him. Lawyers were the chief weapon of the enemy, but I needed a written contract to protect me, and a lawyer to represent my interests.

Craig drafted a fairly standard legal letter, asking that I be given an employment contract for a period of two or three years, with appropriate compensation. He also asked that I be given a producer credit on *Nixon,* with "most favored nation" status with respect to other producers on the project. This phrase is as misleading in Hollywood as it is in Washington. Translated from the Hollywood meaning of the term into English, it meant that I should receive no less than Clayton or any other producer on *Nixon.* This seemed fair and reasonable to me, since I had conceived of and initiated the project, brought it to Oliver, found the writers and worked with them through six or seven drafts of the script (so far). In other words, I had done exactly what a creative producer is supposed to do in Hollywood, despite being shackled with the additional burdens of handling business affairs. I did not see how Oliver could reasonably object to this, but I knew enough to expect a volcanic reaction. I waited.

When Oliver saw the letter, he leapt into a black abyss of rage and paranoia. At the end of the day on a Friday, after a long week, he called me into his office, which was darkened. He sat behind his desk and intoned melodramatically, "This is going to be a tough meeting." At that point, I expected the worst. However, I just shrugged my shoulders and remained silent.

"I'm suspending you from work," he hissed. "This letter from your lawyer is outrageous. . . . I don't trust you anymore."

I tried to remain calm and reasonable.

"Oliver, first of all, I don't even know what this is all about . . . "

"I don't believe you," he yelled, before I could finish my sentence. I waited for a moment and then continued.

"As far as I know, he's just asking for the same thing that any other producer would get on a project—like Don and Jane, or Janet, or Clayton, or anyone else. . . . Anyway, it's a negotiation between two lawyers. If Bob Marshall thinks it's too much, he can come back with a counteroffer, and they can work it out. That's perfectly normal."

I looked at him with an expression of puzzled innocence.

"What's the big deal? All I'm saying is I want to work on this project, and I want to continue to work with you on other projects. That's what we agreed on all along. That's why I came here from Washington—to do a series of political films with you. I thought that's what you wanted to do."

"It is," admitted Oliver. "But this is the good Eric talking. You have to work your way up in this business. Now I've seen the other side of you. I can't trust you, and I can't let you stay here until this is resolved."

I shrugged again. At least I wasn't being fired. The whole thing seemed like a pathetic demonstration of power to me. Besides, I felt I had worked my way up in eight years on Capitol Hill—an experience at least as valuable as working in Hollywood. But there was no point in arguing.

"OK . . . If that's the way you want it. I think it's a waste of time. But I'll talk to Craig and tell him to get it resolved. I'm sure it will be done in a day or two."

"It better be," growled Oliver with menace.

"It will be," I said. "It's no big deal."

With that, we shook hands and I left.

In fact, it took two more weeks of intensive negotiations to get this stupid issue of my deal resolved. Over that weekend, I called Larry Kopeikin, an attorney at CAA whom I had worked with and come to like and trust. In a business full of sharks, Larry seemed to have survived with his integrity and honesty intact. I explained the situation, and I asked him if he would act as an intermediary between Craig and Bob Marshall to help get this resolved as quickly as possibly. Larry graciously agreed to help.

Meanwhile, I stayed home for the next two weeks, going to the movies, reading and relaxing. Chris and Steve could not believe that this had happened. I was their lifeline to Oliver, and they were aghast that I had been treated this way.

"Why don't you just fire your lawyer?" said Chris pragmatically. He had been around Hollywood for years and knew how it worked. The same thought had occurred to me as well, but I didn't want to fire Craig, particularly in the middle of this situation. I felt that Oliver would construe it as a sign of weakness.

Amazingly, Azita called me while I was under "suspension."

"Oliver needs you to draft a statement for a press conference for him," she said. "Something about saving the rain forests."

I was incredulous at his chutzpah, but agreed to do it anyway, partly as a goodwill gesture and partly to show him that I was indispensable. No one else in the office could do this kind of thing for him. Besides, it was for a good cause.

"Don't worry, you'll be back soon," Azita reassured me soothingly. "Oliver is just sending you to your room, like a kid."

She proved to be right. With Larry's help, we finally got a deal worked out. I would be "co-producer" of the film—less than a full "producer" credit but acceptable under the circumstances. I would get a fee that, while more than my normal salary, was much less than other producers got on this and other films. At the same time, I would be relieved of my duties as VP for Business Affairs. Though Oliver may have seen this as punishment, to me it was a relief. It also made Pines and Marshall happy. It was a win–win situation.

But the tension and uncertainty of the whole ordeal had been draining. Never again would I be foolish enough to trust Oliver as I had before. And the feeling was probably mutual. The honeymoon was over. . . .

In retrospect, I don't know why I wasted so much time and energy worrying about trying to get a "producer" credit from Oliver instead of a "co-producer" credit. It was inevitable that it would turn into one of his sick and twisted power games, and that he would withhold it simply because I wanted it. In the real world, nobody knows or cares about the difference between the two, and in fact there is no real difference in most cases. It's just a question of who has more power in Hollywood and can grab the best credit for himself (or for his wife, mistress, agent or hairdresser). There are so many different kinds of producer credits on films now that they have become almost meaningless.

Some people who did little or nothing on *Nixon,* like Danny the Weasel, whose main task was bringing agents and Hollywood types to visit the set, got the same credits as people who did all the work. And Oliver, who did almost no actual writing, grabbed a writing credit for himself and got an Oscar nomination for it! As I see it now, being Oliver Stone's co-producer is like being his co-pilot. The pilot is in charge of flying the plane, but it's good to have the co-pilot there with him—especially when the pilot is drunk or stoned out of his mind....

The Martin Luther King Project and *JFK*, Part 2

Oliver liked to juggle several projects at the same time. While working on one film, he would already be planning ahead for the next one, or maybe the one after that. While he often seemed oblivious to the official Ixtlan projects listed on our development slate, he had his own mental list of projects that he kept in his "back pocket" (to use his own phrase). I think he felt insecure if he didn't know what was coming next. Oliver was addicted to his work. As he said to me one time, "I have to work hard and play hard." This was also his excuse for burning the candle at both ends—partying all night and then getting up early to direct a movie or work on a script.

One of the projects that he had kept in the back pockets of his mind for a long time was the idea of a film on Martin Luther King. He had told me over our initial dinner at his home that he wanted to do films on Hitler, Stalin, Mao and Martin Luther King. I did not see what King had in common with the others, but I liked the idea of doing a film about him. It could be an uplifting, inspiring movie like *Gandhi,* with a message of nonviolence and racial harmony. That was the kind of movie I wanted to make with Oliver.

When I got to Ixtlan, I discovered that while a Martin Luther King project was listed on the development sheet, there was no script, no writer attached and nothing was happening with the project. I gave Oliver a "treatment" on the assassination of Dr. King that I had acquired in Washington. This had come to me in a curious way. After I had told a number of my friends on the Hill that I was leaving Washington and going to work for Oliver Stone in Hollywood, John Kerry's personal secretary and executive assistant, Tricia Ferrone, told me that she knew some people who were working on an investigation of the King assassination, and asked if I would be interested in meeting them. This seemed like a logical connection to make, given the fact that Oliver had just come out with *JFK*. I took her up on the offer, and she put me in touch with a House staffer who I will call "Dave." Dave worked for a midwestern member of Congress, but investigating the King assassination was something he did in his spare time. I talked with him and agreed to meet him and his "partner" at a cafe near Dupont Circle in Washington, away from the Hill.

Dave's partner turned out to be a strange character in a white suit, with a southern drawl and mysterious manner, who appeared to have stepped out of Jim Garrison's New Orleans. There was something about him that I did not like. The two of them claimed to be working with former D.C. Representative Walter Fauntroy on a book about the King assassination. Fauntroy had been the District's nonvoting representative in Congress for many years, until he foolishly gave up his seat to run for mayor, which he lost in a landslide.

Fauntroy had been a member of the House Select Committee on Assassinations in the late 1970s, and had chaired the subcommittee that investigated the shooting of Dr. King. The committee ultimately found that there was the "likelihood" of a conspiracy in the King killing, which it said involved a group of racist St. Louis businessmen. Then, without pursuing the matter further, the committee closed shop and sealed all of its files for the next fifty years.

Unlike the JFK files, the King files had never been unsealed by Congress. When asked why at a press conference introducing the JFK bill, Fauntroy replied succinctly, "Because no one's made a movie about it." This seemed like a royal cop-out to me, but at the same time, it was the truth. It seemed, though, that Fauntroy had personally taken some of the hottest King files home with him and kept them as his personal property, in violation of the committee's vote to seal them. It was these files that Dave and his friend were using as the basis of their investigation and their proposed book.

While I was wary of getting involved with these people, I thought this might be something that would interest Oliver. I agreed to take a summary of their findings to him, in strict confidence, and see if he would be interested in purchasing the movie rights. Their scenario involved a wild mix of military intelligence agents, the Mafia, the Green Berets, the Ku Klux Klan and other elements combining in a plot to assassinate Dr. King. The whole thing was planned by the Pentagon and the CIA, and sanctioned by no less than President Johnson. I gave it to Oliver, and he loved it.

Oliver decided that this would become the basis for our Martin Luther King movie. It would show how King had been assassinated by a conspiracy, not by white racists, but because of his opposition to the war in Vietnam. He would make it right after *Nixon*.

He also decided that the perfect writers to hire for this project were ... Chris and Steve. By the end of 1994, most of their work on *Nixon* was done, and Oliver was working on the script himself. He called me in New York, where I was visiting my parents, and said he wanted Steve and Chris to write the King film. I was surprised, but readily agreed that this was a good idea. I found it very easy and pleasant to work with them, and we had already been trying to come up with ideas for a follow-up project that might appeal to Oliver. Now we had one.

Oliver also had another pet project in mind. This was a sequel of sorts to *JFK*. It might be hard to believe that Oliver would even consider making a sequel to *JFK* after all the controversy of the first one, but he was still obsessed with the subject. Besides, this one would be different. It would be a "down and dirty" account of the events in Dallas, set in bars, back alleys and seedy motels. It would show the assassination from the ground level. I saw it as a black-and-white film noir, following up on the end of Garrison's speech in *JFK* when he says, "Let's speculate what really happened that day, shall we?" To me, Stone's reconstruction of the assassination plot in Dealey Plaza on November 22 was one of the most exciting parts of the movie. I found it very believable.

This film would be based on the book *Oswald Talked* by Ray and Mary LaFontaine, husband and wife researchers and investigative reporters. The LaFontaines lived in Dallas, and were a study in contrasts. Ray was of Puerto Rican birth and had a dry, droll sense of humor, as well as being a terrific writer. Mary had long, flaming red hair, reflecting her Irish ancestry, and had a sharp wit and even sharper skills as an investigator. The LaFontaines had done some groundbreaking research on the JFK assassination, which made them very controversial. Conspiracy theorists mistrusted them, and "lone nutters" didn't like them either. That meant they were probably right.

Mary LaFontaine had uncovered Dallas police files from November 1963, released shortly after Oliver's film hit the theaters. With these, she was able to identify the legendary "three tramps" in Dealey Plaza who were depicted in *JFK*. These three men had been hiding in a railway car in a train yard near the Plaza. They had been arrested, and photographs of them being marched through Dealey Plaza by Dallas police officers had been studied for years by JFK researchers. Many believed that the "three tramps" were among the real assassins of JFK. They had been variously "identified" as Howard Hunt, Frank Sturgis and Charles Harrelson (a Texas hit man and father of actor Woody Harrelson), among others.

Mary found Dallas police records of the arrest, indicating that the men's names were Harold Doyle, John Forrester Gedney and Gus W. Abrams. Further checking revealed that the names were genuine and that the men were in fact tramps. This finding challenged one of the sacred cows of the JFK buffs, and did not endear the LaFontaines to that group of people.

But she also found records of a "fourth tramp" who had been arrested that day. His name was John Elrod. To make matters more interesting, Elrod had apparently been held in a cell in the Dallas jail with none other than Lee Harvey Oswald. The LaFontaines managed to track down Elrod on an obscure island in the Mississippi River north of Memphis. He confirmed that he had been incarcerated with Oswald.

Elrod's tale led the LaFontaines into an investigation with many twists and turns. It ended up with a Cuban exile group called DRE (Directorio Revolucionario Estudiantil, or Student Revolutionary Directorate), a fanatical group of right wing anti-Castro extremists who had been involved with Oswald in the months leading up to the assassination. The DRE had also been supported by the CIA. The LaFontaines came to the conclusion that the DRE had not only framed Oswald, but had been heavily involved in the assassination itself. I had discussed these findings with General Escalante in Cuba, who had confirmed much of their information. I had further discussions about it with Escalante at a conference in Rio de Janeiro in August 1995. A fuller picture of the assassination plot began to emerge.

This was fascinating stuff. Unfortunately, the sequel to *JFK* never got made, despite four excellent drafts of a script by the LaFontaines. They met with Escalante in the Bahamas at the end of 1995. Unfortunately I couldn't go because *Nixon* was opening that week. But we never got to follow up with Escalante until much later. He was removed from his position sometime in the spring of 1996, shortly after an incident in which a small plane piloted by Cuban exiles invaded Cuba's airspace and was shot down. Two men on the plane were killed. This caused a crisis in U.S.–Cuban relations, which were already poor. It also led to a crackdown by hard-liners in Cuba. "Liberals" like Escalante, who had been involved in extensive meetings with Americans, were purged from their jobs. I was told that Escalante was "en casa"— literally "at home," but probably meaning under house arrest. The order had apparently come from Raul Castro, with support from his brother Fidel. I was unable to make any further contact with Escalante, despite repeated attempts.

In my opinion, the Cuban government made a big mistake. Researchers were on the verge of cracking the JFK case. If the contacts and exchanges of information between U.S. and Cuban researchers could have continued, I believe the entire mystery would have been solved by now. Unfortunately, there are still unanswered questions that need to be pursued. We may never know the full truth, but we have moved closer to it. We can now put together a plausible scenario of what really happened in Dallas—one that answers many of the questions and contradictions that have plagued the case for over three decades. And I can't forget that all of this was started by Oliver's film. For that alone he deserves much more gratitude than he has received. I think history will judge him more kindly.

Let me make one final point about the JFK assassination. People often say that this is a "cold case," if not a closed case. In reality, it is not a cold case at all. As a result of the JFK bill, literally millions of new documents have been released. Many new leads have opened up. Many of the people who were involved at the time are still alive. (If Oswald had lived, he would only be in his early sixties today.) And in 2001, one of the bombers of a Birmingham church—a heinous racist act that killed four young black girls—was convicted of murder and sent to prison. Another was tried and convicted in 2002. That bombing occurred in September 1963—*before* the murder of John F. Kennedy. It is never too late to hear the truth, or to apply justice.

Researching *Nixon*

Contrary to popular belief, making a movie is not all fun and games. There is also Serious Research to be done—especially on a film like *Nixon*. This was one of my main areas of responsibility, and Oliver wanted to get things right (and did not want to repeat the experience of getting clobbered with criticism as with *JFK*).

One of Oliver's best attributes as a filmmaker was that he liked to do firsthand research and really dig into the material before he started filming. Part of the process was to meet with as many people with firsthand knowledge as possible. We started by meeting with Alexander Butterfield, a key figure in the Watergate scandal who had revealed the existence of Nixon's taping system in testimony before Congress. This led to the eventual exposure of the Watergate tapes, which were damning to Nixon's case. Butterfield, who lived near San Diego and was in his late seventies, had been introduced to us by Ian Masters, a jovial and politically savvy Australian expatriate who hosted a political talk show on KPFK radio in Los Angeles.

Butterfield's manner of speaking was deliberate and careful, but his mind was still sharp. He told us he was writing his own book on Watergate, but would be glad to help us with the film. Many people do not know that Butterfield sat literally right outside the Oval Office during much of Nixon's term, handling the flow of paper to the president. He had an encyclopedic knowledge of the Nixon White House, as well as a good sense of Nixon the man. He would often speak of Nixon in the present tense, saying "Nixon does this" or "Nixon wouldn't do that." It was clear that Richard Nixon was still a living, breathing presence to Butterfield, although he had died in April 1994, a few months after we began the project.

Oliver decided to hire Butterfield as a consultant to make sure that we got all the details right on how the Oval Office should look, who would have done what, and generally how the place operated. He stayed on the set during most of the filming and was a valuable adviser. He also contributed an essay to a book about the film, which I edited.

We had an even greater stroke of luck in connecting with another, even more important Watergate figure. This was John

Dean. George Linardos, one of the creative executives at Ixtlan, had mentioned to me that he knew someone who played golf with Dean, and asked if I would be interested in meeting with him. I immediately said yes, and George set up a meeting with Dean, who lived in Beverly Hills.

To me, meeting John Dean was like meeting one of the Beatles or the Rolling Stones. Dean was one of my idols from my college days. I had spent the entire summer of 1973 glued to the TV set, watching the Watergate hearings. It was spellbinding to watch this young man, then in his early thirties, who had been counsel to the president, testifying before the Watergate committee in such a cool and unflappable manner. He obviously had a brilliant mind and an incredible memory for detail. He was the only member of Nixon's inner circle who had the guts to take him on and to tell the truth to the country about what had happened inside the Nixon White House. Although the Nixon people attacked him viciously, Dean had been vindicated when the Watergate tapes were finally released by order of the Supreme Court. Everything he had said turned out to be true. His testimony was the beginning of the end for Nixon.

Oliver and I met with Dean in Oliver's office. After about an hour, Oliver excused himself to do other things, but I kept Dean there for another two hours, asking him about one aspect of Watergate after another. I was enthralled by the discussion, and I recommended to Oliver later that we also hire Dean as a consultant. I thought that he would bring credibility to the project, and even if we only talked with him a few times it would be worth it. As it turned out, we did much more. John Dean was an absolute godsend to the *Nixon* film, and a genuine pleasure to work with. He consulted on every aspect of the script, making sure that it was strictly accurate. Along with Steve Rivele, he also did a great deal of annotation of the script, which we published in our book to show that the film was accurate, along with the sources for our information. He even wrote a few (uncredited) scenes for the film. In the process, he also became a friend.

Part of John's motivation for helping us was to make sure that we did not get caught up in an unsubstantiated conspiracy theory. He was involved in a lawsuit against the authors of a book called *Silent Coup,* which alleged that the real mastermind of Watergate had been Dean himself, and that his motivation was to cover up the fact that his wife had been involved with members of a call girl ring based out of the Democratic headquarters in the Watergate building (!). This was obviously an absurd theory, but it had gained credence in right wing circles as a way of absolving Nixon. G. Gordon Liddy, a Watergate burglar and convicted felon turned radio talk show host (only in America!), had spread this theory incessantly on his nationally syndicated show. Liddy had developed an intense and irrational hatred of John Dean and his wife Maureen, and used the book as a club to bludgeon them with. Liddy was also a defendant in the lawsuit.

Chris and Steve and I had looked at *Silent Coup* and found it to be unreadable and incomprehensible. However, its conspiracy theory was initially appealing to Oliver, as one might expect — particularly with its mix of sex, scandal and politics. To his credit, though, Oliver changed his mind after talking with Dean and also with Howard Hunt and Rolando Martinez, both of whom had been involved in the break-in and had firsthand knowledge of the events. We eliminated any references to the *Silent Coup* scenario from the script and the book. I have often thought in retrospect that the movie might have done better at the box office if we *had* included some sex and call girls along with a new conspiracy theory. But it wouldn't have been the truth.

In the process of making *Nixon,* I also got to know "Mo" Dean, John's wife. I had admired her quiet dignity during the Watergate hearings. She was a noticeable presence, sitting in the front row of the hearings during every session while her husband testified. She was a beautiful woman, with her blonde, demurely pulled back hair, and could not help but attract attention. When I finally met her, I found that she looked almost unchanged, although two decades had passed. I also discovered that she was a highly intelligent person and shrewd political analyst. Anyone who has ever met this decent, dignified, elegant woman would understand how preposterous it would be to think that she could have been associated in any way with a call girl ring. These charges had hurt her deeply because, of course, there are always plenty of people who want to believe the worst about a prominent person. To his credit, John Dean felt strongly that his wife had stood behind him during Watergate, and he would stand behind her during this ordeal. After several grueling years of legal battle, the case was ultimately settled on terms favorable to the Deans.

Early on, I suggested to Oliver that we do a "book of the film," to publish the full screenplay with annotation, bibliography, source notes and other material to show that it was factually based. I naively thought that this might help head off criticism of the film by the Washington media elite. There had been a similar book done on *JFK,* but it didn't come out until six months after the film was released. I wanted the Nixon book to come out simultaneously with the film to be available in our defense.

This was easier said than done. I managed to convince Oliver of the idea, but had a harder time with Hyperion, the publishing arm of Disney. They finally went along with it, but put up only

$25,000 as an advance, all of which went to pay contributors of essays to the book. I wanted to ask people with interesting perspectives on Nixon to contribute original essays, like John Dean, Howard Hunt, Frank Mankiewicz, Paul Nitze, Stanley Kutler, Daniel Schorr and others. This approach worked out well. However, most "reviewers" of the film simply dismissed the book and its elaborate footnotes, which were done largely by Steve Rivele and John Dean, with some assistance from Chris Wilkinson and me. We also included actual Nixon documents and transcripts of his tapes, which were far more damning than anything we could have made up for the movie!

In fact, when further tapes were released after the film, we were vindicated on several counts. For example, Nixon intimates claimed that he never drank while on duty as president. Many of the tapes clearly reveal Nixon speaking in a slurred, drunken voice, and often making anti-Semitic remarks. The same righteous defenders claimed that Nixon would never, never have used the word "cocksucker." In fact, this word is sprinkled throughout his tapes in his own voice. (Anthony Hopkins loved to imitate Nixon on the set by hunching his shoulders and muttering "cocksucker!")

It was surprising to me that Bob Miller, the head of Hyperion Press, was so reluctant to do the Nixon book. Hyperion after all is an arm of the Disney empire and this was a perfect opportunity for corporate synergy. He told me that he'd had bad experiences with other filmmakers such as Quentin Tarantino and Spike Lee, who did not meet deadlines and demanded last minute changes in cover art and other details, which made it very difficult to get the books out in time for the release of the films. He also told me that he'd had an unbelievably bad experience on a previous project with Danny "the Weasel" Halsted. Evidently the Weasel, while still an executive at Hollywood Pictures, had come to him at the last minute and persuaded him to do a book of the film *Encino Man*. Miller was talked into it and the book was rushed into print. As the publisher, Miller later looked into the sales figures and was astonished to learn that the *Encino Man* book had sold only two copies—in the entire country! He told me this was unheard of and had never happened before. (He may have been exaggerating, but that's what he told me....) I assured Bob that Danny the Weasel would have absolutely nothing to do with the Nixon book, and that as a former Senate aide I was used to working under time pressure and meeting deadlines. Miller graciously agreed to publish the book.

In the course of researching the film, Oliver and I also spoke by phone with the late John Ehrlichman, Nixon's former domestic adviser. Since leaving the White House and going to jail, Ehrlichman had undergone several changes of identity. He moved to Santa Fe, grew a beard and started writing novels. Later, he moved to Atlanta and became a corporate businessman. It was there that I reached him by telephone.

Ehrlichman was cautiously friendly when I first spoke with him. He said that he expected the film to be an "ax job," and seemed reassured when I told him that we envisioned it more like a Greek tragedy or a Shakespearean drama.

"Good," he said emphatically. "That's exactly the right approach."

He agreed to have a conference call with Oliver and me to follow up, which we did. He told us stories about Nixon and the good old days. He said that Nixon could not hold his liquor, and that Ehrlichman had threatened to resign from his reelection campaign unless Nixon stopped drinking. He also told us an interesting story relating to the "Bay of Pigs thing." He confirmed that Nixon had an obsession with the Bay of Pigs, and had repeatedly ordered him to get the full file on the subject from Richard Helms at the CIA. Helms refused to give it to him. This account is confirmed in Nixon's own memoirs.

Ehrlichman had written an interesting novel called *The Company*, based on the Nixon White House. It revolved around a CIA director based on Helms, and a president named Richard Monckton, who were blackmailing each other over a report relating to the Bay of Pigs debacle. (Ehrlichman's private nickname for Nixon had been "The Mad Monk.") He told me that while he was in prison, investigators from the Office of Naval Intelligence had come to see him, demanding to know where this "report" was. He told them that the book was fiction, and that there was no such report. The investigators then told him that there was such a report, and they were trying to find it. Ehrlichman said he couldn't help them.

In Richard Nixon's own memoirs, *RN*, he wrote the following about the overthrow of South Vietnam president Ngo Dinh Diem in 1963 and the Bay of Pigs invasion (p. 515): "Our efforts to document the role of the Kennedy administration in the Diem assassination and the Bay of Pigs did not prove easy. The CIA protects itself, even from Presidents. Helms refused to give Ehrlichman the agency's internal reports on either subject. At one point he told Ehrlichman on the phone that even he did not have a copy of one of the key Bay of Pigs reports. He also expressed concern about all the people, and specifically Howard Hunt, who he said would like to run around in the agency's 'soiled linen.' Helms finally brought me several of the items after I had requested them from him personally. . . . When Ehrlichman read the materials Helms had delivered, however, he found that several of the reports, including the one on the Bay of Pigs, were still incomplete. The CIA was closed like a safe, and we could find no one who would give us the combination to open it."

In her book *ZR Rifle: The Plot to Kill Kennedy and Castro*, Claudia Furiati wrote this: "Let's get to the final conclusions. The Cuban State Security Department has concluded that those responsible for Kennedy's assassination are [the CIA's] David Phillips, as the promoter of ZR Rifle; and Santos Trafficante, as the coordinator of the Mafia participation in the operation. And those who fired the shots were Cubans from the 'elite troops' in exile. The day of the assassination they were deployed in groups, together or separate, forming a triangle of fire.... And who was the ultimate author of the entire scheme? Richard Helms, the brain of the CIA.... But Helms was invisible, hidden behind four walls." Those are Cuba's conclusions.

General Fabian Escalante told me the same thing when I met with him in Havana, based on his extensive research into secret Cuban intelligence files. Helms, of course, has repeatedly denied any involvement. He was, however, convicted of lying to Congress under oath in a separate matter in the 1970s.

Later, Ehrlichman's seeming friendliness turned to hostility. He had apparently gotten hold of a leaked copy of the *Nixon* script, and was upset by its treatment of him. He threatened to sue us if we didn't make changes. I asked him what specifically he was referring to, and he refused to tell me. I said that if he could tell us what part he had a problem with, we could work with him and try to fix it if it was inaccurate. He still refused to give me any specifics.

I immediately reported the threat to Oliver, and also wrote him a memo about it. Oliver, of course, freaked out as he did at any threat of a lawsuit. He refused to talk to Ehrlichman, but he made changes in the script that made Ehrlichman more of a "moral voice" in the White House. I thought this was ludicrous at the time, but in retrospect I can understand why Oliver did it.

It turned out that Clayton Townsend had turned in a report to the company insuring the film the day after the incident, and did not mention the threat from Ehrlichman. The "errors and omissions" insurance was issued, but Bob Marshall realized that we would not be covered if Ehrlichman sued us, since Clayton had failed to disclose the threat in a timely fashion. Clayton of course tried to blame me, but since I had written a full memo to Oliver the day that it happened, he did not succeed in passing the buck. I began to understand, though, why Don Murphy referred to Clayton as "Satan."

In the end, Ehrlichman didn't sue us. In fact, he wrote a piece in *Newsweek* praising the film, after he saw how he was depicted. He was pleased by the way J. T. Walsh, a superb actor who inhabited his characters with nuance and realism, had played him in the movie. Sadly, J. T. passed away not long after making *Nixon*. He was not only a gifted actor but a humble and decent person. I was flabbergasted when, after the film was released, J. T. asked me to sign a copy of the Nixon book for him. I was too embarrassed to do so. I felt that I should be asking him for *his* autograph instead!

Our research also included a field trip to the Nixon library and birthplace in Yorba Linda, about an hour's drive from downtown Los Angeles. The Nixon library is an Orwellian place that tries hard to rewrite history in his favor. It was aptly and humorously described by historian Stanley Kutler in an essay written for our Nixon book. As Kutler wrote, "The film that museum visitors view at the start of the tour casually dismisses Watergate in about one minute. That tragic, even pathetic, scene of Nixon leaving the White House grounds on a helicopter is transformed into a triumphal exit. Hollywood never did it better. . . . His lies are the heart of his history. Fittingly, Nixon enshrined that legacy in his own memorial."

Artifacts such as a replica of the Woodstock typewriter used by Alger Hiss and a pumpkin like that used by Whittaker Chambers to hide secret documents are included in the museum. Because we had arrived unannounced, the museum staff did not know at first who we were. But by the time we got to the end of the tour of Nixon's boyhood home—with Oliver wisecracking the whole way, making loud comments like "This is complete bullshit"—I think the tour guide had figured it out.

A more ambitious research trip was our excursion to Washington, D.C., to meet with friends, foes and observers of Richard Nixon. I was put in charge of organizing it and rounding up as many people to meet with as we could pack into two days. Oliver and I were originally going to go with Anthony Hopkins, but at the last minute James Woods invited himself along as well, and "Jimmy" was a delightful addition. Some production people also came along to scout locations.

Woods is a highly intelligent graduate of MIT, an independent thinker, a great storyteller and joker, and all-around good guy. His only weakness may be for young women, which he would be the first to admit. He talked Oliver into giving him the part of H. R. Haldeman—the opposite of his own personality—a role that Oliver had planned to offer to Ed Harris (who ended up playing E. Howard Hunt instead). Oliver had planned to go with only Hopkins and me, but "Jimmy" had invited himself along. Woods was about Oliver's age and had made *Salvador* with him in the mid-1980s. They'd since had a falling out when Woods was not given a part in *JFK*, but had made up later.

One big advantage of having Jimmy around was that he was unafraid to talk back to Oliver and regarded him as a peer, not a god (the same was true of Hopkins). Together, they kept Oliver from getting too out of line (most of the time). Other actors sometimes resented Woods for "stealing" scenes, but this usually meant that he made them better. For example, there is a scene in *Nixon* in which Haldeman and Ehrlichman come walking out of the Oval Office after a particularly grim meeting. In the hallway, Woods turns to Walsh playing Ehrlichman and says, unscripted, "You do know we're next, don't you?" That said it all.

In a whirlwind of forty-eight hours in Washington, we managed to meet and talk with Lee Hamilton, John Kerry, Daniel Schorr, Ron Ziegler, Stephen Hess, John Sears, Elliott Richardson, Len Garment, Robert McNamara and Paul Nitze. We also had a private tour of the White House and met with Clinton chief of staff Leon Panetta, who had been fired by Nixon. We saw George Stephanopoulos briefly. Unfortunately President Clinton was away for the day, but Oliver came back another time and met with him separately, as did Anthony Hopkins.

In the White House, we ran into John Deutch, then head of the CIA. Needless to say, Oliver regarded the CIA as his archenemy (and vice versa). Oliver told him to "keep opening up those files." Ironically, Deutch was later found guilty of taking unauthorized files from the CIA to his home. He was pardoned by President Clinton. On a tour of the Senate, John Kerry introduced us to Senator Phil Gramm and Fred Thompson, a senator who appropriately had been both a minority counsel to the Senate Watergate Committee and a Hollywood actor. He later came to a premiere of the film at the Kennedy Center when it was released. After the premiere, I saw a young reporter rush up to Thompson (who is a Republican) and ask him what he thought of the film. Thompson, who had obviously become a politician again, thought for a minute and then said, "Interesting . . . "—probably the most noncommittal comment he could make. He rushed off before she could ask any more questions.

The Washington trip with Oliver has to rank among the strangest experiences of my life. The positive side was that I got to know two very fine people—Anthony Hopkins and James Woods. Both are not only great actors but great human beings. Tony Hopkins is a delightful, unpretentious man who has never forgotten where he came from (a small coal-mining town in Wales). He has won an Oscar, been knighted by Queen Elizabeth and played every major Shakespearean role on the London stage, but you would never know it by talking to him. He likes to joke around and is a hilarious mimic. Hopkins could do anyone from Mick Jagger to the Queen Mother. His impression of Oliver was uncanny and had me on the floor laughing.

We picked up some interesting background material for the movie from the meetings with former Nixon press secretary Ron Ziegler, journalist Dan Schorr and others. One of the most surreal encounters I've ever witnessed was the meeting between Oliver and Robert McNamara. Hopkins, Woods and I were also present but mostly listened. As Woods said later, it was a bit surreal to be sitting in the same room with both Robert McNamara and Oliver Stone! McNamara of course had been secretary of defense for both JFK and LBJ while Oliver had served in Vietnam. His book *In Retrospect* had just been finished and was about to be published, so he showed it to us and discussed it. The book, subtitled "The Tragedy and Lessons of Vietnam," was McNamara's famous and controversial reconsideration of the war as a historic mistake.

The book was written in part due to the urging and support of my father (then head of the Carnegie Corporation of New York), whom McNamara graciously thanked in the acknowledgments. Despite the criticisms of some, the book contains many valid and interesting points. McNamara, who agreed to see Oliver only because of his friendship and respect for my father, actually agreed with Oliver's thesis in *JFK* that Kennedy would never have gotten the United States into the Vietnam War. This is amply documented in the book. Though he disagreed with some of the details in the film that were based on John Newman's *JFK and Vietnam,* he did agree that Kennedy would have pulled out after the 1964 election.

It is a little-known fact that during JFK's three years in office, fewer than 100 Americans died in Vietnam. During the presidencies of Johnson and Nixon, more than 58,000 Americans were killed in Vietnam. Those are the names on the Wall in Washington. The numbers speak for themselves. It was actually Eisenhower who first got America into Vietnam. When JFK became president, there were 15,000 U.S. noncombat troops in Vietnam, which he planned to pull out after the 1964 election. In fact, he removed the first 1000 just before he was killed. Of course, Nixon loved to blame Kennedy for the war, and even had Howard Hunt making up fake cables in the White House to "prove" this. I hoped that McNamara would give us a copy of the book, but at the end of the conversation he put it back in his bag. I guess he thought we could buy it for ourselves if we were that interested.

We also had an interesting conversation with the late Elliot Richardson, Nixon's former attorney general, who was sacked during the "Saturday Night Massacre" after refusing to fire Archibald Cox, the special prosecutor investigating the Watergate case. Richardson was a senior partner with a law firm called Millbank, Tweed—which Oliver found very funny. Richardson's manner of speaking was Boston Brahmin to the extreme, but his observations on Nixon were quite insightful.

Richardson was very nice to us and revealed that he had been a close friend of actor Montgomery Clift. This seemed incongruous to say the least, since Richardson epitomized the WASP Eastern establishment, whereas Clift was more like James Dean than John Dean, but it seemed to make him feel a bond with us raffish Hollywood types. He shared some helpful insights into Nixon that we used in the movie. At one point he said of Nixon, "he had the defects of his qualities." Oliver liked this line, but gave it to Kissinger in the movie. (Richardson was shown only in news clips and was not portrayed by an actor in the film.) We also tried to see Henry Kissinger but he refused, although he later met with actor Paul Sorvino, who played him brilliantly in the film. He did a better Kissinger than Kissinger himself!

I found former press secretary Ron Ziegler interesting although a bit strange. He clearly was very close to Nixon, particularly during the final days. He said he was planning to write a book about the experience and I hope he does. He seemed to be haunted by his days in the Nixon administration. Len Garment, Nixon's former lawyer, was also at a luncheon with us at the Brookings Institution. (We had so many people to see that we sometimes had lunch twice in one day.) Garment almost drove us crazy with his constant interruptions. He called himself a "manic-digressive," which is an accurate description. At one point, he took great offense at a reference Oliver made to Garment's former wife, who had committed suicide. Oliver can be extremely insensitive, but I think this was more of a misunderstanding than a calculated offense. It was cleared up in correspondence between them. In fact, Garment later wrote to Oliver that he had seen the movie again on video and actually liked it!

The lunch with Paul Nitze was also helpful and entertaining. Oliver was obsessed with Nitze and believed he was the father of the Cold War and hence of all evil. He was dying to meet him though, and I was able to arrange this through some connections. Nitze was a distinguished, silver-haired gentleman in his eighties who had served in and out of government since World War II. The definitive biography of Nitze by Strobe Talbott is appropriately entitled *The Master of the Game.* Oliver gave Jimmy Woods strict instructions in advance not to interrupt him or even speak while he was talking to Nitze. When the moment arrived, however, Oliver became tongue-tied and could barely get a sentence out. He finally turned to Woods and said, "Jimmy, did you have any questions for Mr. Nitze?" Jimmy was rarely at a loss for words.

It was also interesting to me that while the waiters at the Metropolitan Club were unfazed by the presence of Nitze, Bud MacFarlane and other political luminaries, they were starstruck by the presence of Oliver, Hopkins and Woods. As we left the restaurant, they asked all of us to sign a menu for them—even me. I'm sure they had no idea who I was, but they knew I was from Hollywood!

At yet another lunch, John Sears made an interesting comment to me. We met with him, Ziegler, Garment and Hess (a former Nixon aide) at the Brookings Institution (which Nixon had once ordered to be firebombed! No one missed the irony of this). Sears had worked in the Nixon White House, and then later as Reagan's campaign chief in 1980, before being replaced by William Casey, who became the head of the CIA under President Reagan.

I asked Sears if he believed that there had been an "October Surprise" scheme in 1980, whereby the Reagan campaign made a deal with Ayatollah Khomeini's Iranian regime to hold the American hostages until after the election in order to defeat Jimmy Carter. Sears said, "I wouldn't be surprised if it happened.... I wouldn't put anything past Bill Casey. It's just the kind of thing he would do."

In light of our luncheon that day, it is interesting to note that Len Garment, who was White House counsel after John Dean was fired, has recently written a book charging that John Sears was "Deep Throat," the mysterious figure who fed information to Bob Woodward during the Watergate unraveling. Sears has denied this, as has Woodward. When we flew Sears out to Los Angeles for a week to act as a consultant on the film, he told me that he knew who Deep Throat was. Of course, he wouldn't tell me the man's name, but he said that he was going to write a book or an article that would reveal it. So far he hasn't done that.

Personally, I don't believe that Sears was Deep Throat. In Garment's book *In Search of Deep Throat,* he described our lunch at Brookings, and the fact that Sears had been a consultant on our film. He concluded that "Sears had shaped the movie much as he had shaped the reporting of Woodward and Bernstein." This is a laughable assertion. While I respect Sears's intellect and found him likable, he had a negligible effect on the film. Perhaps his most important contribution was to appear in a cameo role in one scene. He did contribute an insightful essay to our book entitled "Richard Nixon: The Loner," for which I am most grateful. But he certainly did not shape our movie. If any one consultant had an important influence on the film, it was John Dean, not John Sears.

Oliver's fascination with Paul Nitze was related to another of his pet projects—the "Afghanistan Project." This was to be a film based on Oliver's belief that the CIA had actually induced or tricked the Soviets into invading Afghanistan, and that the war was actually the fault of the United States, not the Soviet Union. He believed that the CIA's "Team B"—a group of hard-line cold warriors assembled by George Bush while he was CIA director in 1976 and 1977—had drawn up this secret plan. Nitze, as a member of Team B, was thus personally responsible for the Afghan War.

The flaw in this theory is that there is no evidence for it. The Soviets did not invade Afghanistan until the end of 1979, by which time Jimmy Carter was president. George Bush and Team B had long since been purged from the CIA, and Nitze was out of government. Furthermore, Mikhail Gorbachev has written in his memoirs that the decision to invade Afghanistan was made by a small group consisting of Soviet leader Leonid Brezhnev and a few other top Soviet leaders. Even Gorbachev, who was a member of the Politburo himself, was not told about the decision until after the fact. Paul Nitze was not included in this decision.

Yet this did not stop Oliver from believing in his theory, and commissioning several drafts of a script based on it. The movie, of course, met the same fate as so many of his pet projects—it never got made.

This trip to Washington was exhilarating, but it was also exhausting. I ended up with a migraine headache that kept me in bed for an entire day. And we hadn't even started shooting the film yet! The worst was yet to come.

I had to make one more trip to Washington before we started filming. This was to meet with Alexander Haig, who had been Nixon's chief of staff during the "final days," and later became Reagan's secretary of state. He was famous for having charged into the White House press room after Reagan was shot and breathlessly announcing, "I'm in control here!"—which only made him seem out of control.

I was originally supposed to go with Powers Boothe, the actor who would be playing Haig in the film. But at the last minute, Boothe had to have an emergency root canal and couldn't go. Oliver insisted that I go by myself; Boothe would take part in the meeting by telephone. This seemed like a complete waste of time to me, since Boothe could have talked to Haig on the phone without me being there in person. But Oliver had made up his mind, so I had no choice.

I found Haig to be just as strange a character as many others have attested. He told me that he had gotten hold of a bootleg copy of our script, just as Ehrlichman had. This was inevitable, given how many copies were floating around Hollywood and elsewhere. Nevertheless, Oliver freaked out when it was eventually leaked to *Time, Newsweek* and other media outlets. I understood part of his reaction, though, when I read their accounts of the script. Some writers claimed that we had Nixon conspiring to kill JFK, which was far from the truth. The lingering controversy over *JFK* was a specter that would continue to haunt us throughout the making of *Nixon* and beyond.

Haig complained that the script showed him advocating a military coup to Nixon. In fact, it did nothing of the sort. His complaints were muted, though, compared to Ehrlichman's, and he did not threaten to sue us. I asked Haig if he was Deep Throat, as some have speculated, and he of course denied it. John Dean had done a very thorough job of analyzing all the candidates for Deep Throat in his 1982 book *Lost Honor.* He believed that, although no one person fit all the points of description in *All the President's Men,* the one who came closest was Haig. After both Haig and Woodward denied it, Dean came to the conclusion that Haig was not Deep Throat. I believe that there was no Deep Throat as such, but that this was a composite character created by Woodward and Bernstein to make their story more dramatic. Haig was clearly a key source for their second book, *The Final Days,* which covered the period when he was chief of staff in the White House.

I also asked Haig about an assertion made in his memoir *Inner*

Circles where he claimed that as a Pentagon officer working on Cuban affairs in 1963, he had seen a report stating that Oswald had been in Havana. There is no credible evidence of this, and no reputable investigator, including those of the Warren Commission and Congress, found any evidence that Oswald had ever been to Cuba. Nevertheless, Haig repeated this claim, and furthermore said he believed that Castro had been behind the assassination! This theory has been examined and rejected by every official body that has looked into the case, as well as by the most respected independent researchers. I don't know if Haig actually believes these things, or was just acting as a provocateur and purveyor of disinformation. There was an extensive effort by CIA sources to blame Cuba for the assassination in its immediate aftermath, and that effort has been revived in recent years as more and more facts to the contrary have emerged. Indeed, Escalante told me that the reason he had begun his investigation was to disprove the frequent efforts to blame Cuba for the crime.

I chose not to argue with Haig, as I sensed it would be pointless and counterproductive. After about fifteen or twenty minutes of conversation, Powers Boothe called from California, and I listened in and took notes as he talked with Haig. Actors like to get a sense of the character they are playing, and I'm sure the conversation was helpful in that respect.

Goodbye Azita, Hello Annie

Shortly after this trip, and just before we started filming, Oliver abruptly fired his loyal assistant Azita. This was a blow to me, as she was my only close friend in the office, and was also a source of valuable information.

Azita Zendel was treated very badly by Oliver. After working for him day and night for four years, she was abruptly ousted for no good reason. I think Oliver was upset because she said she was burnt out as an assistant and expressed a desire to move up in the company (which had been promised to her). This was completely reasonable considering not only her devoted service to him but also the fact that she is highly intelligent, talented and energetic and had contributed a great deal to his films. She had earned the right to move up, but instead he pushed her out without reasonable notice or cause. Oliver's excuse was that he was about to start shooting *Nixon*, and did not want her leaving in the middle of production.

What disgusted me even more was his lack of any sense of loyalty to her after she left. He never lifted a finger to help her get a job, let alone to stay in touch or invite her to screenings or premieres. I got her into a few, but Oliver complained about it.

Her mistreatment and abrupt dismissal by Oliver was obviously a tremendous blow to absorb. But Azita bounced back, taking film classes at UCLA and ultimately making an independent film of her own. She also remained a good friend of mine, even after I left Oliver's office. There were many who did not, which is always the case in Hollywood.

Azita had in fact become more and more dissatisfied with being a mere assistant, despite her uncanny ability to talk on two telephones at the same time, one at each ear. In a sense, she probably wanted to leave. Danny the Weasel had promised her a top job in his new company, but of course he had broken his promise. Azita could see the end coming, and had starting training a "second assistant" named Annie.

Annie came into the office as a sweet young woman just out of college, but things changed after she took over Azita's job. I had noticed on Capitol Hill that many press secretaries and assistants eventually began to think that they were just as important as the senators and congressmen they worked for. The same was true in Hollywood. This tendency had emerged a little bit in Azita toward the end, when she was burnt out. But Annie quickly developed a full-blown case of it. She began to scream orders at interns and even at creative executives and producers. If Oliver wanted it, it had to be done—now! Anything less was a personal insult to her.

Annie also became the keeper of a little black book she inherited from Azita labeled "OS Harem." This was a list of Oliver's women friends carefully organized by city—from New York to Paris to Hong Kong. It was updated regularly. Needless to say, this was a precious (and top secret) document.

I had several fires to put out on the *Nixon* front. First, I found out that Annie had become romantically involved with Steve Rivele. This was supposed to be a secret, but I figured it out when they both told me that they had just come back from vacations in Fiji. Quite a coincidence! Normally, this would be no one's business but their own, but I knew that if and when Oliver heard of this, he would immediately suspect a conspiracy against him. He soon found out, and when he did, it simply fed into his sense of paranoia. Now he couldn't even trust his own assistant! The tension around Annie's office, which was next to Oliver's, was thick and tangible.

A funny but sad episode took place on Annie's birthday. In her honor, some of the women in the office had hired a male stripper to come in and do his act. The entire staff gathered to watch this performance. The stripper turned out to be a long-haired Yugoslavian called Drago, who resembled a male model out of *Vanity Fair*. He brought with him a boom box and appropriate music, and started his act. Annie grew increasingly uncomfortable with his attentions, particularly as he drew her into his act and stripped down to his Calvins. Annie yelled, "I need a drink," and Janet Yang brought in a bottle of vodka from Oliver's office. Annie poured herself one glass after another, and starting enjoying the show. Drago finished his erotic dance, still dressed in his underwear, and made his exit.

Annie seemed to be OK, but when I came back into the conference room a little while later, she was writhing on the floor, violently drunk. She was almost incomprehensible but seemed to be muttering "Call Steve ... call Steve" (with whom she had long since broken up). Not knowing what else to do, I called him. He was very surprised but gallantly rode to the rescue. He literally picked her up and took her home, at which point she kicked him out again. No good deed goes unpunished.

Shooting the Movie

The official start date for shooting *Nixon* was May 1, 1995. Shooting was to run through the end of July. Unofficially, though, there was a week of preshooting at the end of April. This was to get the actors warmed up and to shoot scenes that would be used later as part of a mock "documentary" about Nixon's career that was to be included in the film. This material would be based on an actual television documentary, Nixon's political "obituary," that was broadcast by Howard K. Smith on ABC after Nixon's defeat in the California governor's race in 1962. Obviously, reports of his political death were premature.

I was drafted into "acting" in one scene, although I did not actually appear on camera. The setting was the House Un-American Activities Committee, where Nixon got his first public exposure as a congressman in the late 1940s. Anthony Hopkins was made up as the young Nixon, and sat with other committee members in a congressional hearing room setting. Oliver wanted someone to sit in the witness chair who they could fire questions at. He looked around the room and then barked, "Eric, come up here . . . you're Alger Hiss." I guess he considered me the most "Eastern intellectual" type on the set.

Hopkins glared at me sternly and asked questions like "Are you now or have you ever been a member of the Communist Party?" Since I was off camera and would not appear on screen, I did not take the whole thing seriously and tried to give humorous answers, but Hopkins maintained his stern demeanor throughout. At one point, he asked me something like "Are you aware of any Communist-influenced films that have been made in Hollywood?"

I answered, "Well ... there was a film called *Natural Born Killers* by Oliver Stone. ..." Oliver glared at me, but Hopkins kept his Nixonian game face, stayed in character and kept firing questions. If I'd known in advance that I was going to be drawn into shooting on the first day, I would have done a little homework and maybe even asked if I could appear on camera. But Oliver liked to be spontaneous at times, which seemed to work for him.

Later, I saw Hopkins deliver the famous "Checkers" speech, with Joan Allen made up as Pat by his side. When I heard his rendition, I knew he would make a great Nixon. Hopkins had studied hundreds of hours of Nixon video interviews and speeches to prepare for the role, and he had obviously gotten inside Richard Nixon's skin. Joan Allen was also very convincing as a stiff and uncomfortable Pat Nixon being used as a political prop. I felt that the film was off to a good start.

I asked Oliver if I could go to the set to watch the first "official" day of filming on May 1, but being superstitious about such things, he said no. (Oliver had many superstitions. He also believed August was a lucky month for him, but could not wait that long to start shooting the movie.) I did go on the second day with Steve and Chris, and we had lunch with Oliver there. We toured the set, which was an amazing recreation of the White House—the Oval Office, the Cabinet Room and other White House settings. It was an eerie feeling, like stepping back in time into a Nixon time warp. Even the schedule memo on the secretary's desk outside the Oval Office, which would never be seen on camera, was a reproduction of an authentic Nixon schedule from that period. Oliver prided himself on these kinds of touches in making his films seem real.

It was also exciting to see all of the actors on the set in costume and in character. We watched Hopkins do a scene where he gives a ranting lecture to the Cabinet about leaks, saying, "Halde-man is my Lord High Executioner, and I'll be tougher than he is," and other Nixonian rhetoric. At one point he improvised a line that I had researched for him—"Remember the Rosenbergs? Old Sparky got 'em"—referring to the electric chair. I was happy to see that my research was going to good use.

Oliver had decided that Hopkins would not be made up to look exactly like Richard Nixon. He felt that this would make Hopkins into a caricature of Nixon, and that it was far more important to convey a sense of Nixon the man. This Hopkins did superbly through his speech, gestures and body language. Oliver had told me that Tony was a pleasure to work with—very profes-sional, on time and well rehearsed—unlike some Hollywood actors he had dealt with. I think Oliver liked the fact that Tony was willing to take and follow direction without questioning his authority as director, despite the fact that he was an Academy Award-winning actor (for his role in *Silence of the Lambs*), as well as a knighted British "Sir." Tony took a British approach to acting—he would rehearse his lines at home up to 200 times, then show up on time and do his job. His training combined with his natural talents and prodigious research produced his usual impec-cable results.

Early in the shooting, Oliver had tried to needle Tony by telling him, "You need to loosen up ... have a few drinks." This despite the fact, or because of the fact, that Hopkins had been a nondrinker for the past twenty years—a fact that was well known. Oliver then turned to a makeup girl and said, "Tony looks tense.... Why don't you give him a blow job?" Hopkins brusquely told Stone to get lost, in no uncertain terms. This helped to establish the parameters of their relationship, and Oliver subse-quently treated him with due respect. I think that the presence of

Sir Anthony Hopkins on the set, as well as the nature of the subject matter of the film, created an atmosphere that was more adult and sober than, say, that of *Natural Born Killers*. As Oliver put it, "This is an older man's movie." (That's probably why it didn't make money!)

At lunch with Oliver, Steve and Chris and I discussed the Martin Luther King project, and also the possibility of their writing a script based on *The New Emperors,* a book about Chairman Mao by the late *New York Times* journalist Harrison Salisbury. Oliver had bought the rights but never bothered to get a writer to adapt it. I ended up writing it later.

A couple of days later, they called me in a rage. Danny the Weasel had tried to stab them in the back and prevent them from getting an outside writing assignment with another company. They had met with Laura Ziskin, then head of Fox 2000 Pictures, about writing a script about Aldrich Ames, the CIA spy. Danny the Weasel found out about it and told Ziskin that Steve and Chris had not really written the *Nixon* script—that Oliver had done most of the actual writing. This was a blatant lie and also a stupid thing to say. Ziskin apparently had called their agent at CAA, who in turn told Steve and Chris what the Weasel had done. Steve said he never wanted to set foot in a room with Danny the Weasel again, and would punch him out if he saw him.

A typical day on the set consisted of . . . well, there was no such thing as a typical day on the set. There is, of course, a certain structure to the making of any Hollywood film. First of all, there is the script (or at least there should be a script). Then there are the sets, and the actors and the director. There is a shooting schedule for each day, and a "call sheet" indicating which actors will be needed for what scenes. There is an overall schedule for shooting, whether it is thirty days, sixty days or more (or less). There is, of course, a budget for the film. If anything goes wrong, which it usually does, the film falls behind schedule and goes over budget. As directors go, Oliver was actually pretty good at keeping things moving along on schedule and more or less on budget. Later, on films like *U-Turn* and *Any Given Sunday,* this fiscal and personal discipline would begin to deteriorate as Oliver did.

There are also numerous people who hang around the set with some function or other. These are called the crew. There are also visitors to the set, who must be approved by Oliver. In fact, everything on the set must be approved by Oliver. A film director is a dictator, pure and simple. If he isn't, he will lose control of his own movie. For all his fanaticism, rudeness and general unpleasantness, Oliver managed to retain control of his films and their original vision. This is the difference between *Platoon* and *Halloween Part 3*. Oliver has a vision, and it comes across on the screen. His films are not made by committee. This is what makes them great. They come from one man's vision.

Almost all of the shooting on *Nixon* was done on sound stages on the Sony lot. (Despite the fact that the film was being released by Disney, Oliver had made a deal with Rob Reiner to use his old White House sets from *An American President*.) A sound stage from the outside looks like a nondescript warehouse. It looks the same on the inside, until the set is "dressed" — that is, decorated for whatever the scene requires. Oliver, to his artistic credit, had created a perfect replica of the Nixon White House (actually on several different stages, depending on whether it was the Oval Office, the Nixons' bedroom, their dining room, the Cabinet Room or some other location being depicted).

For one memorable scene, a fake Lincoln Memorial had been

built to full scale on a sound stage. This was used to replicate an actual event in which Nixon got up at four in the morning and went down to the memorial with his faithful Cuban valet, Manolo Sanchez, to "talk to the kids." Some of the bleary-eyed hippies camped out on the steps of the memorial thought they were having an acid hallucination when they saw him. Nixon wanted to talk football, but the students wanted to talk about the war. Finally one young woman, in a moment of revelation, says, "You can't stop it, can you? Even if you wanted to. . . ." Oliver also offered women on the scene $100 each to take off their tops, but unfortunately I missed this. That part of the scene didn't make it into the movie anyway. He probably did it just for fun.

I was always surprised to see how many people could be crowded onto the set, behind the cameras. It would have been very distracting to me to have such a large audience, although I guess actors like playing to an audience. Sometimes, in a particular intimate scene, such as Nixon praying and crying with Kissinger, Oliver would close the set. It was amazing to me how Tony Hopkins could pour out such emotion on cue. But then that's what makes him a great actor.

A few scenes were also shot off the lot. Rolando Martinez was present for a scene in which he had taken part twenty-four years earlier. The scene, depicting the break-in of Daniel Ellsberg's psychiatrist's office, was filmed at the Huntington Library in Pasadena for some reason, even though the actual break-in had taken place at an office building in Beverly Hills. A few other scenes were filmed at outdoor locales around southern California, and a "second unit" crew flew to Washington to shoot background and establishing shots. But most of the film was shot right in Hollywood—just like in the movies!

Problems with MLK

Meanwhile, a controversy had developed over the Martin Luther King project (or MLK, as we called it for short). I had called William Pepper, the attorney for King's accused assassin James Earl Ray, to ask if Steve and Chris could visit with Ray in prison in Tennessee on an upcoming research trip. Pepper lived in London, but somehow still represented Ray, although he had been an associate of Dr. King in the civil rights and antiwar movements of the 1960s. I had called Pepper from my home before I went to work in the morning because of the time difference between Los Angeles and London. Pepper had agreed to let them meet with Ray, since it could help his client if the movie got made.

By the time I got to the office, a crisis had erupted. It turned out that Pepper was writing a book about the case and had made a deal for the movie rights with legendary Hollywood producer Jerry Weintraub, which he had not told me. Evidently Pepper had called Weintraub as soon as he hung up from my call, and Weintraub in turn had called Oliver in a state of agitation. Pepper's book, entitled *Orders to Kill,* was based on theories very similar to Walter Fauntroy's and would obviously compete with our project if developed as a film. Danny the Weasel found out about this and freaked out.

There was one infallible principle in dealing with Danny the Weasel: Whatever he told you, the opposite was true. A corollary to this was that he was lying to you because he had his own agenda, which inevitably involving stabbing you or someone else in the back. Keeping these principles in mind was the only rational way to deal with Danny the Weasel.

Chris and Steve were already highly suspicious of him, but became totally disgusted after he tried to kill their chances for writing the Aldrich Ames film. In the end, they got the job anyway and Danny the Weasel achieved nothing except to permanently poison his relations with them. (After *Nixon*, Chris and Steve became hot writers in Hollywood with high salaries to match. Their next film, *Ali*, was released six years after *Nixon* in December 2001.)

The Pepper–Weintraub situation was a little more complicated. Oliver wanted Steve and Chris to write a script for him about the life and assassination of Martin Luther King, which he would make after he finished *Nixon*. They did write the script, but it never got made. It was based in part on the information I had obtained from Fauntroy and his congressional investigation, plus other sources in the public record. Now it turned out that Weintraub owned the rights to Pepper's forthcoming book, which contained a highly complex and convoluted conspiracy theory about King's death involving the FBI, the CIA, the Mafia and military intelligence. Needless to say, Oliver loved it.

Pepper had actually gotten a lot of his material from the same sources that Fauntroy had, but had fleshed it out into a book. For some reason, he had hooked up with Weintraub, who had worked with Elvis Presley, Frank Sinatra and many other legends in his time. Weintraub was a card-carrying Republican and supposed buddy of George Bush, and I'm sure he didn't believe a word of the Pepper book, if he even read it, but for some reason he had bought the rights.

Oliver wanted to make a deal with Weintraub to join forces and gain access to the Pepper book. Danny the Weasel was opposed to this because he felt that he would be squeezed out as a producer if the much more powerful Weintraub got involved. He tried to spread rumors that Weintraub was connected to the Mafia and could have us all killed, but this failed to persuade Oliver. I was not afraid of Weintraub, but was dubious about some of the assertions in Pepper's book (many of which later proved to be false). Nevertheless I thought it would be better to deal with him than get involved in a battle or a lawsuit that could kill the whole project. My feeling was that if we had the rights to Pepper's book, we could use what we liked and ignore the rest.

Ultimately, Oliver did make a deal with Weintraub and Pepper, but decided not to make the movie. I suggested to him many times that he simply produce it and find a good African-American director like Spike Lee or John Singleton to direct it, but Oliver always rejected such suggestions. He felt that only he could do it properly. . . .

The "New Emperors," on the other hand, was a film project about Mao and Deng Xiaoping based on a much more respectable book by Harrison Salisbury. Oliver owned the rights to this book, but never hired a writer or took any steps to develop it. Even Janet Yang seemed to take no interest in it, probably feeling it was not commercial. I thought it had potential, and tried to persuade Chris and Steve to write a script for us based on the book. That never happened. After the Nixon and MLK projects, they decided never to work with Oliver again, and certainly not as long as he was involved with Danny the Weasel.

In the end, I wrote the Mao script myself as part of our deal when I left Ixtlan. To my amazement, Oliver called me and said he loved the script and really wanted to make it. But of course he never followed up. After the abject failure of his film *U-Turn*, Oliver decided he could not make a commercially risky film about Chairman Mao and company, so he dropped the whole idea.

Oliver Becomes Nixon

Shortly after these events, Chris and I made another attempt to visit the *Nixon* set. Chris was accompanied by his girlfriend, and wanted to show her what we were doing. Unfortunately, Oliver was in a foul mood that day because things were not going well on the set. He snapped at me and then at Chris, and basically told us to get lost. We were both very upset, and Chris felt humiliated by this treatment since his girlfriend was there with him. It was completely irrational of Oliver to lash out at us in this way. We were obviously being made the scapegoats for things that we had nothing to do with. At times like these, Oliver would get a crazed, malevolent look in his eye. I realized then that he was becoming more and more like Nixon himself.

Oliver Stone has many unusual characteristics. One of them is that he is very soft-spoken in person, even when he is saying very crazy things. In this respect, he reminds me of interviews I have seen on TV with Axl Rose, the lead singer of Guns N' Roses. He talks in a soft, quiet voice, which gives you the impression that he must be saying something thoughtful and profound. Usually, the exact opposite is true. Oliver would also get a demented look when he was about to explode (which was often). His eyes would glaze over and I would actually get the feeling that I could see smoke coming out of his ears. When this happened, the best thing to do was to get away from him as quickly as possible.

I decided then to keep my visits to the set to a minimum, although there were times when I had to go there. As anyone who has been on a movie set knows, there are long periods of inaction and boredom between takes and scenes. In Oliver's case, though, he seemed to view the set as a war zone, with himself as general. He would set up a small black "tent" in the corner that covered his equipment and himself. Inside he had a TV monitor so he could watch the action, but no one could see him. You entered his tent at your own risk. This created a very nerve-wracking atmosphere much of the time. Oliver was happiest when he was in charge of the action, barking orders and making decisions. When we were shooting *Any Given Sunday* later, I compared him to the coach of the team. He said, "No, I'm the quarterback. I'm out there on the field, calling the plays, running around, throwing the ball...." That was the feeling he loved.

However, I had to go back the next day, as John and Mo Dean had been invited to visit the set. Oliver was on better behavior, and I had lunch with him, the Deans, Mary Steenburgen (who was playing the young Nixon's mother Hannah), James Woods (who was Haldeman, complete with crewcut), David Hyde Pierce (who was playing John Dean) and Alexander Butterfield. Needless to say, times like these felt slightly surreal but were also part of what made the experience rewarding. There was something very unsettling about seeing the real John Dean (at age sixty) standing next to an actor made up to look just like John Dean at age thirty. Even stranger was to see the entire set of the Watergate hearing room meticulously recreated on a Hollywood sound stage. The young "Mo Dean" (played by Donna Dixon) was sitting in the front row with her blonde hair pulled back in a bun, just as everyone remembered it. It was like traveling backward in time. How it felt for the Deans, I can only imagine.

Another project related to the *Nixon* film reached fruition thanks to John Dean. This was his idea of doing a CD-ROM tied to the film and the book, for which he ended up doing most of the work. His thought was that you could include much more material on a CD-ROM, including Nixon documents, transcripts, biographies, film and interviews, than you possibly could in the film itself or even in a hefty book. It was hard to persuade anyone to take it on, however, and in the end Disney, Sony and other companies all passed on the idea. Eventually it was picked up by Graphix Zone, which had done an excellent Bob Dylan CD-ROM with voluminous archival and supporting material. The Nixon CD-ROM turned out very well, and was narrated by Alexander Butterfield. I was credited as associate producer. Unfortunately, CD-ROMs seem to be a dying art form, and I don't think too many copies were sold. But it's an invaluable resource for Nixon buffs—and Nixon-haters.

Visiting the Set

During the *Nixon* shoot I spent many days at the Ixtlan offices, as there was plenty of work for me to do there researching the film. I would often help actors who were trying to get a better sense of their character by giving them material to read and then discussing it with them. I also avoided going too often because Oliver considered it goofing off for me to be there unless he had asked me to come, or there was some specific reason for me to be there for a given scene. Of course I would sometimes get frantic calls that I must come to the set immediately because Oliver needed me. Once I went there with a whole box full of books because Oliver thought he remembered reading that Kissinger had made some anti-black remarks to Nixon, and Oliver wanted me to find the exact quote. I looked through Hersh, Ambrose, Brodie and about ten other books, and finally said, "Oliver, it's just not here." He was disappointed but accepted it.

I would sometimes try to sneak onto the set for a particularly spectacular scene, but it was risky. Oliver seemed to have eyes in the back of his head and a sixth sense for knowing who was there at any moment in time. For example, I went over to watch the Lincoln Memorial scene, and somehow Oliver saw me slip in the back door. Even though the building was crammed with people, including an NBC film crew, he immediately sensed my presence. He called me over and said, "What are you doing here? What do you want?" I mumbled some excuse, starting with "Well ... I assume ..." Oliver cut me off abruptly. "Don't assume!" he ordered sternly. "'Assume' makes an ASS of U and ME." This was one of his favorite clichés. For a guy who considered himself on the cutting edge of culture, he could be pretty corny at times. The trip to the set turned out to be useful, however. He thrust a paper into my hand.

He said, "Take a look at this," and handed me a threatening legal letter that had been sent to him by Richard Helms, former director of the CIA. "Write a response to this," he barked. So the trip wasn't a total waste after all.

Needless to say, Oliver was agitated by the threat of a lawsuit from Helms. I don't know if the Helms threat was just a coincidence of timing or was somehow inspired by the Ehrlichman threats. I later learned that John Taylor, head of the Nixon presidential library in Yorba Linda, bragged that he had leaked the script to Helms. But like Ehrlichman, Helms never actually sued us. It was another empty threat by a Watergate figure spooked by our film.

As I've mentioned earlier, Oliver was very paranoid and hyper-sensitive to threats of lawsuits from anyone, let alone important people like Helms and Ehrlichman. He actually cut all the Helms scenes from the final version of the film that was released in theaters, although they were included in the video later. Oliver claimed that this was done purely for artistic reasons, but I think he may have been intimidated by Helms. Ironically, there was nothing libelous in the Helms scenes and there was absolutely no legal case there. Sam Waterston gave an excellent performance as Helms but it ended up on the cutting room floor. The only saving grace was that this also eliminated some ridiculous scenes of Helms cultivating flowers and reciting poetry to Nixon, which had never happened. This was Oliver's attempt to combine the crazed spy James Angleton, a poetry and orchid freak, with Richard Helms.

While I never believed that either Helms or Ehrlichman would sue, or had any basis for it, I can see how both of them might have believed that their relatively favorable treatment in the film was due to their efforts to intimidate Oliver. There may be some truth to that. I had actually hoped that they would sue us. It would have been good publicity for the film ... and I would have loved to have the opportunity to question Helms under oath!

I would also visit the set to bring writers who needed to meet with Oliver about other projects. This was the case with John Leone, a writer and journalist living near San Diego, who was working on the "Mexico Project." Leone had sent Oliver a treatment about Subcommandante Marcos and the Zapatista rebellion in Chiapas that he liked, and wanted to hire him to write a script. I met with Leone and we talked on the phone many times. I suggested that he broaden the script to include the many political assassinations in Mexico, the rise of the drug cartels, the widespread corruption and the transformation of Mexico into a "narco-democracy," which still continues. Oliver liked this idea, as did Leone, although it may have been too ambitious in retrospect. It would have been like a fictionalized Mexican *Godfather*. Leone wrote several drafts of a script that were very good, but the project was ultimately killed by Danny the Weasel, who didn't understand it and didn't like it because it wasn't his idea and he didn't control it. This was absolutely typical of him. Later, a very similar movie, *Traffic,* became a major hit. We could have done it first, and should have, but we didn't. Oliver later went to Chiapas and met with Marcos, but still didn't make the movie.

I brought another interesting visitor to the set early on. This was E. Howard Hunt, the former CIA agent and Watergate burglar. Oliver had decided he wanted to meet Hunt, and we flew him out from Miami. Hunt's son David came up from San Diego, and Hunt's friend and lawyer Bill Snyder came down from San Francisco. Although Howard Hunt and I have diametrically opposite political views, we hit it off and ultimately formed a friendly relationship that continued beyond the *Nixon* film. Hunt also contributed a very good essay for our book.

I met with Hunt the day before we visited the set, along with Bill Snyder. Snyder was very friendly, Hunt initially a bit more reserved, but also friendly. We chatted for about an hour. Hunt gave me the piece he'd written for our Nixon book, which was very critical of Nixon, and also admitted that he had lied himself. I didn't press him on the JFK assassination as I wanted to keep a good atmosphere for the meeting with Oliver the next day. We did talk about Guatemala, the Bay of Pigs, Gordon Liddy and other things. Hunt had been involved in the CIA's 1954 coup in Guatemala, as well as in the Bay of Pigs invasion. As one of the Watergate burglars, he had spent thirty-three months in jail. This was a painful subject for him. In addition to his notoriety and prison sentence, he had lost his wife in a plane crash in December 1972 during the Watergate crisis. The whole episode was a chapter in his life that he would rather forget. He felt he had spent his life serving his country, and then been stabbed in the back by Nixon and Helms.

The next day I picked up Hunt, Snyder and David Hunt at eleven A.M., and took them over to the set. We watched the filming, talked some, and then had lunch with Oliver. Later I had dinner with them at L'Orangerie, a fancy French restaurant, which Snyder had suggested. It cost me $424, but luckily I got reimbursed for it later. It was an interesting day, to say the least. Hunt didn't give any ground on the JFK assassination; he basically denied everything. At one point, I asked him if he'd met Oswald in Mexico, and he said, "You'll have to pay me a lot of money to tell you that." He also jokingly told Oliver that he would sign a confession for $5 million—"But you'll still have to prove it." I think he denied a little too much. For example, he told me he'd never heard of Antonio Veciana (a famous Cuban exile leader), which seems doubtful. He also denied knowing right wing extremist Guy Banister, mobster Johnny Roselli and even Ted Shackley (a legendary former CIA official known as the "Blond Ghost"). When I asked Hunt if he had been involved in the 1961 assassination of the Dominican president Rafael Trujillo, he replied, "I'm not Charles Manson, you know!"

Howard Hunt has written books about both the Bay of Pigs and his CIA career, as well as about seventy spy novels. He is a legendary figure who has been accused of many things, including being involved in the assassination of President Kennedy. Some believe he was even in Dallas and was one of the "three tramps" arrested in Dealey Plaza, although this has been pretty well disproved by the research of the LaFontaines.

My own conclusion after getting to know Hunt on this and

other occasions, and also having an extended correspondence with him, is that he was and is a sincere (if sometimes misguided) right wing patriot who believed in the Cuban exile cause. He did not like John Kennedy, but I don't believe he was involved in Dallas on November 22. I do think he knows more than he has ever said about it, though. He obviously has bitter feelings toward the CIA generally and Richard Helms in particular, believing that they betrayed him in the aftermath of Watergate. The Cuban exiles trusted him, which is why Hunt was chosen to recruit the team of Watergate burglars among the exiles in Miami who had worked with him on the Bay of Pigs. I hope that he will write a memoir, even if published posthumously, that will reveal the full extent of his career and his knowledge of the CIA's innermost secrets, as well as the full story of Watergate. I have tried to persuade him to do so, but haven't succeeded just yet ... as far as I know.

Later on in the filming, we also flew out Rolando Martinez and his wife Silvia from Miami. Martinez was another of the Watergate burglars, and the only one who had received a pardon (from President Reagan). He and his wife are both from Cuba, and Martinez had been involved in literally hundreds of clandestine raids on Cuba for the CIA. He is an older man now, about seventy, and I enjoyed meeting him. I had the opportunity to spend about three hours talking with him as I drove them from Santa Monica to Long Beach in bumper-to-bumper traffic in the pouring rain on a Friday afternoon.

I was bringing them to the set at the Long Beach airport, where we were filming a scene. It was meant to depict the Dallas airport on the morning of November 22, 1963. It was eerie to see the scene recreated, the terminal draped with American flag bunting and signs saying "Welcome, Mr. President, to Dallas." On that fateful day in 1963, Nixon flew out on a small plane just before

Kennedy flew in. Many people thought we made this up to make Nixon look guilty, and that this was just another example of Oliver Stone's conspiracy mongering and rewriting of history. It seemed preposterous that Nixon had been in Dallas just before JFK, but it is true. The scene was taken from Nixon's own memoirs.

Martinez was also there to serve as a consultant for an outdoor cockfight scene in which Hunt approaches Liddy about recruiting the Watergate burglars. Strangely, though, Oliver ignored him during the entire shoot. This was fine with me, since it gave me more time to talk with Rolando myself.

I told him that I had visited Cuba twice, which didn't seem to bother him. He said he would like to go back but would never do so as long as Castro is in power. He got upset when I said there was a high rate of literacy in Cuba (which is true). He said, "Yes, but there is nothing to read there!" He was viscerally, emotionally anti-Castro, and his wife even more so. But they were very pleasant people and we got along well.

I had read a lot about Cuba and asked him about some of the Cubans who had been connected by various writers to the Kennedy assassinations. He did not deny that some anti-Castro Cubans may have been involved, but insisted that he was not one of them (and I believed him). He singled out two Cuban brothers, Guillermo and Ignacio Novo, as being "muchachos malos," and hinted that they may have been involved. But he said he didn't know for sure. He did tell me that he had made over 300 raids on Cuba, and had been involved in some secret operations even after the Watergate break-in, which had never been publicly revealed. He was impressed by my interest and knowledge of obscure Cuban figures, and said that if he ever told his whole story he would tell it to me. So far, he hasn't. He was also proud of the fact that he had received a pardon from President Reagan after making a personal appeal to him.

Rolando and Silvia were especially pleased when they got their pictures taken on the set with Oliver Stone and Anthony Hopkins. I took the pictures and later sent them to Miami, for which they thanked me profusely. I heard that Oliver later saw Rolando again on the street in Miami in 1999 while shooting *Any Given Sunday.*

On another occasion, my mother visited the set, and actually ended up in the movie! She had come out to visit, and we drove to Pasadena where Oliver was filming a scene in a large mansion. Inside, the setting was supposed to be a cocktail party on Fifth Avenue in New York circa 1963, where Nixon was discussing politics with John Mitchell and Nelson Rockefeller. Oliver decided that my mother would fit in perfectly as an extra in the scene, and being a good sport she agreed to do it. The wardrobe people outfitted her in a suitable black cocktail dress of the early 1960s, complete with stiff corset, and she mingled with other high society types in the background of the scene. She also had a scene standing right between Pat Nixon and Martha Mitchell (played by Madeline Kahn) as they were talking. Unfortunately, her close-up got cut from the movie, but you can still see her in the background of the scene if you look carefully! Needless to say, this made her day, and mine as well.

Strange Episodes

Around this time, we had a curious episode involving Ben Stein, a writer and comedian. He had called Oliver, and Oliver asked me to call him to follow up. Ben Stein is the son of Herb Stein, the late economic adviser to Nixon who was one of the more respected figures in Nixon's administration. Ben has had a very strange career as a writer, game show host and other things. He is also very close to the Nixon family, particularly Julie Nixon Eisenhower and her husband, David. Earlier I had written to them, offering to meet with them and also asking if they would like to contribute to our Nixon book. We also asked if they would be willing to meet with any of our actors. They never responded to my letter, although we did use Julie's book on her mother as a useful source for Joan Allen's portrayal.

I knew that Ben Stein, who has many Hollywood connections, was close to them and had written an essay called something like "Richard Nixon—The Man I Loved," which had been published in a magazine. I asked him if we could reprint it in our book and he tentatively agreed, but said he would get back to me. He also asked for a copy of the script. I said I would ask Oliver and get back to him about it. Oliver agreed, and I called Stein several times to follow up, but he never returned my calls. My strong suspicion is that he was acting as a front for David and Julie, trying to get the script without letting us know it was for them. When he was able to get it from other sources (there were hundreds of copies floating around Hollywood), he dropped any pretense of further interest. I never heard back from him, and he never sent me his essay, so we could not include it in the book. The last I heard, he was hosting a silly game show on TV called *Win Ben Stein's Money.*

Another odd character that I encountered was the author Garry Wills, who was writing a magazine piece on the film. Garry Wills was one of the strangest characters I met during the whole Nixon experience. He is considered a respected academic who has written a number of books, including one called *Nixon Agonistes*. I read through it and found most of it as incomprehensible as its title. If you want to understand Nixon, there are much better books you can read, starting with Fawn Brodie's excellent *Richard Nixon: The Shaping of His Character*. This was probably the single most important influence on our film as a resource for understanding the man.

Wills visited the set, but seemed to take almost no interest in learning anything about what we were doing. I knew he would be prejudiced against us because he had hated *JFK*. For some reason, Wills had written a book about Jack Ruby early in his career, defending him as a poor, misunderstood nightclub owner who killed Oswald for patriotic reasons and had nothing to do with the Mafia. A likely story.... If you are interested in Ruby, read Seth Kantor's book *Who Was Jack Ruby?* Kantor, unlike Wills, was a journalist who actually knew Jack Ruby personally at the time, and did substantial research on him as well. His findings are fascinating.

As I expected, Wills later trashed *Nixon* just as he had *JFK*. Later, though, he wrote a magazine piece defending *Natural Born Killers* as a cinematic masterpiece on the level of Dostoyevsky's *Crime and Punishment*. . . . As I said, he is a very weird guy.

A stranger episode involved a man who wrote to Oliver claiming to be a member of the JFK "hit team" in Dallas. This became another of Oliver's crazy pet projects. He got a very strange and garbled letter from someone calling himself "Ron" (not his real name), from a post office box in Georgia. He claimed he had been part of the JFK hit team in Dallas and said, "You finally found one of them." After I read the letter, I concluded that he was either a nut or someone deliberately spreading misinformation, or both. Oliver, of course, desperately wanted to believe that he had found one of the real assassins. I did correspond with "Ron" a few times at Oliver's insistence, and became more and more convinced that his story was nonsense. I told him as much, and suggested that if he had any information he should go public with it. Mercifully, after this the letters from "Ron" stopped.

Yet Oliver actually met with "Ron" later in New York, in Central Park across from the Stanhope Hotel, where he liked to stay. By prearrangement, Oliver was wearing a Seattle Mariners baseball cap to add a dash of intrigue (and absurdity). Oliver continued to believe "Ron's" story and as far as I know still does. (There have been many such phony "hit men" who have come forward over the years, for whatever reason, and their stories have been invariably disproved.) "Ron" apparently lives in Bermuda and claims to still work for the CIA. I gave copies of his letters to Jim Lesar and Howard Hunt, both of whom agreed from different perspectives and long experience that they were completely ridiculous and that "Ron" was a phony.

Around this time, we received another letter that proved to be much more fortuitous. Although the letter was about our Nixon project, it turned out to be the beginning of another project—a football movie....

The football idea came up while I was researching *Nixon*. It ultimately turned into Oliver's film *Any Given Sunday,* released in late 1999 and starring Al Pacino and Cameron Diaz. Richard Weiner is a sportswriter for the *New York Times,* and his father Sanford Weiner had been a political consultant for Nixon. Richard had come across some of his father's old papers and thought he might have found some information relating to the identity of Deep Throat. He wrote to Oliver, who passed the letter on to me to look into. I called Richard and had a long talk with him. I told him we were not really dealing with Deep Throat in the movie, but ended up discussing many other things besides. It turned out that

Richard was writing a book with legendary quarterback Joe Montana entitled *The Art and Magic of Quarterbacking*.

I asked Richard if he thought there was a chance of doing a movie based on Montana's story. It had occurred to me that Oliver had never done a sports movie, and that this would be a good subject for him for many reasons. Richard said that he didn't think Joe would agree to such a project for personal reasons. I said I would like to try to develop a football project for Oliver, and could he come up with any other ideas that might work? He said he would talk to a former 49ers player named Jamie Williams, who had just retired and had some interesting stories to tell. I asked him to write up a football treatment with Jamie and send it to me.

This became the genesis of *Any Given Sunday*. It turned out that Oliver was a huge 49ers fan and had been since he was a kid. Y. A. Tittle had been his hero in the early 1950s, when Oliver had collected football cards, and he had prized Tittle's card with a picture of the bald quarterback above all others. I had a sense that pro football was the kind of sport that would make a good subject for an Oliver Stone film. I thought it would combine the macho combat elements of *Platoon* with the big money, media and greed of *Wall Street*. This turned out to be right. Oliver loved the idea, and hired Richard and Jamie to write a script on the basis of their treatment. This was the beginning of a long and tortuous saga, as well as a lasting friendship between myself and Richard Weiner.

As shooting was finishing up on *Nixon*, I was spending more and more time on the Martin Luther King and football projects (or MLK and NFL for short). Richard and Jamie came to Los Angeles to meet with Oliver.

I took Jamie and Richard out to lunch and hit it off with both of them. Jamie had just retired from the 49ers, and had also played for the Raiders and the Houston Oilers. He was a big African-American man who had played tight end for a decade in the NFL, and he had a gentle manner. Both were obviously well educated and highly intelligent. Their concept was to write a film about a black quarterback and his struggles to make it in the NFL. Jamie had wanted to play quarterback, but had been discouraged in his efforts by coaches in high school and college. He felt that there was a lot of racism in the NFL and in sports generally, which was reflective of society at large. I thought that this film would be a good way to deal with those issues and others without being as overtly political as *JFK* and *Nixon*.

Oliver and I also met with Dexter King, son of Martin Luther King, and his business associate Philip Jones, to discuss the MLK project. They wanted to be involved and included in the project, which was good from our point of view, since we wanted to have the King family's support and endorsement for the film if we did make it. I sensed a mixture of motives on Dexter's part—a desire to protect his father's reputation and legacy, an interest in finding out more of the truth about his father's assassination, and a good old-fashioned American desire for "economic empowerment," as Jones put it. I felt that we could work with them. Negotiations with Fauntroy's people had gotten nowhere, and having the King family on our side would be far more valuable.

Oliver was happy with the NFL treatment by Jamie and Richard, and decided to hire them to write a script. This was very good news from my point of view, since it gave me a hot new project to work on. He was less happy with the first draft of the MLK script that Steve and Chris had written, but I knew their abilities and was confident that they could produce something as good as *Nixon* (which had gone through nine or ten drafts before it was done).

I was pretty confident that one of these two projects would be

Oliver's next film, and that I could continue to work with him beyond *Nixon*. I had a sense that Oliver felt the same way too. At the wrap party for *Nixon*, he even said to me, "You're doing a great job!" He was drunk when he said it, but it was still a nice feeling to be appreciated. However, when he saw Azita there, he immediately gave her a dirty look and snapped at her.

MLK, NFL, *Nixon*, Annie and Danny

As soon as shooting on *Nixon* was finished, we had a meeting with Steve and Chris about the MLK script. Oliver went through it page by page and systematically savaged the script. They took it well, but it was a brutal meeting. Chris later compared it to "having your fingernails pulled out one by one." We all took lots of notes for the next draft, but I began to sense that this project was in trouble. Steve and Chris had written a very funny version of James Earl Ray as a bumbling, Elvis-loving redneck hick who was manipulated from the beginning. Oliver hated their take on Ray and wanted the whole thing rewritten from start to finish. He also wanted to show Dr. King as a swinging womanizer, and to include the wild conspiracy scenario of William Pepper (although we did not yet have the rights to his book). In other words, Oliver wanted a page one rewrite.

Meanwhile, the football project was heating up. As soon as Danny the Weasel got wind of the fact that Oliver was interested in doing a football movie, he started desperately looking for another football script, book, story or anything else that he could submit in place of our project. Since he had no original ideas of his own and never had, to anyone's knowledge, his only recourse was to steal other people's ideas—usually mine, since he knew Oliver liked them. In this case, he eventually succeeded, at least partially.

He mysteriously came up with a script that was extremely similar to Jamie and Richard's but by another writer, claiming that it was just a coincidence and he had nothing to do with it. He said it had been sent to him by an agent friend of his as a "spec" script that just happened to be about a black quarterback and had all the same elements as our script, but set in a different city. (The coach was even named Stone in his version.) I felt sure that this story was a complete lie but could not prove it to Oliver's satisfaction. When I told Oliver that Danny was a weasel and a liar, he said to me, "He's in a position of trust, so I have to trust him." The logic of that statement still escapes me.

Eventually even Oliver saw through Danny the Weasel and got rid of him, but not before he had sold him on the "spec" script, which was called *Any Given Sunday*. It was basically modeled after the Williams–Weiner script (theirs had been called *Monday Night*). Williams and Weiner got screwed after working on the project with Oliver for over four years. They knew it, but were still happy to have the connection with Oliver and Hollywood that I had given them. I was credited as "co-producer" on *Any Given Sunday*, as on *Nixon*, after conceiving, originating and developing the project for Oliver. Ironically, Richard Weiner and Jamie Williams, who had brought us the original story and script, never got the credit they deserved, and ended up credited as "technical consultants." So what else is new in Hollywood? The official writing credit went to Oliver and to John Logan, who probably knew nothing about Danny's tricks.

After we got started with the football project, I gave Oliver a new book that I thought he might find interesting as background material. It was a memoir and exposé called *You're Okay—It's Just a Bruise: A Doctor's Sideline Secrets About Pro Football's Most Outrageous Team*. It was written by Dr. Robert Huizenga, who had been one of the team physicians for the Oakland Raiders until he quit in disgust. He had also testified at the O. J. Simpson trial.

Huizenga's book detailed the abuse of medicine in sports, and the ways in which athletes were doped up and drugged so that they could keep playing even with serious injuries, often without any informed consent. I thought it showed a side of pro football that was usually hidden from the public and that should be revealed. Oliver agreed, and wanted to get the rights to the book so we could use it for our movie.

However, the rights were already owned by Richard Donner and Lauren Shuler-Donner, a powerful husband and wife producing team in Hollywood who were personal friends of Huizenga. The book was in fact partially dedicated to them, "for the spark." I knew this meant the rights were probably not available, but I thought he should read it anyway. As it turned out, our project was eventually combined with theirs at Warner Brothers, and the Donners were credited as producers. James Woods played a sleazy team doctor in the movie.

After he finished filming *Nixon*, Oliver took off for Tibet, leaving the editors behind to put it all together. He was accompanied by Richard Rutowski, his buddy and traveling companion, who Jane Hamsher had referred to as "Pimpowski." Fortunately, I was not involved in this aspect of Oliver's life. Oliver and Richard both professed to be followers of Tibetan Buddhism and the Dalai

Lama, although I never saw how this was translated into practice. I'd heard one story from a mutual friend that the two of them went to meet with an important Tibetan lama while high on drugs. It always seemed to me that there was a slight conflict between Oliver's hedonistic lifestyle and the true practice of Buddhist principles, which include moderation in all things and compassion for all living beings ... but I stayed out of it.

While Oliver was away, I took the opportunity to visit the set of *Freeway*, a pet project of Danny the Weasel. Oliver and Rutowski were also listed as producers, along with some outside producers from a small company called Muse Productions. *Freeway* was sort of a campy, low-budget version of *Natural Born Killers*, starring Brooke Shields and based (very loosely) on the story of Little Red Riding Hood. I went to the set with Annie, who had replaced Azita as Oliver's assistant. They were filming at a house in Encino. Shields played a housewife who blows her brains out with a gun in the bathroom. We watched several takes of the scene. She looked like a mess, with her skirt hiked up, hair askew and fake blood and brain matter splattered about. It was not a pretty sight.

Freeway turned out to be one of the worst films I've ever seen. If you haven't seen it, don't! It was so bad that it was released in theaters for about a day or so. It also made no money. In its review, *Daily Variety* referred to *Freeway* as "roadkill." Incredibly, the same people involved later made a sequel called *Freeway 2: Trick Baby* (without Brooke Shields). Luckily I was spared that one and never saw it. I later heard that after Oliver finally kicked Danny the Weasel out of the office and terminated his deal, Danny moved into an office near the sleazy Venice boardwalk with the same people from Muse Productions who had made *Freeway*.

Annie had given an advance copy of the galleys of our Nixon

book to Steve, as both Steve and Chris had written essays for the book. One of the little-known facts about the Nixon book that was overlooked by reviewers was that Steve had named, for the first time, the alleged identities of the CIA assassins code-named QJ/WIN and WI/ROGUE. Their identities had been among the CIA's most closely held secrets, and had been ferreted out of documents released under the JFK bill by Steve and Mark Allen, a Washington researcher. Both men had reportedly been involved in the CIA's plots to assassinate Congolese leader Patrice Lumumba in 1960.

This was a major revelation, but it was a far less significant part of the book that caused a problem. The book also contained an "interview" with Oliver about the film, which had actually been written by the film's publicist, Michael Singer. Oliver had read the questions and answers that Singer had written and had approved them. Among them was one paragraph in which he gave me credit for originating the project. This caused a slight tempest in a teapot. Chris and Steve felt that they should receive recognition for their contributions to the project, which was only fair. At the same time, Bob Scheer had gotten an advance copy of the book through his sources at the *Los Angeles Times,* and felt that he and his son Chris should be mentioned as well. And I felt that if the Scheers were mentioned, John Newman's contributions as a consultant should also be noted. As JFK once said, "Victory has a thousand fathers, but defeat is an orphan." When *Nixon* looked like it might sweep the Oscars, everyone around wanted to take credit for it. Later, that changed. . . .

After multilateral negotiations worthy of an arms control treaty, we agreed on language that everybody could accept. In the end, the passage from the Stone interview in the book reads as follows:

Q: Please discuss the genesis of the project.

A: I had two consecutive projects about strong but fatally flawed political leaders—Noriega and Evita—which for one reason or another I decided not to proceed with. I was interested in doing a character study of a powerful leader against a large historical backdrop, and Eric Hamburg—who had come to me from Representative Lee Hamilton's office in Washington, where he helped draft the JFK Records Act of 1992—suggested Richard Nixon. He asked Steve Rivele and Chris Wilkinson to submit a treatment. The idea appealed to me, and we hired these brilliant screenwriters, with whom I wrote the script. We also had help with research and consultation from Robert Scheer, a political columnist for the *L.A. Times,* and his son Christopher, a fine young writer. Their ideas helped shape the script into its final form. Additional consultation was provided by historian John Newman, who wrote *JFK and Vietnam.*

This is the language that was published in the book, which was agreed upon by all parties concerned. It's also a very accurate description of what actually happened. To me, that closed the matter, and I remained friends with those involved, especially Chris and Steve.

Next, Oliver called me from India, wanting me to draft a response to an attack on him by Gerald Posner (author of *Case Closed*) that had appeared in the *New York Times Sunday Magazine.* He even said he would pay $10,000 to take out a full-page ad in the *Times* if necessary. Later, he thought better of that idea, and called me back at five in the morning (of course my time) to say that he liked what I had written, but wanted it shortened into a letter that the *Times* would print for free.

A few days later, now in France, Oliver called me again. He wanted me to write a 300-word letter to *Buzz* magazine—and heavy on the sarcasm—in response to their naming him as one of Hollywood's "Top Ten Bullies." This would be published under my own name. *Buzz* was a flashy Hollywood gossip magazine, now sadly out of business. It was read by everyone "in the know" in Hollywood. Luckily, another of Oliver's publicists, Stephen Rivers, talked him out of this idea. Stephen had experience in politics and was very media savvy. If Oliver had listened to him more often, he could have avoided a lot of problems. Eventually, of course, Oliver got rid of him. He blamed Stephen for his own bad press, just as he had blamed his previous publicists before he fired them.

I had more problems before the book was done, though. First, Oliver decided at the last minute that he wanted Bob Scheer to write an essay for the book. This was way past the deadline, as the book was getting ready to go to press. But I managed to talk the editors at Hyperion into agreeing to a short foreword by Scheer, providing I could get it to them in forty-eight hours. Scheer wrote it, and they published it. Ironically, Oliver got upset when he saw it, because the essay praised the performance of Anthony Hopkins but made no mention of Oliver.

Then Stephen Rivers and Arthur Manson, two of Oliver's other publicists, got upset because I had put a picture of the real Nixon on the cover of the book, instead of using Disney's poster art of Anthony Hopkins as Nixon. I explained that Disney had not gotten the artwork to me in time to meet the publishing deadline, so I had used a collage sent to us by a college student (who was thrilled, of course). Stephen and Arthur were insistent that the cover should be changed. I finally told them that they could talk to Bob Miller at Hyperion about it. If he would agree to the change, I would go along with it. I knew full well that he wouldn't, and he didn't. Nixon's face stayed on the cover.

MLK and NFL Revisited

When Oliver finally got back to California, we had another meeting about the MLK project. Oliver liked the second draft much better, which was a big relief to Steve and Chris, and to me as well. Oliver had wanted to include more of King's alleged womanizing in the script, which we thought would be a mistake. As Chris said later, "He wants to do the 'Guns N' Roses on tour' version of the civil rights movement!" They put in as much as they felt comfortable with, which was still not enough for Oliver. I think part of the appeal of figures like Kennedy and King to Oliver was that they had both been moral leaders in public and "immoral" womanizers in private. He saw himself the same way. At one point in the meeting, Oliver was talking about King's womanizing, and Danny the Weasel said, "But what's his motivation?" Oliver turned to him and said, "If you had a penis, you'd understand!" It was all we could do to restrain ourselves from bursting out laughing.

But Oliver was still pursuing the football project as well. Around this time, I went to San Francisco with Oliver, his son, Sean, and Chris Renna for a weekend. Renna, a licensed M.D. who had been the "set doctor" on many of Oliver's productions, also came along. *Spy* magazine had run a lengthy piece once on

Renna's excesses in dispensing drugs to Oliver and his actors, to which Renna sent a tongue-in-cheek response that did not deny the charges, but expanded on them. But of course, his drugs were "legal." (We called him Oliver's "Dr. Feelgood.")

We went to a party at Jamie Williams's house on a Friday night, which happened to be Oliver's forty-ninth birthday. Jamie had organized a big party for him with many local celebrities. Of course, Jamie had also stocked the party with plenty of attractive women for Oliver's benefit. There would be no point in going all the way to San Francisco to see a football game if you couldn't party and have a good time, after all. . . .

The next morning we went to the 49ers headquarters in Santa Clara and watched a practice session. We met star quarterback Steve Young, lineman Harris Barton and a bunch of other players. Oliver always had a thing for Asian women, so Saturday night we had dinner with Jamie and Richard, plus Betsy Chin, who was a production manager for an independent film that Jamie was doing, and also another Asian woman who was a friend of Oliver's and a Polynesian dancer. After dinner we had a drink with Betsy at the hotel and stayed up till two A.M. talking. He came on to her of course, but she resisted. This was typical of Oliver's lifestyle—constantly on the move, drinking, partying, hanging out with stars and lowlifes alike, trying to pick up women, staying up late, then waking up with a hangover, taking a few of Dr. Feelgood's pills, and getting back to work. He was constantly burning the candle at both ends, and often trying to light it in the middle as well. Chaos was his normal biorhythm.

On Sunday we went to Candlestick Park for the 49ers game with the Patriots. The Niners won 28–3, which made everybody happy. We were in Eddie DeBartolo's box (owner of the 49ers). He wasn't there, but I met his daughter Tiffanie. She lived in Santa

Monica and was a writer/director. She had made one independent film already and was planning another. She seemed smart and interesting. I also talked quite a lot with Roger Craig (former star running back for the 49ers), who was very friendly and praised Bill Walsh to the skies. Walsh's attorney was there as well. He suggested we hire Walsh as a consultant for the NFL project, which was a good idea, but it never happened. Oliver idolized Walsh and later met him briefly for a drink in Palo Alto, but Walsh did not want to get involved with the project. Bill Cosby was also there, sitting by himself in a corner. He seemed to be in a strange mood, and we left him alone.

A few days later, I had lunch with Tiffanie DeBartolo in Santa Monica to discuss her film projects. She wanted to show her film to Oliver and me. Tiffanie, only twenty-four years old, had made a beautiful and touching independent film called *Dream for an Insomniac*. It starred Jennifer Aniston (of *Friends*) and Ione Skye. I saw it on video and was impressed. It was picked up by Columbia Pictures, but for some reason was never released in theaters, which is too bad because I think it would have done quite well. It is now available on video. If you ever see it on your video store shelf, rent it and watch it!

Meanwhile the King movie was running into more problems. Oliver told executives at Fox that he wanted to make it for $45 million, with no stars. After giving this some thought, Fox executives said no. There were also several competing civil rights projects. Rob Reiner was doing a movie about the Medgar Evers case (which became *Ghosts of Mississippi*). Jonathan Demme was planning to make *Parting the Waters,* based on the Taylor Branch book about the civil rights movement. And Warner Brothers was still planning to make a film with Weintraub based on the Pepper book about the conspiracy to kill Dr. King.

None of which deterred Oliver. He wanted to start shooting *Memphis* (the working title for the MLK film) in April, three months after *Nixon* would be released. He said, "It's a race" to see who can finish first. He had to transform it into a battle in his own mind—otherwise it would be no fun. . . .

At the same time, he was also editing *Nixon,* which had to be in theaters by the end of the year. It was now mid-October, and the picture wasn't done yet. Or rather, there was too much of it. It was already three and a half hours long.

Notes on *Nixon*

That afternoon I saw a rough cut of *Nixon* for the first time. It looked good but it didn't move me as much as it should have. I think it needed a lot of editing. It was over three hours long and seemed disjointed and rambling. I thought Oliver should cut it down and make it more linear. I was probably overly influenced by the fact that I was sitting next to Annie in the screening room when I saw it, and she kept making negative comments. I did not realize then that she had already broken up with Steve and was taking her anger out on the film. My thought was, "If an intelligent twenty-five-year-old woman can't understand this film, then we're lost."

I gave Oliver my notes on the film the next day. They were pretty frank and tough on the film. I said I thought he should cut half an hour from the film—for example, scenes from Nixon's childhood—and put it in chronological order. The film had a complex structure with many flashbacks, and seemed hard to follow for anyone who was not an expert on Watergate. I thought that if all college-age students reacted as Annie did, the film would sink.

Oliver wasn't too happy.... He came into my office and said, "Jeesus—you hated it!" I denied that and said I was trying to give an honest opinion. He asked if it was my own reaction or how I thought an audience would react. I said it was a bit of both, but I was more concerned about the audience. He seemed to accept this. He at least respected me for saying what I thought, even though he didn't like it. Annie said her respect for me went up "two thousand percent. ... You didn't try to kiss his ass," as she delicately put it. I doubted that he'd take most of my suggestions, but I hoped they would influence him a little in that direction. He said my comments were the most radical of anyone's. I was worried, but at least he didn't threaten to fire me for disagreeing with him.

I felt that I was getting a little too close to the line for comfort, though. After seeing a revised cut of the movie a few days later, I wrote a much more positive set of notes, which put me back into Oliver's good graces. But I was still worried about the length of the film. I had seen other instances where friends of his came out of an advance screening praising a film to the skies, only to see it bomb in the theaters. This had happened to *Heaven and Earth,* and I didn't want to see it happen to *Nixon.*

A few days later, we got the first attack in the press on the film, which had not even been finished yet, let alone released. It came from Chris Matthews, a columnist, talk show host and former staffer for House Speaker Tip O'Neill. He was upset about our film and wrote a column attacking it because of our reference to Haldeman's book *The Ends of Power* and our portrayal of Nixon's phrase "the Bay of Pigs thing" as a code word for the Kennedy assassination. Matthews said that he had interviewed Haldeman once, and that Haldeman told him he never wrote this and that it had been put into the book by his co-author, Joseph DiMona.

While I don't doubt that Haldeman may have in fact said this to Chris Matthews, I very much doubt that Haldeman was telling the truth. First of all, he was known as the ultimate control freak, and would never have allowed such a thing to be slipped into his memoirs without his knowledge. I tracked down Joe DiMona and spoke to him myself on the phone. He told me he was essentially a ghostwriter and that he had gone over everything in the book many times with Haldeman. In addition, Haldeman had gone over it again several times with his editors at Times Books in New York. Sadly, Joe DiMona passed away in 1999. In his obituary in the *Los Angeles Times*, he was quoted as telling one interviewer: "You don't write anything for Haldeman. He changed my book right down to the end. He rewrote, revised, edited for five drafts. He's very meticulous." Joe DiMona wrote much the same thing in a letter to Dr. Gary Aguilar, a San Francisco physician and JFK researcher, who had helped me track him down.

As I pointed out in our Nixon book, there was also a paperback edition published of *The Ends of Power*, in which Haldeman addresses the various controversies about it. Nowhere did he disavow his earlier words about the Bay of Pigs. He described Joe DiMona as a "collaborator," and also said that "the writing style is essentially DiMona's. The opinions and conclusions are essentially mine." Nor did Haldeman disavow the earlier book in the foreword he wrote to *The Haldeman Diaries*, which were published shortly after his death in 1994.

Haldeman may have changed his tune when talking to Chris Matthews, but it should be remembered that this was a man who had already been convicted of perjury. So his words in an interview years later, when not even under oath, should perhaps be taken with a grain of salt. Oliver also told me later that Matthews had told him he was upset because he had just written a book of his own on Kennedy and Nixon, and our film had killed his chances of selling it in Hollywood. Whether this was true or not, I don't know. For whatever reason, Matthews never mentioned Haldeman's explosive revelations in his own book, nor did he ever talk to DiMona to get his side of the story, to my knowledge. This would seem to be a basic requirement of journalistic fairness.

I went to another screening of *JFK* on November 4, 1995, which happened to be a Saturday. The date was significant because the night before Oliver's girlfriend Chong had a baby—a little girl named Tara (after a Buddhist deity). She weighed 8 pounds, 2 ounces—quite big considering that Chong was quite small. Chong was an actress/model from Korea whom Stone had met in a nightclub somewhere. I think he was looking for a companion after his divorce, and liked Asian women, whom he regarded as submissive. And he also wanted to have a baby girl. Chong fit the bill. She was a nice person, but never said anything unless spoken to, and even then not much. As Azita bluntly put it, "Oliver bought her." At least he bought her a house near his and brought her mother over from South Korea to live with her. Oliver was handing out cigars and was in a very good mood. I think he felt that was a good omen for the movie. Like I said, he was very superstitious. And the film looked better to me this time, too.

The following weekend, I made a trip to Dallas with Oliver and Sean to go to a 49ers–Cowboys football game. This was part of our research for the NFL project. I survived the trip to Dallas with Oliver—barely. Just being around him raised my stress level and probably my blood pressure as well. He just made me nervous. He was too moody, irrational and unpredictable for me to enjoy his company anymore. Plus he moved at a frenetic, nonstop pace that was exhausting. The night before the game, Oliver, Jamie and Richard went out late to a topless bar, but I declined and went to bed early at the hotel. When they got back at about three A.M., Oliver banged on my door and yelled to wake me up, just for fun. The 49ers won the game 38–20 (which no one expected since star quarterback Steve Young was out injured). So Oliver should have been in a good mood.

But the stress of traveling with Oliver was just not worth it. He couldn't let himself relax and have a good time. He had to create some crisis and make everyone else miserable. A prime example was the trip home.

This was one of the most insane performances I have ever witnessed, by Oliver or anyone else. We were all in a great mood after watching the 49ers upset the Cowboys. Suddenly, in the middle of the fourth quarter, Oliver decided he wanted to leave immediately. I tried to call our limo driver, but couldn't reach him. We went outside to the designated area, but we couldn't see him anywhere. It was dark outside the stadium, and the limousine area was packed with hundreds of black limos. Oliver went berserk. He started screaming at me and throwing an incredible temper tantrum, in front of his son Sean and everyone else in our party. I prevailed on another driver to let me use the phone in his car, and tracked down our driver, who arrived a few minutes later. Oliver then started screaming obscenities at him. It was one of the most bizarre and unbelievable mood swings I have ever seen. I could only guess that the darkness, noise, crowds and confusion had somehow evoked the fog of war, and had provoked an episode of post-traumatic stress disorder. Either that, or his drugs were wearing off fast....

We raced to the airport, with Oliver screaming abuse at me

and at the driver the entire way. He told me, "You're down to an associate producer now," and called the driver "a stupid mother-fucker." The poor driver was in shock, but did his best. (I slipped him a $20 tip to make up for it when we got there.) Unfortunately, we missed our flight by two minutes. Luckily, we had a backup reservation on another flight leaving forty-five minutes later. Once on the plane, I pointed out to Oliver that we would arrive only thirty-seven minutes later on this flight than we would have on the other one. He screamed at me, "That's thirty-seven minutes I could have spent with my new baby daughter!!" I felt like saying, "It's also thirty-seven more minutes that you can spend with your son Sean," but I restrained myself. I can only imagine how Sean felt, seeing and hearing this display. Of course if Oliver had really cared, he could have stayed home and spent the whole weekend with Tara and Chong. But I didn't offer this observation either.

When we got back, I had to do more damage control for Oliver. He had taken offense at an essay about *JFK* by historian Stanley Karnow in a book called *Past Imperfect* published by the American Historical Association. He was even more offended by a review of the book by *New York Times* literary critic Michiko Kakutani, which took shots at Oliver and *JFK*. He asked me to draft a blistering response for him, which I did, even though I doubted the wisdom of responding at all. Oliver always felt that the *Times* was out to get him and he wanted to get back at them. Then he changed his mind and decided it would be better to send the letter under my name rather than his. I did not like this idea but had no choice but to agree under the circumstances. Luckily, the letter was never printed.

In the midst of all the hoopla surrounding the release of the movie, Oliver insisted that I go to New York to take his place in a debate with Stanley Karnow, sponsored by the American Historical Association. Given that Karnow had admitted in his essay that he was not competent to discuss the assassination and was not knowledgeable about the facts, I was not too worried about this aspect of the confrontation. What he wanted to do was dispute Oliver's contention that JFK would have pulled out of Vietnam, unlike LBJ (and Nixon).

I was a little intimidated by having to debate a famous and respected historian in front of an audience of his peers, including luminaries such as Arthur Schlesinger Jr. However, the actual debate went pretty well. My mother and sister were in the audience, which may have helped. Among other things, I pointed out that only 79 Americans were killed in Vietnam during Kennedy's presidency, whereas more than 58,000 were killed under Johnson and Nixon. There was simply no comparison. Kennedy was already pulling troops out of Vietnam before he died—a fact I had pointed out in an essay that I ghostwrote for Oliver that was later published in *Newsweek*.

I also mentioned that Karnow was misleading the audience by pretending that *JFK* was a movie about the Vietnam War, when everyone knew it was about the assassination. If Karnow had sincerely wanted to discuss Vietnam, he could have written about *Platoon, Born on the Fourth of July* or *Heaven and Earth*—Oliver's great Vietnam trilogy. But he didn't. On the way out of the auditorium, Karnow hissed at me, "I think what you're saying is total bullshit—but I defend your right to say it." I responded, "The feeling is mutual." I do respect Karnow's books on Vietnam and the Philippines, but don't look to him for insights on the Kennedy assassination. (*JFK* was also criticized by historian Stephen Ambrose, who hated it. I feel that his criticisms of *JFK* and *Nixon* were wrong, but I won't kick a man when he's down.)

On the Cover of *Newsweek*

In general, *Newsweek* was very good to us on *Nixon*. In the December 11 issue, they ran a picture of Anthony Hopkins as Nixon on the cover, with an amazingly positive eight-page cover story by Stryker McGuire (their West Coast correspondent) and David Ansen (their film critic).

Among other things, they wrote: "Prepare for a surprise. On the verge of 50, Oliver Stone has discovered complexity, ambiguity, and even a measure of restraint.... This is no whitewash of Nixon.... But his bitterest enemies won't like it, either, for it forces the viewer to acknowledge the twisted humanity of the man. Stone's *Nixon* is appalling and strangely moving, a man whose private and public demons bring him down with an almost Shakespearean thud.... Stone immersed himself in research, with the help of Eric Hamburg, a former Washington Congressional aide...." The rave review ended by saying, "You won't have Stone to kick around anymore. And maybe, finally, that's why *Nixon* is as strong and surprising and empathetic as it is, because Stone has made the imaginative leap any true artist must: he's seen himself in Nixon."

This was about as good as we could possibly have hoped for. The only negative note was the sidebar by Evan Thomas, a Washington editor for *Newsweek,* who wrote, "Oliver Stone can't resist linking Nixon to JFK's assassination. But he's wrong." In fact, Thomas was wrong. We did not link Nixon to the JFK assassination—in fact we went to great pains not to do so. I am convinced that much of the coverage by Thomas and others was colored and simply biased by the fact that Oliver Stone had made *JFK*, a film they did not like and did not agree with. I am convinced that if *Nixon*—the exact same film—had been directed by Francis Ford Coppola or Martin Scorsese instead of Stone, we would not have gotten this kind of criticism. The media also did not like the fact that Stone could go over their heads and reach his audience directly with his films. That took away some of their power.

In his piece, Thomas repeated the baseless criticisms of Chris Matthews regarding the Haldeman denials. He also gave a plug to his own book, *The Very Best Men,* about the founding fathers of the CIA. These were the men who planned and plotted such disasters as the military coups in Iran and Guatemala, the Bay of Pigs fiasco, and the bungled assassination plots against Fidel Castro, to name several of their more colorful achievements. I would have called it *The Very Worst Men*!

Thomas insisted that Nixon had nothing to with the plots against Castro, even though they were originated while he was vice president in 1959 and was the "action officer" for Cuba in the Eisenhower administration.

I had pointed out to Thomas on the phone before he wrote his piece that CIA Director Allen Dulles had authorized these plots in writing in December of 1959, and that this was documented in the Church Committee report. Thomas ignored this. I had also pointed out that such respected historians as Fawn Brodie, Michael Beschloss and Arthur Schlesinger Jr. were our sources, and that they agreed that there was a "Track 2" (that is, a plan to kill Castro), and that Nixon had very likely been the person who authorized it. I also mentioned some other books that discussed the links between the CIA, the Mafia and the plots against Castro and Kennedy. Predictably, Thomas replied, "Well, those are conspiracy books...." Of course! There was no conspiracy, because the only books that discussed it were "conspiracy books." That made sense to him, but not to me.

In his book *The Crisis Years* historian Michael Beschloss wrote, "Throughout the invasion planning, *the CIA had been quietly working on another track.... Track Two was the assassination of Fidel Castro...*" [emphasis added]. Beschloss also includes an extensive explanation of how Jack Ruby was connected to the Mafia, and how these Mafia plots might have led to the assassination of President Kennedy. I pointed these facts out to Evan Thomas, but he blithely asserted that he had talked with Beschloss, and that Beschloss agreed with him (!). I was disappointed that Beschloss, who seems to appear on TV at the drop of a hat to discuss anything "presidential," never defended our film in print or on the air. In fact, he never made any public comment as far as I know. I think he was afraid to be seen defending an Oliver Stone film, even though he knew we were right.

Enough said. I would just add that for those interested in the subject, there is an excellent chapter in Fawn Brodie's Nixon biography called *The Assassination Track,* which lays out all of this history in detail. I have never understood why people like Evan Thomas insist that Kennedy must have known about the Castro plots, but that Richard Nixon was as pure as the driven snow. In his piece, Thomas did concede that "Stone has published an annotated script of his historical sources, most of them mainstream biographies and histories of the period, even before the movie arrives on the screen." So maybe our book did some good after all—at least for the people who read it. I respect Evan Thomas and Chris Matthews, but I think their hatred of Oliver Stone and *JFK* clouded their judgment on *Nixon.*

Most of the other reviews were very positive. *Entertainment Weekly* proclaimed *Nixon* "the best movie of the year," and reviewers Siskel and Ebert called it "Absolutely riveting! Two thumbs up!" Over fifty film critics put it on their top ten lists, including the *Washington Post*, NBC-TV, Siskel and Ebert, *Sneak Previews* and *Good Morning America*. Not bad for a director who had been consigned to the trash heap of cinematic history after *JFK*!

The Press Junket

The days before the official release of *Nixon* were exhausting—a nonstop round of trips back and forth across the country from L.A. to N.Y. to D.C. and back again. I went with Oliver on a press junket to New York with the stars of the film, then back to L.A. for the Ixtlan–Illusion Christmas party. Oliver gave a special toast to me, which was nice, and I reciprocated. I also gave him a 49ers jacket as a Christmas present. He loved it.

Then it was back to New York and Washington again. It was a whirlwind publicity tour. We had screenings at the Kennedy Center in Washington and the Museum of Modern Art in New York. Bob Woodward came to the D.C. screening, as did Dan Schorr and others. Joe Califano, a former aide to LBJ, was there also. The Eastern media elite seemed to be fascinated with Oliver. In between, Oliver did interviews with Dan Rather, Charlie Rose and others. I have to say that Rather was probably the stiffest and most tightly wound person I have ever seen. Oliver tried to tell him about the LaFontaines' book, but Rather said he knew about it already (which I doubted). He was pleased that we had brought with us a copy of his own Nixon book, *The Palace Guard*. I had checked it out of the Santa Monica library in preparation for the interview. Rather commented, "Well, they must have a good librarian there!" That warmed him up for the interview.

I accompanied Oliver to the interviews and other events. He asked me how he had done with Rather. I said I thought he had done well, which was true, since Rather had mostly asked softball questions. I said, "He respects you because he sees you as a tough guy, which is how he sees himself." Oliver nodded. I think I was right about that.

I stayed on for a few days of rest but ended up spending a lot of time on the phone dealing with Nixon stuff. *This Week with David Brinkley* did a whole show on the film. John Dean represented us ably, under some hostile questioning at times. Bob Woodward also wrote a long piece on the movie in the *Washington Post*, calling it "borderline slander" in part. Strangely, he had praised the movie to me when he saw it at the Kennedy Center premiere with his daughter, and even suggested that we follow it up with a movie about the end of the Cold War. The controversy went on and on, and most of the criticism was wrong-headed or misleading. At least in my opinion. . . .

After the film was released, the Nixon family issued a statement strongly criticizing it as "character assassination," which was quoted in the *New York Times* and other publications. Oliver, Steve, Chris and I were singled out by name for special condemnation. I was disappointed by this, since the family had not even seen the film, and had also refused to talk to us or cooperate in any way. I think if they had actually watched it, they might have been surprised and even liked it, at least in part. However, I have to admit that I was pleased in one respect by their statement—the fact that they mentioned my name. I felt that I was finally getting some recognition for my efforts.

Oliver sent me a suede leather jacket as a Christmas present with a very complimentary note that read: "Dearest Eric, You have been incredible and beyond generous. My affection for you grows and grows. I wish you and your family the happiest holidays and a strong 1996. Love, Oliver." I called him at his house in Telluride to thank him.

Nixon Bombs

Unfortunately, despite all the publicity and good reviews, *Nixon* was a disaster at the box office. My own theory is that people just didn't want to see a three-hour movie about Richard Nixon. They never liked the man, and they just wanted to forget about him. I think it would have helped us if the movie were shorter, but I had no control over that. Probably in Hollywood terms, an actor like Tom Hanks or Jack Nicholson would have helped "open" the movie—that is, give it a bigger gross on the opening weekend, which is now considered crucial in the film industry. But for my money, Anthony Hopkins is the greatest living actor in the world today, and his performance as Nixon was brilliant. So how could we have done better than that?

The box office failure of *Nixon* killed any chance that Oliver would make "Memphis" his next movie. While shooting *Nixon*, we had met with Cuba Gooding Jr., who Oliver had wanted to play Martin Luther King. This was before Gooding won an Oscar for *Jerry Maguire* and was not well known, but Oliver always did have a good eye for casting.

We met with Cuba and he was impressive. He wanted to do it and would have made a riveting Dr. King. We also met with Donzaleigh Abernathy (daughter of the civil rights crusader Ralph Abernathy), an actress in Hollywood who had been close to the King family. She gave us a wealth of inside information, and would also have made a powerful Coretta King in my opinion. But after *Nixon,* Oliver lost his enthusiasm for the project. I was disappointed because I felt that the film could have been another *Gandhi,* something really inspirational that would have educated a new generation about the principles of nonviolence, as well as the history of the civil rights struggle in this country. That's what I went to Hollywood to do. But that's not what sells in Hollywood these days.

I was truly surprised that there was so much controversy over *Nixon.* I felt that we had really done our homework and that we had thoroughly documented our sources in the book. Unfortunately, the Oliver-haters ignored all of that and tried to make it into *JFK* Part 2—which it clearly wasn't. As John Dean said, "The movie is a portrait, not a photograph." In that sense, I think we succeeded. The irony was that, as *Newsweek* predicted, the Nixon-haters didn't like it any better than the Nixon-lovers. Which I guess means we got it about right.

We had an absolutely rave review of the film in *Entertainment Weekly* (which also gave the book an "A+"). Most of the newspaper reviews around the country were also highly favorable. Many of them compared the film to the Orson Welles classic *Citizen Kane.* While this surprised me at the time, in retrospect I can understand the comparison. Both are extravagant, classic American stories about epic characters, brilliantly acted and directed. It is reassuring to know that *Citizen Kane,* which was made in 1941, is still being watched and enjoyed today, as well as being studied in film classes everywhere. And I don't think anybody remembers what it grossed on its opening weekend! In fact, I read recently that it took *Citizen Kane* fifty years to turn a profit. Maybe *Nixon* will earn its deserved appreciation in coming years.

Oliver was devastated by the failure of *Nixon* at the box office. He said to me, "I feel like McGovern in 1972. I feel like we lost an election." I think this wounded him psychologically, just as the torrent of criticism and abuse did after *JFK* (which he also did not expect). He had already called me after the failure of *Heaven and Earth* at Christmas in 1993 and said, "They're trying to drive me out of the country." He felt that the critics and the media were out to destroy his career. He saw himself being driven into exile, like Charlie Chaplin in an earlier era.

Ironically, I heard rumors after Oliver's arrest in 1999 that he was thinking of moving to New York, or even to Paris for a Roman Polanski-style exile. Actually, it might not have been a bad idea. His mother is French, he had spent summers there as a youth, and still speaks fluent French. Maybe he would do better in Paris. The French are more tolerant and take a laissez-faire attitude toward his kind of indiscretions. And he would be outside the long arm of the law in America. In France, Oliver might be regarded once again as a great auteur and artist—maybe even on a par with Jerry Lewis!

The Beginning of the End

I had a talk with Janet Yang after *Nixon* came out. We shared our (negative) thoughts about Danny the Weasel. I suggested we do an "intervention" with Oliver. I also suggested that she talk to Lisa Henson, head of production at Columbia and a close friend of hers, about trying to get us a studio deal there. I thought probably nothing would come of it. Still, I wanted to keep up a good relationship with Janet—even though Oliver told me she had tried to get me fired a year earlier, when he "suspended" me from work.

My conversation with Janet did lead to some results, although not quite the ones I expected. Ironically, Lisa was soon ousted as head of Columbia in an executive shuffle. As often happens in Hollywood, she was given a golden parachute in the form of a "producer deal" on the lot. She started a company called Manifest Films, and Janet joined her as a partner. Naomi Despres, one of Ixtlan's creative executives, went with Janet. This was the beginning of the end as far as I was concerned. After they left in the fall of 1996, the situation in Oliver's office became intolerable, with Danny the Weasel running Illusion and Ixtlan essentially defunct. Soon after that, things went from bad to worse.

Oliver had earlier promised to take me with him to Asia when *Nixon* opened there, since I had never been there. Oliver loves Asia—especially its women. But when the time came to make the trip, he reneged. It was just as well. After the New York, Washington and Dallas trips, I had vowed to myself never to travel with him again.

His next trip was even more exotic. Oliver decided to go to Chiapas in southern Mexico to meet with Subcommandante Marcos, the Zapatista guerrilla leader. He had already decided not to make the Mexico film based on John Leone's script, but wanted to meet Marcos anyway. He also wanted to be out of town at the time of the Oscars, since he didn't expect to win any (he had been nominated for best screenplay, along with Steve and Chris). He offered me the opportunity to go with him to Mexico, but I politely declined. I had been run down and exhausted ever since *Nixon* was finished, and had somehow ruptured a disk in my back, which was causing me great pain. I could not see myself riding around on a donkey in the Mexican jungle. Oliver took Rutowski and Renna with him instead.

Steve Rivele had offered to get me tickets to the Oscars, but somehow didn't get them in time. I had resigned myself to watching them on TV. Both Anthony Hopkins and Joan Allen had been nominated, along with John Williams for the musical score. I doubted that we would win anything since the film was so controversial, but I hadn't totally given up hope.

Then I ended up going to the Oscars after all. The situation was a bit messy but it worked out well in the end. Steve decided to take his son Eli instead, and Annie unexpectedly got hold of an extra pair of tickets on the morning of the event, which had been sent to Oliver's office for some reason. She appropriated them for herself, then changed her mind and decided not to go. She offered them to me if I would buy her a dress! I agreed (I ended up giving her $500 instead). I invited Azita's cousin Jacqueline, who I'd been seeing, to be my date.

At literally the last moment, I rented a tuxedo and Jacqueline got herself dressed up. The Disney people even sent a limo for us! It was fun, but disappointing that none of our nominees won an Oscar. Clayton Townsend and Sandra Noriega were sitting next to us, but left halfway through the ceremony for some strange reason. I think they were miffed that we were there. Bob Scheer and his wife were sitting in front of us.

Afterward, Jackie and I went to the dinner and dance at the Governor's Ball, which was set up in a tent outside the hall. We sat with Steve and Chris and their respective "dates"—Steve's son and Chris's nephew! The legendary Hollywood columnist Army Archerd was also at our table.

We talked with Joan Allen and commiserated a little. She was brilliant as Pat Nixon, and if anyone deserved an Oscar, she did. But the awards are often given for political and personal reasons, not always for artistic achievement. *Nixon* was too controversial for too many of the stuffy Academy members, and Oliver was not popular in Hollywood. Still, we had a great time and a taste of real Hollywood glamour. And it was much more fun than chasing Oliver through the jungles of Chiapas on a braying donkey!

Life After *Nixon*
● ● ● ● ● ● ● ● ● ● ● ● ● ● ● ● ● ●

After *Nixon* was over, life got very boring for me in the office. Oliver decided to develop a movie based on the book *Young Men and Fire* by Norman Maclean, the author of *A River Runs Through It*. Like so many projects, he ultimately dropped the idea.

Meanwhile I decided to try my hand at writing a script. I had always wanted to write, and this seemed like a good opportunity. I had offered to write many projects for Oliver, but he always refused for some reason. I think he felt threatened, or just didn't want to pay me extra money to write a script. Or he just wanted to be negative. I long ago gave up trying to psychoanalyze him. I started to work on my "Uzi Falafel" script without telling him.

At the same time, Oliver had also undertaken a writing project of his own. For some reason, perhaps from frustration over *Nixon,* he had decided to resurrect an autobiographical "novel" that he had written when he was nineteen, entitled *A Child's Night Dream.* He had started writing this more than thirty years before, then thrown part of it away in disgust and kept the rest in a shoe box. He now had hauled it out and started working on it again, with the intent of publishing it as his first novel.

Oliver started spending much of his time at home working on his manual typewriter (he had never become very computer literate). Because the project was top secret, I never really knew what he was up to, but evidently he was editing the original manuscript and adding some revisions and new material along the way. The result was published in 1997 by St. Martin's Press. It was a dud, and roundly panned by critics. Most agreed that it should have stayed in the shoe box.

An article by Bruce Newman published in 1999 in the *New York Times,* shortly before the release of *Any Given Sunday,* described the sensational and weird nature of the book. "In the wildly autobiographical novel ... Stone writes of his hero—who is named Oliver Stone—dreaming of sexual ecstasies with his mother, who is French. 'And it was my mother's face staring down at me,' he writes in one passage, 'as she was doing this to me and me to her, both of us entwined like snakes of desire.' Then comes the transforming moment of consummation: 'O how thrilling! How exciting! Against all rules! Against all flags!'"

Stone told Newman, "It was very bizarre, as a boy, to be introduced to women through my mother." In an interview by Lloyd

Grove in the *Washington Post*, both Stone and his mother Jacqueline admitted that something like this had in fact occurred, although they differed on the exact details. Perhaps this helps account for Oliver's strange attitudes and behavior toward women in later life.

In the *Post* article, Grove quotes Oliver's ex-wife Elizabeth: "'Jacqueline told me'—Elizabeth mimics a husky voiced French woman—'"He couldn't relax and I had to show him." I was shocked that she loosed her wiles on a child—a little, sad, lonely, pitiful figure. So she robbed him of any chance to take possession of his own sexuality.' Elizabeth claims that Jacqueline Stone touched her teenage son's genitals and masturbated him. Jacqueline heatedly denies it.... In any event, Elizabeth theorizes that his mother's raw sexual power over him—along with his father's hiring a prostitute for him when he was 16—seriously damaged his [Oliver's] psyche."

I met Oliver's mother myself on several occasions. She lived in New York, where Oliver had grown up. One time, I asked her which one of Oliver's films was her favorite. Her reply surprised me. "*The Doors*, of course." I asked why. "Because I knew Jim Morrison," she replied. I didn't ask any more questions....

After the firefighter project fell through, Oliver started casting about for his next film, and briefly reconsidered doing "Memphis." One day, I received a call from Danny the Weasel, who was calling from his car. "Guess what," he said cheerfully. "I've got good news for you." I was skeptical as to what this could mean, but listened politely as he continued. "Oliver's going to do the movie about the shmoogie!"

I was totally puzzled. "The what?"

The Weasel was exultant. "The shmoogie. You know, the black guy!"

I began to get the idea, although I had never heard this term before. "You mean 'Memphis'?"

Halsted obviously thought I must be slow on the uptake. "Yeah, the King project ... the shmoogie! Isn't that great! I'll talk to ya later." And so the potential producer of a film about Dr. Martin Luther King hung up and took another call.

But Oliver quickly dropped the "Memphis" idea again, and starting looking around for his next film. He never cared very much about the films he "produced," only the ones he directed himself. He liked to have his next film lined up before the last one was released. But that hadn't happened this time, and he was frustrated. Since he was rarely in the office, it was hard to know what he was thinking or planning, but I do know he spent much of his time traveling around the world, occasionally stopping to relax at his $8 million vacation home in Telluride, which he was trying to sell (I heard later that he had). He was always complaining that he was "broke" from his divorce, but seemed to be quite wealthy by any normal standards. He had a constant stream of income from his old movies, which were always being shown on cable TV, and from video rentals—not to mention the multimillion-dollar directing fees he commanded for making them.

But Oliver's cheapness was legendary. On one infamous occasion, he had taken his young son Sean to a sci-fi movie at a theater on the Santa Monica Promenade near our office. After the movie was over, Oliver checked his ticket stubs and noticed that they had charged the full adult price for Sean, who was only about seven at the time. Always one to stand up for his rights, Oliver marched back to the box office. He shoved the stubs at the kid in the ticket window.

"What the hell is this?" Oliver demanded. "You charged me

full price for a child's ticket." The kid in the booth gave him a bemused look and examined the stubs.

Oliver was now enraged that the young clerk did not trust his word. "Goddamn it! This says seven dollars. Kids are half price. You owe me $3.50, you idiot!" Oliver looked around. "Where's the manager of this fucking place?" he asked menacingly. The ticket clerk could see that he was dealing with some kind of a nut.

"OK, OK … I'm sorry," he stammered, as Oliver continued to glare at him. "We made a mistake. I'm sorry. I apologize." He groped in the cash register drawer, pulled out $3.50, and handed it to Oliver, who grabbed it and stuffed it in his pocket.

"This is the last time I come to this fucking theater," growled Oliver. Having set a good example for Sean, Oliver marched off in triumph, his son trailing behind.

Oliver's ex-wife Elizabeth had kept their house in Santa Monica as part of the divorce settlement, where she lived with their two boys. She also got another vacation home that they owned in Santa Barbara—a Mexican-themed dream house that had been featured in *Architectural Digest*. Oliver bought another house for himself in Santa Monica, and yet another house for Chong and Tara that was nearby. Chong lived there with her mother and other relatives, who helped her take care of the baby. Chong was a down-to-earth person with good family values. I liked her and never understood how she had gotten mixed up with Oliver. But they had their own arrangement, which seemed to work for them. Oliver once defined it by saying, "I'll see you when I see you"— which was not all that often. He was frequently in the company of other women, yet at times Chong would accompany him to social events. It was also not clear whether they were actually married. This, too, was a secret.

Another Fiasco—Oliver's *U-Turn*

Following his repeated tilts toward making "Memphis," Oliver returned to the idea of making the NFL movie. The situation became more and more complicated, though. The film had been set up at Turner Pictures. When Turner Broadcasting merged with Time Warner, Turner Pictures went out of business, and many of their projects moved to Warner Brothers, including this one. However, there was already a football movie set up at Warners—the one owned by the Donners and based on the book by Robert Huizenga, the former doctor for the Raiders. They had commissioned a script called "Playing Hurt" based on this book.

Warners, understandably, did not want to make two football movies. Ultimately, Stone joined forces with the Donners, got the rights to the doctor book and script, and combined them with "Any Given Sunday" as well as "Monday Night," the original script written by Richard Weiner and Jamie Williams.

However, Oliver also wanted Robert DeNiro to play the coach of the team. Apparently, DeNiro wanted $15 million, which would have brought the total budget up to about $55 million. This was deemed to be too high, and Oliver was forced to once again drop the project. Eventually, DeNiro was replaced by Al Pacino as the coach, but the project was set back by about three years in the meantime.

Oliver had always had an obsession with Alexander the Great, and now decided the time had come to make a movie about him. He commissioned a script, and spent much of the summer of 1996 in Greece researching and working on it. Ultimately, though, the project fell apart. Oliver wanted Tom Cruise to star, and he wanted him to play Alexander as a gay or bisexual man, which Cruise did not want to do for some reason. The film also would have been very expensive to make, with a budget of perhaps $100 million for period costumes and location shooting around the world. At this point, Stone was not that bankable as a director. He later dabbled with the idea of making "Mission Impossible 2" with Cruise, but that didn't work out either. Having already worked with Oliver once, on *Born on the Fourth of July*, I think Cruise was reluctant to repeat the experience. (Stone later announced in 2002 that he would make the Alexander film in India with another actor.)

While in Greece, Oliver was also making phone calls to Stanley Weiser, who was working on a rewrite of "Media"—the Maureen Dowd project. But he could never get a script that satisfied him, although Weiser did an excellent job.

Ultimately, Oliver chose the worst of all the available options. This was a script brought to him by Danny the Weasel called "Stray Dogs," by a writer named John Ridley. The script was a second-rate imitation of Quentin Tarantino's style, and was also a complete theft of the plot of *Red Rock West*, the film noir directed by John Dahl and starring Nicholas Cage. (The title of the film was eventually changed to "U-Turn," because the late Akira Kurosawa, the great Japanese director, had made a film in 1949 called *Stray Dog*.) When Kurosawa read the script of this one, he refused to let his title be used. (Unlike book titles, film titles can be registered and copyrighted. Even a similar title cannot be used without permission.)

I could not understand why Oliver wanted to make this movie. Out of a pile of a hundred scripts, this would have been about the ninty-ninth that I would have chosen. It had no political or social content, and seemed to be at best an inferior version of *Natural*

Born Killers. Like *Killers,* it was set in the American Southwest and involved a thoroughly despicable set of characters with no redeeming virtues. It seemed to represent Oliver's current view of the world, in which everyone was selfish, dishonest, disloyal and just waiting to stab each other in the back.

I think another motivation was that Oliver wanted to lower expectations after *Nixon* and make a quick and dirty film that would just make money without generating a lot of heat. Danny the Weasel was quoted in a magazine as saying, "I wanted Oliver to make a film that wouldn't be reviewed on the op-ed pages." In that, he succeeded. The film was ignored not only by pundits, but by audiences, who stayed away in droves. The film was probably Oliver's biggest failure, both critically and commercially, since the beginning of his career.

The respected film critic Roger Ebert wrote, "Only Oliver Stone knows what he was trying to accomplish by making *U-Turn,* and it is a secret he doesn't share with the audience. This is a repetitive, pointless exercise in genre filmmaking." Other critics reacted similarly, and the film grossed almost nothing at the box office. Amazingly, Danny the Weasel then hired the same writer, John Ridley, to write and direct another film for Illusion, called *Cold Around the Heart* (later shortened to *Cold Heart*). This was another cliché-ridden film noir, starring David Caruso of *NYPD Blue* fame. Like *Freeway,* it was so bad that it was barely even released in theaters. It made no money and went straight to video. Oliver also had a falling out with Ridley over the writing credits on *U-Turn* and stopped speaking to him.

Luckily, I was not involved in any of these films and did not visit the set of *U-Turn.* From what I heard, it was a disaster. Sean Penn, who starred in the film, was later quoted in the *New York Times Magazine* as saying that making *U-Turn* with Oliver was like making *Dr. Doolittle*. When asked why, he said it was because trying to communicate with Oliver was "like talking to a pig." (Actor Joe Pesci had made a similar comment after working with Oliver on *JFK*. Pesci said, "Oliver Stone may be a great director, but as a human being he's a piece of shit.")

In retrospect, there may have been a reason for these spectacular failures. I think that Oliver, consciously or unconsciously (or semiconsciously), wanted to lower expectations. After the tremendous critical and commercial successes of *Salvador, Platoon, Wall Street,* and *Born on the Fourth of July,* Oliver wanted to go further, to push the limits, just as Bob Dylan had done by going electric after becoming known as a social protest folk singer. Unfortunately, Dylan then proceeded to make a series of inferior albums like *Self-Portrait* and *Street Legal,* probably on purpose.

With *JFK* and *Natural Born Killers* and *Nixon,* Oliver had found out what the limits were, with a vengeance. He grew tired and burnt out, no longer wanting to be the film world's self-appointed conscience, or the voice of a generation. He decided to remove the burden from his shoulders by making two quick and dirty projects, a film and a book, which essentially had nothing to say and would not be taken seriously. In this, he succeeded. But in doing so, he lost much of his stature both in Hollywood and in the real world. He became both uncommercial *and* uninteresting. Oliver always wanted to have it both ways—to be controversial, and also to be popular. Now he was neither. Like Dylan, he had purposely diminished himself as an artist.

I wonder whether, in those dark days, he thought of his anti-establishment hero Jim Morrison. At the height of Morrison's career, he had quit his band, degenerated into an alcoholic and drug addict, moved to Paris and ultimately killed himself. Morrison was one of Oliver's idols, which is why he made *The Doors* as a movie just before *JFK*. I always assumed that Oliver had chosen Morrison as a subject because of his own obsession with self-destruction and death. Otherwise, why choose the Doors? If you wanted to make a movie about a band of the 1960s, the obvious choice would be the Beatles, or else the Rolling Stones (my personal favorite). Or if you wanted to make a movie about a California band and the hippie culture, you would obviously pick the Grateful Dead. But why make a movie about a macho poseur from L.A. in black leather pants like Jim Morrison? The answer, my friend, is blowing in the wind....

The End of Ixtlan

Unfortunately, I was beginning to have the same experience that Sean Penn had. I began to find it impossible to communicate with Oliver on any meaningful level. I was not on the set of *U-Turn* at all, which was shot in Arizona, since I was not involved as a producer. I was mostly taking care of business at the office, where things were getting worse and worse. Azita was long gone. Janet Yang and Naomi Despres were gone. George Linardos, the other creative executive, had left to do his own writing and work on projects with Uma Thurman and Ben Stiller. Yang's assistant, Janet Monaghan—a girl from a big Irish family, very honest, open and down to earth, had also left. She had been one of my favorite people in the office.

Danny the Weasel had achieved the first part of his master

plan, which was to destroy Ixtlan and become the master of Oliver Stone's domain. Since I was never a part of Illusion, this left me in limbo. And since Oliver was never in the office, and never liked running a company anyway, he left this to the Weasel, giving him plenty of latitude and discretion to do as he liked. This was a big mistake on Oliver's part. It was clear to me and to everyone else who was left that Danny the Weasel had become Oliver's new favorite toy, at least for the time being. Sooner or later this would wear off and Oliver would tire of him, but it hadn't happened yet.

I knew that after Janet and the others left, it was only a matter of time before I would feel compelled to leave also. The atmosphere in the office had completely shifted, and now had a weird, dishonest and sleazy feeling to it. Oliver's erstwhile partner at Cinergi, Andy Vajna, was under federal investigation by the IRS for tax evasion. And I had heard some bizarre rumors about the financial machinations going on at Illusion as well. . . . I was also concerned by the fact that druggies and other lowlifes were passing in and out of the office on a regular basis, and some were even involved in Oliver's film projects. I did not want to be associated with this kind of operation. I tried to convey these facts to Steve Pines, Stone's junior lawyer Nanette Klein and Annie, but it was clear they didn't want to hear it. They were afraid they might lose their own jobs if they told Oliver anything he didn't want to hear.

It was never clear to me why Oliver was so suspicious and vindictive that he drove away everyone close to him. The nearest I can come to explaining it is through this passage about Stalin from Alexander Solzhenitsyn's classic novel, *The First Circle*:

> Mistrust was [Stalin's] determining trait. Mistrust was his world view. He had not trusted his mother. And he had not trusted that God to which he bowed his head. . . . He did not

trust his intimates. He did not trust his wives and mistresses. He did not trust his children. And he always turned out to be right. . . . He had trusted one person, one only, in a life filled with mistrust, a person as decisive in friendship as in enmity. Alone among Stalin's enemies, while the whole world watched, he had turned around and offered Stalin his friendship. And Stalin had trusted him. That man was Adolf Hitler. . . . He had believed Hitler. It had almost—but not quite—cost him his neck. So now, once and for all, he mistrusted everyone.

That was Oliver Stone. . . .

His affinity for Danny the Weasel was hard to understand. As quoted earlier, Chris Wilkinson theorized that after being bullied himself in his career, Oliver needed someone to abuse and dominate as well. That may very well be true. I think there was also a psychological affinity. Both seemed to have sociopathic personalities, with no concern for anyone except themselves, and almost a compulsive, pathological need to lie and deceive other people. And of course, they shared an infinite craving for money. These are not uncommon traits in Hollywood.

To mix animal metaphors, Danny the Weasel reminded me of the old story about the scorpion and the frog. The scorpion asked the frog to carry him on his back from one side of the river to the other. The frog agreed, but said, "You won't sting me, will you?" The scorpion assured him that he wouldn't. Halfway across the river, though, the scorpion stung the frog. As he felt the poison spreading through his body, the frog cried out, "Why did you do that? Now we're both going to die!" The scorpion simply replied, "Well, you knew I was a scorpion when you took me on your back. . . ." That was Danny the Weasel—riding on the back of Oliver Stone.

I draw a distinction between Oliver the filmmaker and Oliver the man. Like Picasso, Oliver Stone was a monster as a human being, but a genius at his craft. I was fascinated watching the film *Surviving Picasso*, which Anthony Hopkins starred in after making *Nixon*. It was obvious to me that Hopkins had picked up many of Oliver's mannerisms and used them in his portrayal of Picasso. The two men were very similar in many ways. They would draw creative people to them, use them for their ideas and their energy, and then discard them when no longer needed. The poet Arthur Rimbaud said, "Talent imitates—genius steals." Like Picasso, Oliver would steal the ideas of others and make them his own. Their sexist and misogynist attitudes were also similar. They were both masters at using people—men and women.

Good News and Bad News

Around this same time, some good things were happening for me. In September of 1996, my father was awarded the Presidential Medal of Freedom, the nation's highest civilian honor, by President Clinton. Our whole family attended the ceremony and I flew out for the occasion. Jacqueline, Azita's cousin, who I had been dating and become close to, joined us. President Clinton gave a very nice speech about my father's lifetime of achievements in helping children, in philanthropy, in conflict resolution, in medicine and in other important areas.

Afterward there was a reception, and I had the chance to speak briefly with the president. My father told him that I had produced the movie *Nixon,* and Clinton's face lit up. He said he had not yet seen it but planned to very soon. Evidently a screening had been scheduled at the White House, and then a crisis arose on that particular night. I said I would send it to him on video so he could watch it at his leisure. We also chatted about a mutual friend from his Arkansas days, Merideth Boswell, who had worked on the film and had helped arrange our access to the White House. It was a pleasant conversation. (In another meeting after leaving office, Clinton told my father that he had since seen *Nixon* and enjoyed it very much.)

I also accompanied my father to a conference called the State of the World Forum in San Francisco, and had the chance to talk with Mikhail Gorbachev. His memoirs had just been published in English, and I raised the idea with him of doing a film about his life. He liked the idea, and asked me to get in touch with him after I had read the memoirs, which I did. I also sent him a copy of *Nixon.*

I of course reported these activities to Oliver, but I think they just made him more suspicious. He did not like Clinton, and in fact called me on election night in November 1996 to complain about his reelection. This despite the fact that Clinton had opened the White House to him and shown him every courtesy, while Clinton's opponent Bob Dole had attacked Oliver over *Natural Born Killers*! Oliver was always suspicious of my Washington background (though it was this same background that had attracted him), and my meeting with President Clinton only exacerbated that. I think he also resented my meeting with people like Castro and Gorbachev on my own without his help. I was getting too independent for Oliver.

My complaints about the shady activities going on around Oliver's office also got back to him. The last straw was when I returned from lunch one day and discovered a fax that had just come in on the office fax machine. It was a letter from Nanette Klein to Danny the Weasel about one of my projects, a documentary about Bobby Kennedy and Martin Luther King. It had occurred to me that since we had already done all this research for the MLK film, and also a possible RFK film, we might as well put it to use.

I had written up a treatment called "1968: The Death of a Dream," and given it to Oliver, who liked it. Danny the Weasel and I then met with executives at Turner Broadcasting System, who also liked the idea, but wanted some changes. I then put together a long list of people who should be interviewed and questions that should be asked, as well as ideas and themes for the documentary. I believe that 1968 was a watershed year in America, and that the assassinations of RFK and MLK, coming after the shock of JFK's assassination, led to a sense of cynicism and disillusionment in American politics from which we have never fully recovered.

When I picked up the fax and read it, it was clear to me that Danny the Weasel had gone ahead and negotiated a producing deal for the documentary with Turner Broadcasting for himself and Oliver, and had left me out entirely. I was outraged. Since Halsted was not in the office, I called Nanette Klein to ask her how this could have happened. She said innocently, "Well, Danny never told me that you were involved with the project. He never even mentioned your name." He had cheated me.

I got Steve Pines and Halsted on a conference call, and gave them both a piece of my mind. I told Halsted that he was a liar and a thief, and that I could not work with someone who was consistently dishonest. This enraged him, since I had said it in front of Pines, who was close to Oliver. He screamed at me and banged down the phone rather than explain or defend what he had done, since I'd caught him red-handed.

I heard nothing further for a week or two. Danny the Weasel, like a small child, had stopped speaking to me. Oliver was in Arizona making *U-Turn* and could not be disturbed. I later learned that after this confrontation, Danny the Weasel had flown to Arizona in a state of hysteria and convinced Oliver that I was working for the U.S. government, spying on him for the Justice Department, and conducting a secret investigation of him for the IRS. Or something along those lines. Danny claimed that I had "opened his mail," when I had actually picked up a fax off the machine about my own project. This is what Goebbels called the "Big Lie" technique. But Oliver was just crazed and stoned enough to believe it.

I then got a phone message from Pines, who had also been in Arizona along with Bob Marshall and Halsted. All of them had long wanted to get rid of me, and this was their chance. I called back Pines and said, "What happened to my contract?" This was supposedly being negotiated between my lawyer and Stone's, but nothing had happened. "We're terminating your contract," he replied. "What do you mean, terminating—there is no contract!" I responded. "Well, you better talk to Oliver," he said. I would have thought that Oliver, the macho man, would have had the guts to confront me himself, but he didn't.

I then tried to reach Oliver in Arizona. He was on the set shooting, but called back a couple of hours later. He was obviously drunk, stoned or both, and was frothing at the mouth. "You motherfucker," he shouted. "You lied to me." I was stunned. "Oliver, what are you talking about?" I managed to reply. He accused me of making threats against him, of spying on him for the IRS, or maybe the Justice Department, or the FBI or the CIA. "You're working for the government. You always were...." Then he started screaming obscenities at me and hung up. I realized then that it was time to go. I lifted my personal computer off my desk, lugged it down to my car, and drove home.

I was hurt, disappointed and shocked. Even from Oliver, I would have expected better treatment. After all, I had left Washington, given up a good career and come to Hollywood to help him. I thought he owed me some thanks, or at least an explanation. But there was no rational explanation, so none was offered. And he didn't even have the courtesy or the courage to meet with me face to face.

Life After Oliver

By mutual agreement it was time to part company. This should have been the end of the story, but it wasn't, at least not quite. After further discussions between various lawyers, Oliver realized that he owed me certain things, like my salary and fees on pending projects. He offered me a lump sum of money, but I declined. I preferred to reach an agreement that would be mutually beneficial. I also wanted to try to work things out with him in a way that would preserve some semblance of a civilized relationship if possible.

I offered that, instead of taking the money, I would write a script for him for WGA scale. This way, we would both get something of benefit, and I could also become a member of the Writers Guild. It would also enable me to start on a new or additional career as a writer, which I had always wanted to do. Oliver agreed to this. We entered into a mutual legal agreement concerning a number of the projects that I had worked on as a producer, including *Any Given Sunday*. I would receive co-producer credits and fees on these films if they were made.

To my surprise, Oliver insisted on a provision in the contract that I be available on a "nonexclusive" basis to work on "Memphis," which he still hoped to make. When the contract was finished, he even wrote me a note saying that he had a new script of "Memphis" by a writer named Kario Salem (who wrote *The Rat Pack* for HBO about Frank Sinatra and his friends), and that he hoped I would work with him on it. I wrote back and said I would be happy to—but he never sent me the script. The Kennedy/King documentary was eventually made by some outside producers and shown on TBS, and later on *CNN Perspectives* in two parts. I was credited as a co-producer, despite Danny the Weasel's efforts to cheat me out of a credit. While the film was a good introduction to the subject for high school or college students, I was a little disappointed that it did not really provide new insights or perspectives into these two men. Still, I'm glad it got made and shown on television.

I did write a script for Oliver as promised, based on the book *The New Emperors* by Harrison Salisbury about Mao, Madame Mao and the history of modern China since the revolution. I didn't think he would make it, but this was the project he wanted me to write, so I did. I learned a lot about China in the process. In addition to the Salisbury book, I read several other books about Mao, Madame Mao, Deng Xiaoping and Zhou Enlai to prepare myself. The most interesting of these was a book by Mao's former doctor, who spent twenty-two years with him. The more I read about Mao, the more he reminded me of Oliver. Mao, like Stalin, had become increasingly paranoid as he grew older, and gradually destroyed everyone around him. I could see Oliver doing the same thing. In fact, I modeled the character of Mao in my script after Oliver to a large extent. As I thought about the psychological similarities between Mao, Stalin, Nixon and Oliver, I realized how fortunate we all were that Oliver was only a filmmaker, and not running a country....

I was surprised when I got a call from Oliver in the fall of 1997—the first time in almost a year that we had talked. He said, "I like your script a lot—it's much better than I expected." He said that he wanted to make it, but that it would be difficult to get it financed. I knew that, and suggested he look for financing in Taiwan, but he said he didn't want to do that. He also told me that he had a "very smart girl" working for him now who would write up a set of notes on the script, and that he would send them to me. He added, "You left a few things out." I said, "I know—I'm trying to cover fifty years of history here."

I told him I had read the doctor's book, and he replied, "That's just a bunch of disinformation." I have no idea where he got that impression, which I think is totally wrong. I didn't argue the point. I just said that I didn't use much of it because we didn't own the rights. Oliver said he would send me his notes and would be in touch soon. Needless to say, I never got them. It turned out that he wanted me to do the rewrite for free, which I was not willing to do, particularly after the way I had been treated in the past. When he found out he would have to pay me scale, he dropped the whole idea.

Eventually, Oliver circled around again to the idea of making the football movie. I thought it was a good idea for him, but I knew there was going to be trouble when I heard that he had moved the setting to Miami. The original scripts had been set in either Chicago or San Francisco. The most logical place to shoot it would have been Los Angeles, where there were plenty of empty stadiums and the costs would have been lower. But Miami was where Oliver liked to go to party.

I contemplated trying to visit him on the set in Miami, not to hang out or see movie stars, but to try to have a serious conversation with him and clear the air. But I realized this would be impossible. The reports from Miami sounded bad, with Oliver shooting all night long, and then going out to party in the wee hours of the morning. But he was getting a little too old to live like a rock star. The *National Enquirer* even ran pictures of him drunkenly carousing in a bar with Cameron Diaz, and tried to imply that they were having an affair. Oliver looked terrible, and the whole idea was a joke to those who were there. The idea might have appealed to Oliver, but certainly not to Cameron Diaz, who was half his age and considerably more attractive. He had better luck "auditioning" the cheerleaders in his trailer. James Woods said that Oliver was "popping Viagra like candy corn." Another actor told me he saw syringes in Oliver's trailer.

An article by Lucy Kaylin in the September 1999 issue of *GQ* magazine, written after Stone had finished shooting, pretty well summed up the situation:

> At a paunchy 52, wearing his glasses low on his nose and clutching a rumpled copy of the script, Oliver Stone looks positively battle fatigued.... Sleep deprivation, plus whatever substances he ingested last night, has caused his face to sag like an old jack-o-lantern. But there is a glow. At the very least, Stone looks pleasantly postcoital. ("I spent the night with the most incredible woman," he later confirms.) ...Stone is only mildly bemused to find that he somehow lost his tuxedo along the way.... A connoisseur of such things, Stone ranks New York right up there with Hong Kong, Miami and Paris in terms of night life.... Even worse is when he pleasure-seeks like a 19 year old—for instance, getting himself arrested last June for allegedly driving drunk and being in possession of illegal substances, man, like an overgrown Phish fan.

There were also reports of fights on the set, and at one point the police were called to settle matters between actors Jamie Foxx and LL Cool J. Puff Daddy, the original star quarterback in the movie, had been fired because "he throws like a girl." He also had a huge entourage and an ego even bigger than Oliver's. Reportedly, Al Pacino gave Stone an ultimatum—"Either he goes, or I go." Puffy went, and was replaced by Foxx as quarterback. Pacino and James Woods both walked off the set at various times. Longtime Stone associate Victor Kempster quit altogether in the middle of filming over Oliver's abusive behavior. Victor, a true gentleman, did not appreciate being screamed at and humiliated in front of the entire cast and crew, after all his contributions not only to this film but to many of Oliver's other films over the years. Stone's accomplished cinematographer, Bob Richardson, had already quit before production started.

After it was all over, Danny the Weasel also parted ways with Oliver. Stone announced in the trade papers that he was shutting down Illusion, and would only direct his own movies in the future. He would no longer be a producer or run a company. In true Hollywood fashion, Danny the Weasel put out a phony statement to the trades with Stone saying how happy he was about this, that it was the best of all possible worlds, an amicable parting, and that now he could do what he really wanted to do, which was produce movies. This posturing was such Hollywood cliché that it was laughable.

Danny the Weasel did go on to produce other movies. He produced a movie for television called *Witchblade*, based on a comic book. It was so bad that Oliver announced in advance that he was taking his name off the film. *Daily Variety* called the movie "a gigantically overblown cliché.... All promise and no payoff." Danny also produced a film called *The Art of War*, which the *New York Times* called "Ludicrous, impenetrable and headache-inducing.... It is also racist ... Chinese water torture would be preferable." The *Washington Post* called it "So convoluted it's incomprehensible, and dull enough to put Sominex out of business."

Clayton Townsend was also ousted, for "betraying" Oliver in some way. (Evidently, he told Warner Brothers that *Any Given Sunday* was over budget, which was true.) And Annie was also gone. By this time, no significant person who had been with Oliver when I arrived in 1993 remained. In a way, it was kind of sad. And then he got arrested. I had not realized it at the time, but I had witnessed the meltdown of Oliver Stone.

Fast Forward—June 1999

"I was not <u>involved</u>."

Director Oliver Stone Arrested for
Drunken Driving, Hashish

—Los Angeles, June 11 (AP). Oscar-winning director Oliver Stone was arrested by Beverly Hills police on suspicion of drunken driving and possession of hashish, a police spokesman said on Friday.

Stone, 52, who won Academy Awards for *Platoon* and *Born on the Fourth of July*, was stopped just before midnight on Wednesday after officers had followed him for a while.

235 / JFK, Nixon, Oliver Stone and Me

Stone was arrested and taken to the Beverly Hills police station. He was released Friday morning after posting $12,500 bail. He is due to appear in Beverly Hills Municipal Court on July 16.

"The driver of the vehicle committed multiple traffic violations, and an enforcement stop was made. A subsequent investigation culminated in the arrest of the driver and sole occupant, Oliver William Stone," the police statement said.

Beverly Hills police Lt. Edward Kreins told reporters that Stone's alcohol level was above the legal limit of 0.08, and a search of Stone's black Ford Mustang turned up an unspecified amount of hashish as well as some pills and an unknown liquid. If they prove to be narcotics, Kreins said, other charges would follow.

I have to admit that it gave me some pleasure to read this item. Not that I wanted to see Oliver go to jail. I thought the best thing for him would be to be sentenced to thirty days in a drug treatment facility, something like the Betty Ford Center. I wrote him a letter after his arrest: "It is sad to see what has happened to you. To put it bluntly, you are an addict and an alcoholic. You need to stop drinking and using drugs, and start going to AA meetings. Then you will feel much better. Otherwise, you will continue to self-destruct."

It felt good to write the letter. I needed to unburden myself of some of the feelings that had built up around Oliver—very mixed feelings that developed over the course of working with him for more than three years, producing two movies together, going through battles together over *JFK* and *Nixon,* defending him repeatedly, and gradually becoming disillusioned with Oliver and his craziness.

In a way, I was glad he was arrested. At least it was nice to know that in America, even an Oscar-winning director can be arrested and forced to spend the night in jail. Maybe there is some justice after all.

I didn't really expect Oliver to write back. He had sent me a nasty letter about three weeks earlier, implying that I was spying on him for the government, secretly opening his office mail, and other high crimes. When I read that, I realized there was no point in responding—that his paranoia had taken over completely and he had lost touch with reality. I decided to ignore his letter, although it was upsetting, and just cut off any further contact with him.

But after the arrest, I couldn't resist writing back. Not just to counterpunch at him, although that felt good. But also because I felt that he needed help. The problem with being someone like Oliver Stone is that you are surrounded by sycophants and flunkies, and no one will tell you the truth. Certainly not about things like your drinking and drug use. And that's what he needed to hear.

However, my message obviously did not sink in, because I was surprised to receive a response from him by return mail. It was an unsigned memo on the letterhead of his company Ixtlan. I found it offensive, but I remember his words clearly. It read in part, "Your language is extreme, and your accusations random and non-pertinent, as I was not <u>involved</u> in the incident" Stone went on to say, "It's surprising that you are so ready to believe what you read in mainstream media...."

Of course! The "mainstream media"! What a delicious phrase, so familiar, so reminiscent of Oliver Stone. How could I have forgotten? Obviously, Oliver had been framed by the "mainstream media." He was a patsy, just like Lee Harvey Oswald. There was a conspiracy, maybe even an Oliver impostor, a second Oliver, an Oliver Stone impersonator, driving his car ... quite possibly an agent of the CIA, or military intelligence. How could I have been so stupid, so naive? Now it all made sense.

Of course, if it were me, arrested in my car after midnight, weaving my way down Benedict Canyon Drive into oncoming traffic, drunk and stoned, if I had been booked and spent the night in jail, I would call that involved. But that's just me. Obviously, Oliver saw it differently. (So did one of his lawyers, who later wrote to my publisher to complain that the "incident" Oliver had referred to was not his arrest, but rather the conduct he had falsely accused me of. But I don't believe this for a minute.)

How else to explain the following item?

Director Stone Pleads Innocent to Drugs, Drunk Driving Charges

—Beverly Hills, Calif., July 15 (Reuters). Film director Oliver Stone, who was arrested last month for allegedly driving drunk, pleaded innocent on Thursday to charges of driving under the influence and possessing controlled substances.

Stone was charged with possessing a small amount of Hydrocodone, a strong pain medication, and a small amount of concentrated cannabis, prosecutors said. He also faces a misdemeanor count of possessing small quantities of fenflu-ramine, phentermine and Meprobamate and two misde-meanor counts of driving under the influence.

Oliver appeared in court wearing dark sunglasses like a Holly-wood star, presumably to show his indifference to the proceed-ings. Outside, he mugged for the cameras, then took out a small camera himself and starting taking pictures of the photographers.

"I'm going to sell them to the tabloids," he explained.

Of course, Oliver Stone is entitled to a presumption of innocence like anyone else. If I hadn't seen him act drunk, stoned, irrational, paranoid and just plain crazy on so many occasions, I might even have believed in his innocence myself. But the drugs found on Oliver were just a daily snapshot of his portable pharmacy. The same drugs, or others, could have been found on him on any given Sunday—or any other day of the week for that matter. I had often heard that Oliver was using "synthetic heroin," but didn't know exactly what this meant. Evidently this referred to the hydrocodone, which is a painkiller somewhat similar to morphine.

Next, this article appeared in the newspapers:

Director Oliver Stone Agrees to Drug Treatment

—Beverly Hills, Calif., Aug. 24 (Reuters). Hollywood film director Oliver Stone agreed on Tuesday to enter a drug treatment program as part of a plea bargain with prosecutors over his arrest in June on drug and alcohol charges.

Stone's lawyer, David Wood, told a court hearing that as part of the plea bargain he expected prosecutors would drop several charges related to drug possession.

He said the Academy Award-winning director had also agreed not to contest two misdemeanor charges of driving while intoxicated, which would be erased from his record once he completes the drug rehabilitation program....

His attorney had intended to enter the plea on Tuesday on Stone's behalf, but Beverly Hills municipal court judge Judith Stein said she would not accept it without Stone being in court.

Stein said she wanted to be sure Stone personally understood the legal consequences involved in the plea. ...

Between Stone's plea of innocence in July and his guilty plea in late August, a significant event had occurred. On August 5, actor Robert Downey Jr. was sentenced to three years in prison for violating his probation on drug charges. Downey had starred in Oliver's film *Natural Born Killers,* playing an Australian tabloid TV reporter. After working with Oliver on the druggy set of that film in 1993, Downey's problems had accelerated. In 1996, he was convicted on drug charges after police pulled him over and found cocaine, heroin and a pistol in his car. A month later, he was found passed out on a child's bed in the home of a neighbor. Apparently, Downey had wandered into the house thinking it was his own home. Three days later, he was arrested for leaving a recovery center, and was then sentenced to probation and community service.

Downey was sentenced to a three-year jail term in August 1999 after admitting that he had violated his probation by using drugs. This episode probably caused Oliver to conclude that he would be better off admitting his guilt and making a plea bargain deal than taking his chances in a court trial. Downey was released after a year, and then was arrested again in November 2000 for possession of cocaine and other drugs.

Finally, there was this:

Director Stone Admits Drug Possession

—Los Angeles, Aug. 31 (Reuters). Academy Award-winning director Oliver Stone dodged reporters and photographers on Friday to plead guilty without publicity to charges of drug possession and drunk driving, authorities said on Thursday.

. . . Instead, Stone, 52, slipped quietly into the court on Friday afternoon, long after the media circus of TV crews, photographers and reporters had packed up and gone home.... Stone pleaded guilty to a single misdemeanor charge of drug possession, and no contest to driving under the influence.

He was ordered to attend drug and alcohol treatment programs and was placed on probation for three years. During his probation, Stone can only drive to and from work and the drug rehabilitation program. Under a plea bargain agreement, if Stone successfully completes the programs, the charges will be expunged from his record....

The Oliver Zone

I recently was surprised to receive a letter from Oliver, or rather a handwritten note in his inimitable handwriting, on one of his gray Ixtlan note cards. It read as follows: "Eric Hamburg—Saw this in Greece. Thought you might get a kick out of it. O."

Enclosed with the note was a neatly photocopied article from a British newspaper. The headline was "Why Washington is still drooling over Katharine: Eulogizing is all rather sickening, says Mark Steyn." Mr. Steyn, the author of the piece, devoted his article to trashing Kay Graham, the recently deceased publisher of the *Washington Post,* and deriding those who praised her after her death.

The article also included the following passage: "One writer stood head and shoulders above the rest. The anonymous editorialist at the *Pittsburgh Tribune-Review* evidently returned from lunch drunk and momentarily forgot himself.... He started off conventionally enough, but then wandered deplorably off-message.... 'She married Felix Frankfurter's brilliant law clerk, Philip Graham, who took over running the *Post*.... Graham built the paper but became estranged from Kay. She had him committed to a mental hospital, and he was clearly intending divorce when she signed him out for a weekend outing during which he was found shot. His death was ruled a suicide. Within 48 hours, she declared herself the publisher.'"

Mr. Steyn then rhapsodically went on. "That's the stuff! As the *Tribune-Review*'s chap has it, Mrs. G got her philandering spouse banged up in the nuthouse and then arranged a weekend pass with a one-way ticket. 'His death was ruled a suicide.' Lovely touch, that. Is it possible Katharine Graham offed her hubby? Who cares? To those who think the worst problem with the American press is its awful homogeneity, the *Tribune-Review*'s deranged perverseness is to be cherished. Give that man a Pulitzer!"

To be fair, I should emphasize that those particular words were not written by Oliver Stone, but by someone named Mark Steyn. They were merely sent to me by Oliver with a note saying "Thought you might get a kick out of it." Nevertheless, both the note and the article it accompanied were puzzling, to say the least.

First, I found it strange that Oliver would write to me at all. I had not seen or spoken with him for more than a year and a half, since the premiere of *Any Given Sunday*, and had not corresponded with him for two years, since our exchange after his arrest. And that exchange had not exactly been friendly. Even before that, we had not exactly parted on friendly terms. He had essentially accusing me of being a disloyal, spying government agent and abruptly dismissed me from his employment.

Furthermore, he had obviously not taken my advice about

going into AA or into rehab, or to stop drinking and using drugs. I had heard many reports in the two years since his arrest of Oliver sitting in his office smoking dope, or lighting up a joint in his limo, his home or even in a public park. I also knew that he had not stopped drinking tequila, rum, wine or any other of his favorite beverages.

So why the friendly note? Perhaps he was trying to reach out, to reconcile, even to apologize in his own limited way. Perhaps he felt lonely and isolated, having lost his old office and his entire staff, other than one flunky of an assistant. Or perhaps he had simply forgotten everything that had transpired between us. Who knew?

I had long ago realized that it was impossible to figure out Oliver's motives, because he simply did not act rationally. He lived in what I called the "Oliver Zone" (or for short, the O Zone). The Oliver Zone was like a weird anti-matter, anti-gravity, magnetic force field that warped the reality around it. Usually, events in the real world happen in a somewhat normal, predictable manner most of the time. But when you were around Oliver, these rules were suspended. Strange things would happen, and you often felt like you were the one who was on drugs, not him. I can't explain this phenomenon, but I experienced it many times. Time seemed to move either faster or slower than normal, and people around him seemed to act in abnormal and sometimes surreal fashion.

Part of it was probably due to his celebrity. People in America act differently when they are around famous people, and cease to act rationally when around someone they have seen on *Entertainment Tonight*. They have been unwittingly brainwashed by the cult of celebrity that exists in this country. Oliver often took advantage of this cult of celebrity. He would assume an intimacy with total strangers, and would ask them for personal favors that he fully expected to be granted, and they usually were. These could range from the trivial to the highly personal.

But it was more than just celebrity. I had been around my fair share of Washington political celebrities, and many of them turned out to be pretty normal people when you got to know them, albeit normal people with large egos. Even in Hollywood, I had met stars like Anthony Hopkins who were modest, genuine and down to earth. Oliver was anything but down to earth. He lived somewhere in the O Zone.

I gave the note some further thought. At first I decided not to respond. I had been burned too many times by Oliver's mind games. After working with him on two films, I felt like Charlie Brown in the old Peanuts comic strip, when he would run up to kick the football and Lucy would pull it away at the last minute, causing poor old Charlie to land flat on his back. I had landed on my back for Oliver Stone one too many times.

Next, I wondered if there was a hidden agenda. One of the projects I had worked on with Oliver was called the "Media Project," whose premise was based on the takeover of a fictional version of the *New York Times*, with a Maureen Dowd-like character as the villainess of the piece (more about this later). The script had been written and rewritten, but the movie had never gotten off the ground. Maybe, I thought, Graham's death and his cynical take on it had provoked him to consider reviving it. If so, he might want me to work on it, since I had worked with the writers and contractually stood to get a producer credit and a fee if the film was actually made.

It seemed unlikely that the "Media Project" film would ever get made. Its time seemed to have come and gone (although you never knew with Oliver). And while Oliver was undoubtedly obsessed with the *New York Times*, which had attacked him relentlessly over *JFK*, I didn't think he felt quite as strongly about the *Washington Post*. I had never met Mrs. Graham myself, though I admired her accomplishments. And I was quite sure that she did not murder her husband.

But on the other hand, I thought this might be just the kind of conspiracy theory that would appeal to Oliver. After all, Phil Graham had been a personal friend of President Kennedy, and had shot himself in 1963, not long before Kennedy's own death. Could there be a connection there? Could it be sinister? Could there be a movie in it? If nothing else, it would certainly be controversial, which Oliver loved. He knew that the media loved covering the media, and also loved attacking him. Could this be another *JFK*, propelling him back into the spotlight?

I knew that Oliver did not care for Bob Woodward (who had called his film *Nixon* "borderline slander"), but I don't recall him ever saying anything about Kay Graham. And I knew that Oliver detested George Lardner of the *Post* for an article he had written ten years earlier attacking *JFK* before it was even released. I would have been much less surprised if Oliver had sent me an article that Lardner had written in the *Post* on March 26, 2001, which started off by saying, "The House Assassinations Committee may have been right after all: there was a shot from the grassy knoll." This was based on a new forensic study of the evidence that had just been published in a British scientific journal.

Oliver must have jumped for joy at this seeming vindication, but I never heard a word from him about it.

Then I had another conspiratorial thought. Perhaps Oliver had gotten wind of the fact that John Dean and I had written a script about the Pentagon Papers case, which treated the *Times*, the *Post* and Kay Graham favorably. Maybe he was trying to signal me that he knew about it, and wanted to warn me not to do it. The project was already set up at a cable network with Alec Baldwin, but I doubt that Oliver knew about it. In any case, he was never one for subtlety.

I finally decided that Oliver was being the usual inscrutable, irrational, unpredictable person he always had been—friendly and charming one minute, foaming and frothing at the mouth the next. But the very fact that I had wasted so much time trying to figure out what he meant by sending me this strange newspaper clipping told me something: That I had been right in vowing never to work with him again, and to avoid any contact if possible. Still, there was a caveat in my mind. If Oliver would get sober, if he would go to the Betty Ford Center, or Hazelden, or any other rehab facility—or simply break through his denial and start going to AA meetings—things might be different. But that was a very big *if*, for Oliver is nothing if not unpredictable.

The famous screenwriter William Goldman wrote something to the effect that once you became rich and famous and successful in Hollywood, you had to realize that no one would ever tell you the truth again. That had been my mistake. I had told Oliver Stone the truth too many times. I think Oliver appreciated that I was from Capitol Hill, that I was the antithesis of a Hollywood operator in every respect, and that I felt it my duty to tell him the truth as I saw it, especially when I knew that nobody else would. But perhaps I had gone too far.

Oliver operated on many levels. On one level, he was intellectual, highly intelligent, well read, interested in history and interesting to talk to. On another level, he was highly paranoid, suspicious of everyone and constantly seeing conspiracies all around him. In the script of *JFK*, he had written, "Like Caesar, he is surrounded by enemies." That was how Oliver saw himself. On yet another level, he was a self-destructive and reckless hedonist, and gradually destroyed all the important relationships in his life until only his mother and children were left in his camp. Despite being one of the biggest names in Hollywood, because of his increasing reputation for legal and drug problems he could not even get financing from a major studio for the movie project "Beyond Borders," which he had planned to make. They went with another director instead. I began to see him as an Ernest Hemingway figure, traveling the world in search of himself, drinking more and more, rehashing his own work and becoming a self-parody, until the inevitable tragic end. As one of his close friends said to me, "I keep waiting for that phone call." I saw him as being like the character portrayed by Tommy Lee Jones in Oliver's film *Heaven and Earth*—a Vietnam veteran haunted in his dreams by the horrors that he has seen, by the people he has killed, the atrocities he has committed, until he can no longer stand it and turns the gun on himself. I hope it doesn't come to that.

And yet, there was something likable about Oliver. He had a crazy sort of charisma, a combination of childlike innocence and demonic evil, that was fascinating and at times attractive. I still felt a bit of sympathy for the old devil. But he had been corrupted—if not by Vietnam, then certainly by Hollywood. The fame, the flattery, the wine, women, money and drugs had gone to his head. I doubted that he would ever recover, or return to "normal"—if he ever had been normal. I believe that Oliver had been shocked and traumatized by the wave of virulent and negative criticism and abuse he received in response to his films, and especially to *JFK*. To my knowledge, this had never happened to a filmmaker before. I think he expected the normal sort of reviews from film critics—good, bad or indifferent. But I don't think he was prepared for the mugging he received from the "mainstream media"—some deserved, some not—which was unprecedented in its scope and ferocity. After all, he was a filmmaker, not a politician. And it was only a movie.

Before *JFK*, he had been idolized for *Platoon*. He had also won Academy Awards for the screenplay of *Midnight Express* and for directing *Born on the Fourth of July*. He had ascended the highest heights that Hollywood had to offer. And then it all came crashing down on him after *JFK*. I also think that *Natural Born Killers* was his way of responding to his critics—his way of saying "Fuck you" to the media as blatantly as possible. And naturally, they responded in kind. From being an honored and respected filmmaker, he had turned into both a menace and a joke. Oliver Stone had become a caricature, a symbol of excess, a kook and a nut. At least that's the way he was portrayed. And he could not see, or admit, that at least some of it was his own fault.

And yet . . . I haven't given up hope. I admired Oliver for his guts in making *JFK*. I still think he was right about a lot of things (and wrong about a lot of others). And no one else could have galvanized support for the passage of the President John F. Kennedy Assassination Records Act of 1992, as he did. No one else could have opened up perhaps the most taboo subject in American history, as well as literally millions of hidden and secret documents that will be invaluable to historians for years to come. Maybe if he had made a less provocative and controversial film, he wouldn't have accomplished these things.

I remember going to see a film called *Ruby*, about Jack Ruby and the assassination, which came out shortly after *JFK*. There were about three people in the theater. I can assure you that *Ruby* would not have caused the release of even one sheet of paper, let alone the avalanche of secret documents produced by Oliver's film. And I still feel that this was a very valuable and historic accomplishment. I remain grateful to him for it, even after all the abuse I took from him later. I'm proud to have been a part of it. After all, it was our shared interest in uncovering the truth about Kennedy's assassination that brought me into the Oliver Zone in the first place.

John Dean and the Pentagon Papers

After I made my exit from Oliver Stone's office, one of the first people I called was John Dean. Half jokingly, I said, "The same thing that happened to you just happened to me...." John was sympathetic and understood immediately. He graciously offered to work with me on other projects. My father had suggested that I write a script with Dean on the Pentagon Papers case, thinking that it would be a perfect vehicle to tell a story about the Supreme Court and the First Amendment. He was right.

I presented the idea to John, who was taken with it and immediately wrote up a detailed treatment. Dean of course had been involved in these events at the time as counsel to the president, and had later become quite friendly with Dan Ellsberg, the man who leaked the papers to the *New York Times*. They'd had a series of discussions of these events years after the fact. This became the basis for our script, with flashbacks to the actual events.

The Pentagon Papers case involved incredible drama: Ellsberg's tortured and conscientious decision to leak the papers, the difficult and hotly debated decisions to publish them by the *New York Times* and then the *Washington Post,* and the Nixon administration's decision to prosecute first the *Times* and then Ellsberg himself. The latter also involved an illegal break-in of Ellsberg's psychiatrist's office in Beverly Hills by Howard Hunt, Gordon Liddy, Frank Sturgis and Rolando Martinez—the same people who broke into the Watergate a year later. The case against Ellsberg was thrown out two years later when it was revealed that Nixon and Ehrlichman had essentially tried to bribe the trial judge by offering him the directorship of the FBI.

The whole affair, which took place in 1971, was a precursor to Watergate in many ways, and was really the beginning of the end of the Nixon administration. Amazingly, this incredible story has never been told on film, and is little known in comparison to Watergate and the events that followed. John and I went back and researched the full story, with Ellsberg's knowledge, and wrote the script ourselves. Through my friend Janet Monaghan, who had left Ixtlan, we got it to Alec Baldwin, who read it and wanted to make it. He took it to a cable network and set it up there. Especially in the light of more recent political scandals, this is a story that needs to be told. It is scheduled to be made sometime soon, hopefully . . .

I also followed up on my promise to Mikhail Gorbachev by writing a script about his years as general secretary and president of the Soviet Union from 1985 to 1991. Entitled "Revolution," it told the story of Gorbachev's incredible efforts to transform his country and to end the Cold War. Although he ultimately was forced by Boris Yeltsin to leave office, I believe that Gorbachev succeeded in many ways that are still not fully understood. He is one of my personal heroes, and I'm glad that now, ten years after the fall of the Berlin Wall, he is beginning to get the recognition he deserves for his role in bringing about these crucial events.

My father, who had worked with President Gorbachev and his advisers over the years in his role at the Carnegie Corporation of

New York, saw Gorbachev again at an event in New York in early 1999. He gave a copy of my script to Gorbachev, who took it back to Moscow with him. We later got a call from his translator, Pavel Palazhchenko, who said that Gorbachev had read the script and liked it, and would be happy to cooperate. Unfortunately, the world of Hollywood has been less cooperative. I spoke personally with the head of one major cable television network, who told me that he had read the script and couldn't put it down. "But there's no way we could make this," he told me regretfully. "We just don't get the rating on political and historical movies anymore, and we just can't do it."

I also wrote a script about another president who I believe has not received sufficient recognition or appreciation—Jimmy Carter. My father serves on the board of the Carter Center in Atlanta, and I had met Carter several years earlier at a conference at the Carnegie foundation in New York. With President Carter's permission, I wrote a script called "The Blood of Abraham" about the Camp David agreements, based on Carter's own memoirs and subsequent writings. The Camp David Accords were probably one of the greatest and most dramatic achievements of any president, yet they have been largely forgotten or taken for granted as time has passed. Again, I was incredulous when I discovered that these events had never been dramatized in a film.

After I finished the script, my father took it to Atlanta and gave a copy to President Carter at a board meeting. To my delight, I received a letter in May of 1999 in which he said, "I have read your script about Camp David, and it brought back a flood of memories. You have done a fine job of encapsulating what occurred during those days, now about 20 years ago. . . . You've done a good job." He also provided three pages of detailed notes on the script, suggesting changes that would make it more accurate. I was stunned and flattered to receive such a letter from a former president of the United States. He obviously had actually read the script, taken it seriously and given it careful thought. His notes were also more insightful and useful than any I had received in the past from Hollywood "creative executives"!

I made the changes he suggested, and sent him a second draft of the script with my sincere thanks. President Carter was then kind enough to send a copy of the script with his endorsement to the head of a major television network. Unfortunately, the reaction he got was the same as the one I got to the Gorbachev script—"We'd love to make this, but we just can't, because it won't appeal to a young audience." I think TV executives are wrong about that, and I also think that a network has an obligation to the public beyond just getting ratings and making money. But it's hard to convince them of that.

These experiences have led me to realize that the climate in Hollywood at this time is just not conducive to making the kind of films that I want to make and that I feel should be made—films that deal with social, political and historical issues. What sells in Hollywood are action movies, cartoons, sex, violence and anything that is sufficiently weird, but not intellectually challenging. What doesn't sell, with rare exceptions, are meaningful films about real issues and events. It takes a director of rare power and vision, like a Stone or a Spielberg, to even get a film of this kind made. And even then they often don't succeed. Stone was very jealous of Spielberg for his financial success; his many commercial movies had made him a billionaire. But I think Spielberg was also envious of Stone for his Oscars and his serious, political films. I'm sure this is why Spielberg decided to start making films like Schindler's List, Amistad, and Saving Private Ryan.

At the end of 1997, I was in New York visiting my family over the Christmas holidays. To my great surprise, I got a message through my father that Kofi Annan, the secretary general of the United Nations, wanted to meet with me! I was a little stunned and intimidated, but of course accepted. Evidently he had seen *Nixon* and liked it, and wanted to discuss how the United Nations could make greater use of the media and the film world to promote its causes and ideals. On the afternoon of New Year's Eve, my father and I went to the secretary general's residence and spent a very pleasant hour or so talking with him, his wife and his aide Shashi Tharoor.

I made a number of suggestions, and told him that I would love to make a film about the United Nations, if I could only get it financed, but that it would probably be very difficult. His wife, Nane, who is from Scandinavia, suggested the idea of a film about Dag Hammarskjöld, the former UN secretary general who was killed in 1961 under mysterious circumstances in a plane crash in Africa while on a Congo peacekeeping mission. This could be a fascinating story, also involving the U.S. efforts to assassinate Prime Minister Patrice Lumumba of the Congo during the Eisenhower–Nixon years. I hope someday it will be made into a film. But I doubt it. . . .

Strange Encounters with Oliver

I saw Secretary General Annan again in Los Angeles in the spring of 1998, when he made a visit to Los Angeles for the purpose of visiting with the Hollywood community and lobbying them on behalf of the UN. At a reception sponsored by Jack Valenti at the Beverly Hilton, I ran into James Woods and Marley Shelton, who had played Tricia Nixon in the wedding scene of the film. We had a very nice reunion.

Later that night, there was a dinner for the secretary general at Greenacres, the palatial home of billionaire financier Ron Burkle, which was once owned by the silent film star Harold Lloyd. It was sponsored by the Center for International Relations at UCLA, and I attended with my father. To our surprise, who should we run into but Oliver Stone! This was the first time I had seen Oliver since I had left his office over a year before. He seemed very uncomfortable, especially to see my father, for whom he had great respect. He also seemed very drunk. He was wearing a black suit and black shirt with no tie, and looked as if he might have slept on a park bench. Oliver was with a tall, African-looking woman. We chatted briefly, but it was impossible to have a real conversation under the circumstances.

When I was working on this book in late 1999, I ran into Oliver again, also at a dinner at Greenacres. This one was in honor of George Shultz, who had served in the cabinets of both Nixon and Reagan. I knew Oliver had been invited, but was surprised that he showed up. Ironically, he was seated next to my wife Jacqueline at dinner, while I was across the table. Since it was a large, round banquet table with ten or twelve guests, I could not have talked to him even if I had wanted to, which I didn't. I said hello and exchanged pleasantries, but that was about it.

Jackie, though, had a fairly long and friendly conversation with him. Again, he was clearly drunk when he arrived, and drank red and white wine throughout dinner. At one point, he left the table for a lengthy period of time, and his plate was taken away. I assumed that he had left for some reason, but he eventually returned, sweating profusely and wiping his face with a bandanna. This was a sure sign that he had been in the bathroom doing drugs (he had done the same thing at the Kofi Annan dinner). The only other person who I have ever seen sweat like that was Marion Barry, the former mayor of Washington, D.C.

Jackie and Oliver talked about their shared interest in Tibetan Buddhism, and also about Iran, where she grew up. He said he wanted to make a movie about Iran someday. Oliver asked her if he looked bad, and she diplomatically told him he should take better care of himself. In fact, he had gained a lot of weight and looked haggard and blowsy, like an old hooker who has been on the streets for too long. At one point, he asked to borrow my cell phone to make a call. I handed it over, and jokingly said, "This isn't a long-distance call, is it?" He gave me a dirty look and growled, "Yeah—to Timbuktu!" Then he turned to Jackie and asked, "He's not going to be able to trace who I called, is he?" She assured him I wouldn't. "Good," said Oliver emphatically. He leaned over to her and whispered, "He's a spy, you know." Oliver also ate all the dessert off Jackie's plate without asking, and made a drunken pass at another woman at the table, which was declined.

It was sad to see Oliver in this condition, particularly after he had already been arrested and sentenced for drunk driving and possession of drugs. It was clear that nothing had changed. I hoped for his sake that he at least had a limo and driver outside waiting for him. It was near this very spot, on Benedict Canyon Road, that he had been arrested only a few months earlier, weaving in and out of traffic lanes, driving on the wrong side of the road and heading into the direction of oncoming traffic. Luckily, he hadn't killed anyone.

In December of 1999, Oliver's film *Any Given Sunday* was released. As on *Nixon,* I was credited as co-producer. This seemed to be my fate. I hoped the film would do well, and it did. I also hoped that Oliver Stone would not only resurrect his career, but, even more importantly, get his life back together. At the table with Jackie, he had told her that it had been a tough two years for him, and that he had split with many of his closest friends. There is no doubt that he brought this on himself. There is also no doubt in my mind that the reason was his increasing consumption of alcohol and drugs, combined with the culture of Hollywood.

The weekend before Oliver was arrested, he was in Las Vegas staying at the Bellagio Hotel. Eyewitnesses said that he stayed up all night, going from one club to another, accompanied by an entourage of increasingly sleazy hookers and Mafia types. "These were people who should not have been around Oliver," one observer commented sadly. The following week, he went out to dinner with Lorenzo Di Bonaventura, the head of production at Warner Brothers. As usual, Oliver drank heavily. After dinner, he got into his Ford Mustang convertible and headed off for the home of his old friend Sergio, with whom he often shared the pleasures of life. On the way there, his car was pulled over and he was arrested. Oliver Stone, the Academy Award-winning director, spent the night in the Beverly Hills jail. . . .

I had hoped, when Oliver was arrested, that he would be sentenced to the Betty Ford Center, or perhaps the Hazelden Clinic in Minnesota. I felt, and still feel, that this is what he really needs—to clean the alcohol and drugs out of his system, and get into a recovery program. I felt that if this could happen, and if he would attend recovery meetings on a regular basis, he would become a different person. On that basis, I think we could reconcile and maybe even become friends again. Stranger things have happened. . . . But as in so many cases in Hollywood, the judge let him off lightly because he was a celebrity—because he was Oliver Stone. She may have felt that she was doing him a favor, but she wasn't.

I have many feelings about Oliver Stone. I am grateful to him for giving me the chance to come to Hollywood and to make two great films with him—*Nixon* and *Any Given Sunday*. This was an unforgettable experience and one of which I am very proud. On the other hand, I also feel that he treated me very badly in many ways. I often thought that working for Oliver was like being part of a dysfunctional family with an alcoholic parent. You never knew what his mood would be from hour to hour or day to day. You never knew how he would react to any situation, but you learned to expect the worst. He was capable of kindness, but more often of irrational and volcanic rages. Paranoia was a given with Oliver.

In his 1995 biography of Oliver, James Riordan offers an interesting theory to explain Oliver's lifelong suspicion. He thinks it was due to the shock of his parents' divorce at age fifteen. "This was the turning point in Oliver Stone's life," writes Riordan. "To this day the shock from this sudden devastation colors nearly all of his decisions. It turned him forever from the innocent expectation and hope of youth and propelled him like a rocket straight for the dark side. Most of those close to him agree that he never recovered."

Stone himself has confirmed this view of the event. "I felt like shit, like nothing," he told Riordan. "Everything was metallic. All the adults were dangerous, not to be trusted. I reassessed everything. I had a sense that everything had been stripped away. That there was a mask on everything, and underneath there was a harder truth, a deeper and more negative truth."

To this was added the trauma of Stone's subsequent service in Vietnam. His experiences there have been fully chronicled in the film *Platoon,* as well as its sequels *Born on the Fourth of July* and *Heaven and Earth.* They require no further explanation here. I will say, though, that whatever traumas Oliver may have suffered in Vietnam are no excuse for his often brutal and selfish treatment of others in subsequent years. My former boss, Senator John Kerry, also served in Vietnam during the same period as Oliver. He endured experiences just as horrific as those of Oliver Stone, including serving in combat, being wounded and seeing men die. Yet he emerged from that experience as a courageous, honorable and decent person, dedicated to helping others and treating people fairly and honestly. So have millions of other veterans of the Vietnam War and of other wars.

I often thought as I got to know Oliver that he believed you had to be nasty, brutal, tough and ruthless to succeed in this world. I think he still believes that. But I know that isn't true. The best example to the contrary that I know of is my own father. He has been highly successful in the fields of philanthropy, academia, public policy and medicine, and has achieved great honors and recognition for his contributions and accomplishments. Yet he has always treated the people around him with decency and kindness and the highest humanitarian values. He would not know how to live any other way.

The same is true of my former boss in the House of Representatives, Lee Hamilton. He served in Congress for thirty years, and rose to the position of chairman of the House Foreign Affairs Committee. He also commanded the greatest respect and admiration from everyone around him, including not only his own staff but also his political opponents. Lee Hamilton was the epitome of fairness, honesty and decency in government. Perhaps it stems from the fact that both Lee and my father grew up in Evansville, Indiana—far from Hollywood and Washington.

Shortly after Oliver's arrest, I happened to have lunch with Anthony Hopkins and a mutual friend. Hopkins, reflecting on Oliver, shook his head sadly and said, "He's going to wind up like John Belushi." He may very well be right. Or he may wind up like Elvis, or Ernest Hemingway or many others. But I hope not. Some people really do have to hit bottom before they can start to recover. Evidently Oliver has not reached that point yet.

Alcohol and drug addiction is a progressive disease. It doesn't get better. It only gets worse. It's also the only disease that tells you that you don't have a disease. It generates denial. When Oliver wrote to me and said, "I was not <u>involved</u>"—that's denial. But I've heard much worse stories of people who have hit bottom and then, in a moment of clarity, decided to change their lives. It's never too late to change....

I wrote much of this book as a visiting scholar at UCLA in the Center for International Relations. I was also involved there in research and writing on issues pertaining to Hollywood and international relations, the entertainment industry, the media and globalization. To me, this was far more enjoyable than sitting through Hollywood development meetings. I was back in the world of ideas, the world I grew up in on the Stanford campus, where knowledge and intellectual curiosity mattered more than box office grosses, back-end deals and backstabbing producers. I liked talking to and being around the students, drinking coffee outside at the student coffeehouse, sharing ideas, going to the occasional seminar and even giving some myself.

If I learned anything from Oliver Stone, I learned that you can have all the fame, fortune, talent, adulation, wine, women and wealth in the world, and still be miserable. And make everyone around you miserable, too! That's not the way I want to live.

At the beginning of *Nixon*, Oliver included a quotation on screen from the Bible. It read: "What shall it profit a man if he shall gain the whole world and lose his own soul?" Those words were written a long time ago, but they're still true today. Or as Richard Nixon put it in his farewell address to his staff: "Always remember, others may hate you. But those who hate you don't win unless you hate them—and then you destroy yourself."

Final Cut—The Premiere

I had not planned to go to the premiere of *Any Given Sunday*, even though I had originated and co-produced the film. For one thing, I dislike glitzy Hollywood events and rarely go to parties and premieres. Second, I did not think an invitation would be forthcoming from Oliver's office, and did not relish the prospect of seeing him and all of his cronies even if it did. Besides, I would have preferred to see the film with a "real" audience in a theater, where you could get a better sense of their reaction.

But when I got a call and a fax from a pleasant woman at Warner Brothers, offering me eight tickets to the premiere and the party after, I reconsidered and decided to go after all. It gave me a chance to invite some of my friends and colleagues from UCLA, and also for Jacqueline and me to invite her sister Jila and her cousin Azita. It was Azita who had worked most closely with me in Oliver's office, and who had also brought Jacqueline and me together, so this seemed particularly appropriate. Perhaps it would even provide some "closure" to the whole experience.

As usual with these events, the premiere was a zoo, with all kinds of strange creatures wandering around. Steve Pines, Oliver's business manager, came up to me and struck up a friendly conversation. For some reason I had always liked Steve as a person, even though we had clashed many times, not least over my leaving the office. I knew that whatever he did, he was merely carrying out Oliver's wishes, however insane they might be, so I didn't hold it against him too much. We chatted about all the people who had left, and about Oliver's arrest. Steve made excuses for him, saying that he was just "in the wrong place at the wrong time." But he added, "He loves his pot and his hash." I knew nothing had changed. Probably Steve would be the next to go. But it was good to see him, and he seemed glad to hear that I was now at UCLA.

The movie itself was entertaining. It was strange to see it on the screen after almost five years since we started. The basic characters and concepts were still there, and the film was pretty much as I had envisioned it from the beginning. I enjoyed it, but felt that it suffered from Oliver's usual habit of cramming in too many characters and too much material, resulting in a movie that was too long but still felt somehow incomplete. I couldn't put it in the same category with *Platoon* or *Nixon,* but it was a good, entertaining, commercial movie that managed to make some good points about racism, commercialism and other ills of our society that are reflected in professional football. Even Jacqueline and Jila, who are not exactly football fans, enjoyed it. And I have to admit it was nice to see my name on the screen at the end, following the image of Cameron Diaz....

The after party was held in the courtyard of the Armand Hammer Museum and was also a bit of a zoo. Many of the old Stone hangers-on were there, like Richard Rutowski and Sergio Premoli. Richard's role as sycophant and supplier seemed to have been supplanted by a sleazy Italian named Paolo, who followed Oliver around wearing a strange little hat and dark glasses. There was also a copious supply of actress/model/bimbo types, just as there were in the film itself.

I ran into Janet Yang, whom I hadn't seen in three years since we both left Ixtlan, and had a friendly talk with her. I also caught a glimpse of Danny the Weasel lurking in the corner, but didn't talk to him. He seemed to be avoiding all of his former colleagues and associates from the Ixtlan and Illusion era. I didn't see Clayton at all, which was just as well. But Richard Weiner and I had a nice reunion with former 49ers star Y. A. Tittle, a real gentleman. He had played in the era before astronomical salaries in football, and was now selling insurance in Palo Alto.

The reviews of the movie were generally good, although mixed. David Ansen of *Newsweek* called it "Stone's most entertaining movie in years" and praised its realistic violence: "the most earth shaking game of football ever put on film." But he also wrote that "his view of women (bitches, whores) is as enlightened as ever." Similarly, Kathleen Craughwell in the *Los Angeles Times* wrote: "The problem? Even the most sympathetic female character, Lela Rochon, is a bit of a harridan. The others include an alcohol and drug addict (Ann-Margret), a cast-iron witch (Cameron Diaz), a hooker (Elizabeth Berkley) and even a husband abuser (Lauren Holly)."

Variety loved the movie, while the *Hollywood Reporter* trashed it. Similarly, Stephen Holden in the *New York Times* dismissed the film, saying, "Oliver Stone is Hollywood's R-rated answer to P. T. Barnum. . . . He parades his own hyper-macho vision of modern American life as a primitive bread and circuses carnival of power, greed, lust, fame and violence (especially violence)."

Kenneth Turan in the *Los Angeles Times* wrote: "Who better

than Stone, after all, to deal with the orgiastic frenzy of violence, hysteria and macho posturing that has given America's undying passion for professional football the feel of the last days of the Roman Empire?" And according to Richard Schickel in *Time* magazine, "Director Oliver Stone ... may be momentarily in a non-political mood, but that does not mean he has given up his preoccupations with paranoia, greed, and the brutality of American life."

Foreign reviewers, not fond of American football, were less than kind to the film. The *Daily Yomiuri* of Japan wrote: "Penalize Oliver Stone 15 yards of footage for too many clichés on the field and fine him six months' box office receipts for unnecessary stupidity. *Any Given Sunday* is the most hackneyed football movie— nay, sports movie—every made. Why, oh why, did he do it?"

And the *Financial Time*s of London: "*Any Given Sunday* aspires to be a film about America. With padded shoulders and don't-stop-me intensity, Stone barges through every national issue ... from race to drugs to feminism. Finally, though, this film is more than a film about America: It is America. It manifests a demented worship of the winner, thinly disguised as an endorsement of play for play's sake."

Two other reviewers offered the kind of delirious blurbs that make publicity people dizzy. Michael Wilmington of the *Chicago Tribune* wrote that it was "a screaming rocker of a movie. It blasts right over the line." And Ann Hornaday in the *Baltimore Sun* went even further, calling it "as good as movies get."

My own view may be summarized by yet another column in the *Los Angeles Times,* this one by sportswriter Larry Stewart: "The casting and some great cinematography make up for a weak story line and a predictable ending. But the problem, as usual with a Stone film, is everything is overdone.... The movie rambles, and you begin to wonder if it will ever end. . . . Overall, the movie is entertaining. But it could have been just as entertaining if it had been edited into two hours instead of nearly three."

More importantly for Oliver, though, the movie opened well at the box office. It made $14 million for the weekend, and $21 million since its Wednesday opening, according to Warner Brothers. This was a record for a Stone film, and made it his biggest opening weekend ever. His previous best opening was $11 million for *Natural Born Killers* in 1994, which went on to gross about $50 million. But that film also spawned a series of copycat murders, for which Stone was still being blamed and sued. By contrast, *Nixon* grossed $13.7 million domestically, while *U-Turn* made an even more measly $6.7 million. In 1993 *Heaven and Earth* grossed only $5.9 million. If *Any Given Sunday* had flopped, Oliver would have been out of business. Now he was back in business.

The box office numbers continued to be good throughout January, up to the Super Bowl. After that, they would drop off. But the film ended up grossing over $75 million domestically, Oliver's best showing since *Platoon*. Despite the fact that the film had gone way over budget (in excess of $60 million), it would turn a profit with video, foreign sales, DVD and cable revenues added. It wasn't quite *Titanic*, but by Oliver's standards it was a hit. The video release of the film in September 2000 opened in the number two spot on the charts, taking in $8.3 million in rentals in its first week. *Entertainment Weekly* commented, "This was quite a score for Stone, whose last film, *U-Turn*, didn't even crack the rental charts back in 1998."

Oliver was a bankable director again. It would probably be good for his career, but not necessarily good for him as a person. At the premiere he looked puffy and unhealthy. Azita, who hadn't seen him for several years, said he was almost unrecognizable. To me, his dyed orange hair transplants gave him a strange resemblance to Strom Thurmond. . . . And a friend of mine who saw him the next night at the New York premiere said he was completely out of it and had to be almost propped up as he was leaving.

To me, this was both a sad ending as well as a happy one. The price of fame, celebrity, Hollywood and all the rest just did not seem worth it. Stone had made some great films that would be remembered, and I was proud to have been a part of two of them. To me, it proved that the power of an idea can move mountains, just as we had done in Washington with the JFK bill. But I would not want to pay the price that Oliver Stone had paid for his success.

I did speak with Oliver briefly at the premiere. He was surrounded by the usual parasites, but when I saw Azita talking with him I went over to say hello. I shook his hand and said, "Good movie, man." He looked at least halfway out of it but said, "Thank you, Eric," and nodded. At that moment it seemed that a glimmer of something inside him recognized and acknowledged what I had done for him, and that I had done it with the best intentions. That was enough. I said, "Good work," then turned and left. There was no point in trying to have a real conversation with Oliver when he was stoned. And besides, a blonde model in a bright red dress was bearing down on him. . . .

Postscript—
The Bay of Pigs Thing Revisited
• •

WARNING: The following material is recommended for *JFK* fans, conspiracy theorists, assassination buffs, lone nuts and truth seekers. It presents information from highly classified government documents that some may find disturbing. For mature audiences only—parental discretion advised!

Sometimes life brings you full circle in unexpected ways. For me, this happened in March 2001, when I found myself back in Cuba, meeting again with Fidel Castro, reunited with my old friend Fabian Escalante, and even visiting the actual Bay of Pigs, with a group including Arthur Schlesinger Jr. and Jean Kennedy Smith— the sister of John F. Kennedy. This was an unexpected visit that had all come together in a few days' time. Because Nixon's cryptic remarks about "the Bay of Pigs thing" on the Watergate tapes had provided the inspiration for our movie—the link between Cuba, Dallas and Watergate—it seemed fitting that I should finally visit the real Bay of Pigs. To be in the company of those who had taken part in the original events was an added bonus.

I had been wanting to return to Cuba ever since my two visits there in 1994 with Rick English. I found the country fascinating and the people warm and friendly, even to Yanqui gringo imperialists like myself. I had been deterred from going for the last six or seven years because I knew I would not be able to see Fabian Escalante, who was out of favor, and continue our mutually fruitful discussions on the Kennedy assassination. I also had left Oliver

Stone's office, gotten married, become a visiting scholar at UCLA and undergone a few other changes in my life. Nevertheless, I wanted to go back. For one thing, I had promised Jacqueline that I would take her there someday, and I wanted to keep the promise.

The opportunity arose rather suddenly and unexpectedly, partly out of coincidence and serendipity, and partly from my own initiative. I had kept in touch over the ensuing years with David Deutschmann, my guide and companion on my previous Cuban trips, who was based in Melbourne, Australia, but frequently visited Cuba. I would check in periodically to let him know of my interest in going back, and to see if there was any chance of seeing Escalante. I was always politely told no, that it would be impossible to see him even socially if I went to Havana.

I had last seen Fabian Escalante at a conference in Rio de Janeiro in August of 1995, and had planned to see him again that December in the Bahamas for another JFK conference in Nassau with other JFK researchers. I felt that our collaboration was really beginning to bear fruit, given the facts that we had been able to open up the U.S. archives on the assassination and that Escalante had access to the Cuban archives. Unfortunately, I had to cancel the Nassau trip at the last minute because *Nixon* was about to be released on December 20, and there were too many last minute things to do. I could just imagine Oliver looking for me and screaming something like "The Bahamas!! . . . What the hell is he doing in the Bahamas—taking a vacation??"

There had been some vague talk about returning to Cuba for a conference on the thirty-fifth anniversary of the Bay of Pigs invasion, which would have taken place in March or April of 1996. Unfortunately, just at that time two small planes carrying Cuban exiles were shot down over Cuban airspace. This was a provocation by the Miami exiles that had its intended effect—to ruin any chance of improving U.S.–Cuban relations under President Clinton. It also meant that the conference was canceled and, even worse, Escalante was removed from his position and effectively disappeared.

In early 2001, when the fortieth anniversary of this historic fiasco was approaching, I contacted Deutschmann to see if there would be a conference, and if there was any possibility that I could get myself invited. I was not really that interested in the details of the military invasion or the mechanics of the Bay of Pigs operation, but it would be a good excuse to go back to Cuba. However, while confirming that there would be a conference, Deutschmann said that it was by invitation only, was mostly for scholars, and that it was unlikely that I could be invited.

I e-mailed him back, and suggested a completely different idea—that Ocean Press, his publishing house, put out a new edition of a book by my friend Donald Freed entitled *Death in Washington: The Murder of Orlando Letelier*. Letelier was a Chilean diplomat in the 1970s under Marxist president Salvador Allende. Allende had been overthrown and killed in a CIA-sponsored coup, and Letelier had taken refuge in the United States. In September 1976, Letelier was killed in a car bomb attack as he was driving down Massachusetts Avenue in the heart of Washington, D.C. His assistant, Ronni Moffitt, had also been killed in the attack, which occurred in front of the chancery of the Chilean embassy, and her husband was seriously injured.

Incredibly, one of the persons charged with involvement in the bombing was Guillermo Novo, a name I had first heard from Escalante in connection with the Kennedy assassination. He was a Cuban exile—one of those described to me by Rolando Martinez as a "muchacho malo," a bad boy. An American, Michael Townley, was also eventually arrested and convicted of the crime. He struck a plea bargain, served a short sentence and then disappeared. Officially, the assassination was blamed on DINA, the Chilean secret service under General Augusto Pinochet, who had taken power after the coup and murder of Allende. Strangely, though, the assassination of Letelier had happened during the short one-year period that George Bush served as head of the CIA. I found this to be an interesting coincidence. There were also rumors that David Phillips, recently retired from the CIA, had been involved. Phillips, you may recall, had reportedly met with Lee Harvey Oswald shortly before the Kennedy assassination.

Deutschmann was very interested in the idea of republishing the book. In the course of discussing this idea, he mentioned to me that Peter Kornbluh of the National Security Archives in Washington was involved in organizing the Bay of Pigs conference, as well as having uncovered new documents and evidence in the Letelier case. I decided to call Kornbluh.

I had never met him, but had heard his name in the context of both Cuba and Chile. It turned out that he had worked in the Senate the same time that I had in the middle to late 1980s. He had worked for Senator Tom Harkin while I worked for Senator John Kerry. Harkin and Kerry had made a notorious trip to Nicaragua in 1985 to meet with Daniel Ortega, then the leftist president of that country. Kornbluh had been along on the trip and had been greatly impressed with Kerry as a natural leader. He had also become friendly with Dick McCall, one of my friends on Kerry's staff, and knew Jonathan Winer and other mutual friends from the Hill.

From this lucky coincidence, it became clear to him that I was a credible and serious person, not a flaky Hollywood producer. After we talked further, he mentioned that he was interested in making a movie about the back-channel discussions between

Kennedy and Castro. He arranged to have me invited to the conference as an observer, and Jacqueline as well.

This all happened so fast that I barely had time to decide to go, get a ticket to Miami and pack my bags. The next thing we knew, Jackie and I were arriving late at night at the Miami Airport Hotel. The next morning the whole group assembled for a charter flight to Havana. We were given a preparatory pep talk by Peter Kornbluh, who reminded me of a younger and smaller version of Steve Rivele. I had not known who would be on the trip, but it turned out that the list included luminaries such as Schlesinger, Richard Goodwin (who had been an aid to JFK), Samuel Halpern (an old CIA hand from Operation Mongoose—the CIA plot to kill Castro) and Wayne Smith, a Cuba expert who had served in the U.S. embassy in Havana during the revolutionary period of 1958–1960, and then returned as the official U.S. representative in Cuba under President Carter. Wayne was a big, friendly man who I had met at the Rio conference. I knew that he was not only very knowledgeable about Cuba, but also very interested in the JFK assassination.

Other participants included scholars on Cuba from various leading universities, and also Saul Landau, a longtime Cuba expert and father of Valerie Landau, who had befriended Rick and me on our first trip to Cuba. There were also a number of "observers," such as myself, who had the luxury of attending the conference without having to actually participate. In addition to Jacqueline and me, these included, among others, Jean Kennedy Smith, the sister of JFK who had been President Clinton's ambassador to Ireland (accompanied by her famous son William Kennedy Smith), Haynes Johnson (a prominent Washington journalist who had written the first book on the Bay of Pigs) and Daniel Schorr, who was an old friend of our family as well as a distinguished journalist. He had written a fascinating chapter for our Nixon book called "Nixon's Secrets." At age eighty-five, he was still going strong, doing regular commentaries for National Public Radio.

There were a number of foundation types present, and also an aide to Senator Ted Kennedy, Sharon Waxman, who was there on his behalf. To my surprise, another Hollywood person attended the meeting—Sarah Bowen, who worked for Imagine Entertainment. Imagine was one of the major production companies in Hollywood, headed by Ron Howard, formerly of *Happy Days* and probably the most clean-cut, all-American, white-bread, boy-next-door type to ever exist in fact or fiction. His company had made *Apollo 13*, and later *A Beautiful Mind*, but normally specialized in such heavyweight fare as *The Grinch That Stole Christmas*, which had been a huge hit for them a few months earlier.

Howard had read the memoirs of Grayston Lynch, the first American to land at the Bay of Pigs, and wanted to make a movie telling the story from his point of view. This of course would be the exact opposite of the Cuban perspective, but since the Cubans hadn't seen the script, they didn't know what was in it. Even Sarah admitted that it would be a mistake to make a movie with such a limited and wrongheaded point of view, but she was there anyway. She was a young, blonde Hollywood creative executive of a type I was familiar with from my time at Ixtlan—intelligent, well-dressed (in black), hip and ambitious. After I introduced myself, she said, "You probably don't remember, but I worked with you on *Nixon*." I didn't remember, but it turned out she had worked with Victor Kempster, whom I did know, in the art department of the film. She had then moved onward and upward to a good job at Imagine. I was impressed by her accomplishments, although I hoped their Bay of Pigs film would not get made in its current form.

I had been on junkets like this before when I worked in the House and Senate, usually in deluxe Jamaican resorts with a mix of senators and congressmen, scholars and experts, and the occasional odd staffer/observer such as myself. But this trip was different. For one thing, Fidel Castro was there, and took part in the entire conference. His presence alone was riveting. The Bay of Pigs had obviously been one of the highlights of his life, and he delighted in reliving it forty years later. Out of the twenty or so hours of meetings spread out over two days, Castro probably spoke for at least ten of them. His energy and charisma appeared to be undiminished. His memory was incredible.

The participants also included a number of Cubans who had taken part in the actual fighting, and even some courageous members of Brigade 2506, the anti-Castro Cubans who had launched the invasion and had been taken prisoner after it failed (they were released a year later and returned to the United States). Their leader, Alfredo Duran, was obviously a man of integrity and sincerity who wanted to see a reconciliation between the Cuban government and the exiles in Miami. For his efforts, he and the others were rewarded by being kicked out of Brigade 2506, which still exists, as soon as they returned to Miami. As William Faulkner once wrote, "The past is never dead. It's not even past."

The actual participants in the conference were seated around a large oval table, with the Cubans on one side and the Americans on the other. The observers sat behind the participants, or off to the side of the large conference room. Castro sat in the middle on the Cuban side, while Arthur Schlesinger Jr., as the de facto leader of the American delegation, sat across from him. Jacqueline and I positioned ourselves behind Schlesinger, which put us directly across from Castro and in his line of sight. I thought I detected him glancing at Jacqueline from time to time. He always did like exotic young women. His personal translator, Juana, sat behind him. Oddly, she bore a slight resemblance to Jacqueline.

All the participants and observers were equipped with earphones that provided simultaneous translation. I was fortunate to be seated next to Alexandra Schlesinger, wife of Arthur, who was a very friendly and gracious woman. My father knew Arthur Schlesinger from New York, and I mentioned to her that I had worked with their son Andrew on a failed attempt to do a documentary on the presidents of the twentieth century when I was with Stone. We agreed that we would try to revive the project, as Schlesinger was now editing a series of books on all of the American presidents.

At one point during the conference, I pulled a copy of Claudia Furiati's *ZR Rifle* out of my bag to check on a certain point. Mrs. Schlesinger saw me reading it. When I put it away, she asked me politely, "Could I take a look at that book?" Thinking she must mean something else, I pulled out a copy of another book on the Bay of Pigs. She said, "No, I meant the other one, on the assassination. I used to have a copy, but I've lost it." Amazed, I handed over Claudia's book, which she studied with interest. She wrote down all the pertinent information and said, "I'll have to order this again." She leaned over and confided, "I'm sure this book is right. I'm absolutely convinced there was a conspiracy." She then nodded in the direction of her husband sitting in front of us and whispered, "He's an agnostic, but I'm not." This endeared me to her to no end. I didn't have the nerve to ask what her good friend Jean Kennedy Smith thought about the subject, though I wished later that I had. After the conference was over, I saw the two of them walking down the beach together at Varadero, deep in conversation. I wondered what they might be discussing. . . .

The conference itself dealt at great length with the details of the Bay of Pigs planning and invasion, which were not of great interest to me. It did not deal at all with the assassination, which was not surprising since this was not the topic of the meeting. In addition, it had been made clear to me by Peter Kornbluh that he and the other organizers of the meeting did not want to get anywhere near this subject. Even Fabian Escalante, who spoke for only a few minutes at the conference, did not directly address this subject.

The only person who had the nerve to bring it up was Wayne Smith. He made a very interesting comment. Wayne said, "I guess it's inevitable that everyone will look at the Kennedy assassination through the optic of their own experience. For Oliver Stone, that was Vietnam. For me, it is my experience in Cuba. . . . I am convinced that the assassination was carried out by the 'cowboys' of the CIA—men like David Morales, who I knew well from my days in Cuba." I would have liked to hear more, but the U.S. moderator abruptly cut him off. Wayne later told me that he did not mean to specifically state that he knew for a fact that Morales was involved, but only that people "like Morales" were involved in killing JFK. I'm sure he was right about that. Wayne Smith had hit the nail on the head. Oliver Stone was obsessed with Vietnam. That's where his movie about JFK had gone wrong. The cause of the assassination was Cuba, not Vietnam. The Vietnam War was the *result,* but not the cause.

During a break in the proceedings, I managed to have a few words with Fidel himself. Castro had suggested having another meeting in 2002 for the fortieth anniversary of the Cuban missile crisis. I felt that this subject had been wrung dry by the many conferences that had already been held on the subject. I told him that I thought Wayne Smith was exactly right in his comments, and suggested to Castro that he add a section on this topic to the program. I said to him in my high school Spanish that Escalante had been right when he wrote that elements of three groups were involved in the assassination—the CIA, the Mafia and the "gusanos," meaning the most fanatical anti-Castro Cuban exiles in the United States. Castro nodded and said, "I know." I later saw him talking in the hall with Escalante. I could not hear what they were saying, but I was glad to see that Fabian was back in the good graces of Fidel.

At the opening reception before the conference, Jacqueline had spotted Escalante, wearing a suit and tie. I could not believe that he was there. I rushed over and greeted him by saying "Amigo!" We exchanged Cuban abrazos, and he said to me in Spanish, "You still look young." I had not seen him in six years, and did not expect to ever see him again. I asked what he had been doing, and he handed me his card. It turned out that he had become the Cuban representative for the Citroen car company! This would be approximately equivalent to the head of the CIA being fired and becoming the owner of an auto dealership. Nevertheless, he seemed to be in a good mood and happy to be there.

I rushed up to my room in the hotel to get my camera, but needless to say it wasn't working. But I did give him video copies of *Nixon* and *Any Given Sunday* (the latter with Spanish subtitles). He said that he had seen *Nixon* and liked it. He had not seen *Any Given Sunday,* but was impressed when I told him that it starred Al Pacino. I also mentioned that Cameron Diaz was "Cubana," but he corrected me. "She is only part Cuban," he said, which was right. But it was a good part.... I said to Escalante that I was aware what had happened to him and said in Spanish, "If you want, I will talk personally with Fidel." Escalante smiled indulgently and said, "No ... that could be dangerous."

Later, I saw him talking with Ricardo Alarcon at the reception. Alarcon, whom I had met on a previous trip to Cuba, was head of the National Assembly and probably the second or third most powerful man in Cuba. He also spoke good English. I moved in their direction, but Peter Kornbluh stopped me. "Let them talk," he said wisely. After they had finished though, I went over to Alarcon and introduced myself. I reminded him of our previous meeting, and told him I had worked on *JFK* and *Nixon* with Oliver Stone. I told him I was very glad to see that Fabian Escalante was present. I said, "He has written a very important book which should be published." This was Escalante's own book on the plots against Castro and Kennedy, which had been sitting in limbo for five years while he was out of favor and selling Citroens. Alarcon lit up and said, "Yes—we were just talking about that." I told him I thought that if we could work together, we could solve the whole thing in one year. Alarcon looked surprised and laughed. "What do you mean, solve it?" I said, "Everything—who fired the shots, from what positions, who was behind it—the whole thing." This was a bit of hyperbole, but I wanted to impress on his mind how close we were to cracking the case. He said, "I hope so," and left it at that. I didn't want to push him too far.

I almost got to talk to Fidel again during another break in the proceedings, but it turned out he was more interested in talking to Jackie. Naturally, people would cluster around Fidel during the breaks, hoping to talk with him or at least hear what he had to say. During one such interval, he headed straight in our direction. I assumed he wanted to have a word with Arthur Schlesinger, or perhaps one of the CIA types, but instead he approached Jacqueline. "Are you a Norteamericana?" he asked. "No, I am from Iran," she replied. Fidel nodded knowingly. He had an eye for the ladies. "I see . . . Yes, because you don't look like an American. You have a very special look. . . ." Coming from him, this was of course a compliment.

Jackie, who seemed to feel perfectly comfortable chatting with Fidel Castro, said that she could sympathize with him because her country had also been the victim of a CIA coup, in 1953. He nodded again. "Yes. I know all about that," he replied. There wasn't much he didn't know about, it seemed. "I think you are a true leader," Jackie replied. "I hope you live a long time." Castro smiled. "That is because you come from the East," he replied. "You have an Eastern way of thinking." We were left to ponder this cryptic remark as others around him grabbed his attention. It may be a coincidence, but a few weeks later Castro made a trip to Iran—the first in his forty-two years in power. Later, the Cuban Interest Section in Washington sent us a set of very nice glossy color photographs of Jackie conversing with Fidel.

Jackie had not even planned to sit in on the meeting, as she preferred to be a tourist and see Havana, but decided to stay and listen to Castro, to see him perform in person. The two days of the conference were long and somewhat grueling, lasting from early in the morning to well after dinnertime. We did get a chance to see a little bit of the "real" Havana, though. One night we were taken to a special performance of the Cuban National Ballet. Unfortunately, being exhausted and jet-lagged, I fell asleep during parts of the performance. This was especially embarrassing as we were seated close to Alicia Alonso, the former Cuban ballerina who had become head of the ballet company and something of a legend in Cuba. She didn't seem to mind, though. At one point during the intermission, she patted me on the shoulder and said something like "Tu descansa" ("You should rest")—I needed it.

Following the conference a bus trip was organized to the actual site of the invasion—the Bay of Pigs itself. Castro did not join us, but we stopped along the way to see a crocodile farm that he had recommended. We also visited a museum commemorating the battle, and found ourselves surrounded by a crowd of international news correspondents who had been tipped off to our presence. I commented to one of them, "This is the second invasion"—a quip that was later replayed on Cuban television.

The actual site of the invasion was a beach called Playa Giron, which did not look any different from most other beaches. But the thought of standing at this historic place, with the men who had fought there, as well as with the sister of President Kennedy and his top advisers, was mind-boggling and a thrill in itself.

Later, we were treated to a dinner at the Presidential Palace at Castro's invitation. In addition to a delicious multicourse meal, we were entertained by Cuban singers and dancers. There was also a waiter in black tie carrying an entire glazed cooked pig on a platter around the room. I think it was in honor of the Bay of Pigs.

The palace is a beautiful place inside, designed by Castro's lover and fellow revolutionary Celia Sanchez, who had died in 1980. It was full of plants, stones and flowing water, as well as a large abstract art mural on one wall. It felt more like being in nature than in a formal setting. As we were getting on the bus to leave, Jackie noticed Fabian Escalante standing on the steps of the palace. I leapt off the bus and ran up the steps to give him a farewell greeting. Despite his background and whatever he may have done, I had developed warm feelings toward him and wished him well.

After the meeting was over, Jackie and I went to Varadero, a popular beach resort, for a couple of days of relaxation. It was a two-hour drive to Varadero (which cost us $80 U.S. in a taxi!), but I was glad to see that Cuba seemed much better off than it had appeared in 1994. The old colonial-style houses in Havana were being repainted and spruced up, thanks in part to UNESCO, which had declared it a historic site. There seemed to be more housing and construction along the way, and Varadero was much more developed. Dollars are legal in Cuba, and there were signs of private enterprise and nascent prosperity. I hoped it wouldn't go too far, though.

One of the things I liked most about Cuba was that it was unspoiled and uncommercialized, still free of the creeping blight of McDonalds, Starbucks, Burger Kings and the like that afflicts America and other countries. Coca-Cola was readily available though, and I drank this to be on the safe side. I also saw a few women on the street in Havana and along the way wearing scanty Lycra clothing, who appeared to be prostitutes. We did not stop to take a closer look, but others did. I'm sure that eventually Cuba will come to resemble every other Caribbean island, with their jet skis and tacky resorts, but I'm glad it hasn't happened yet. Going to Cuba is like going back in time, and I was sorry to leave.

Ironically, in February 2002, Oliver Stone traveled to Cuba to make a documentary about the island. He had dinner with Fidel Castro and filmed a long interview with him. They hung out together for three days and bonded. Stone also met Fidel's brother Ramon and toured around the island with a Spanish film crew. He and Fidel visited Hemingway's favorite bar at Cojimar, before Fidel saw him off at the airport. In a way, I felt a sense of personal vindication. After several years of trying to get Stone interested in doing a Cuba movie, he had finally begun. I only hope that he does it justice. The Cuban people have already suffered enough. But I think Oliver still has a few good films left in him. I hope so, anyway....

Coda

· · · · · · ·

In 1999 the historian Neal Gabler wrote a book called *Life the Movie: How Entertainment Conquered Reality*. He argues that in today's society, "life itself is an entertainment medium." He says, "The new relationship between entertainment and life" means that "we need never leave the theater's comfort. We can remain constantly distracted.... We have finally learned how to escape from life into life."

In other words, life is a movie, and the movies are life. Entertainment "is arguably the most pervasive, powerful and ineluctable force of our time—a force so overwhelming that it has finally metastasized into life." According to Gabler, entertainment has become "the primary value of American life."

It is no wonder, then, that showbiz and politics have effectively merged. Since the age of Reagan and his "producer," Mike Deaver, the presidency has been reduced to a set of scripted scenes, of sound bites, photo-ops, and thirty-second ads. There is no reality in the Rose Garden—only the virtual reality of an actor playing the president.

But this triumph of Hollywood, of style over substance, extends beyond the White House. In 2000 the China scholar Orville Schell wrote a book titled *Virtual Tibet: Searching for Shangri-La from the Himalayas to Hollywood*. In Schell's view, Tibet exists as virtual reality—as a Hollywood creation. Martin Scorsese's *Kundun* and Jean-Jacques Annaud's *Seven Years in Tibet* have literally put that country on the map. Without them, it would not exist.

In a chapter entitled "Tinseltown Tulkus," Schell describes

how Tibetan Buddhism has become the flavor of the month in Hollywood. Stars from Richard Gere to Sharon Stone to Steven Seagal are now Tibetan Buddhists. And right along with them is Oliver Stone. Schell, a friend and sometime adviser to Stone, quotes him as saying, "I'm happier just living my life and meditating every day on the concept of emptiness."

But Schell also notes, "Even when he is talking about Buddhist compassion, there is a brooding, tense quality to Stone that suggests inner struggle. A part of Stone always seems on the brink of losing control, a part he refers to as his 'reptile brain,' as if an unreformable segment of his psyche lived in a constant state of friction. . . . For him life is 'continual conflict,' 'a raging sea,' 'a war.'"

Schell writes that Stone "finds Tibetan Buddhism a little more forgiving of his 'wild Western practices' than Vietnamese or Japanese Buddhism. 'I don't subscribe to the asceticism of Buddhism,' he says, a sly, gap-toothed smile creeping across his face." Free Tibet!

Perhaps there is something to be learned here. If Tibet can become not only a spiritual force but a political cause owing to the power of Hollywood, then what lines are left to be drawn? Where does Hollywood end and reality begin? Where does politics leave off and virtual reality take over? Perhaps only the Dalai Lama could answer these questions.

My own spiritual journey from Washington to Hollywood has not led me to enlightenment, or to inner peace. But neither has it killed off the idealism I started with. I still believe, perhaps naïvely, that the power of Hollywood, like that of Washington, can be used for good as well as for more cynical purposes. I still believe that one person can make a difference. And I still believe in the power of an idea.

The ancient Greek philosopher Archimedes said, "Give me a lever and a place to stand, and I will move the world." I don't claim to have moved the world, or even perturbed its orbit. But Hollywood and Washington each gave me a place to stand, however small, and the leverage, however slight, to change things just a little. I feel good about that, but also humble, because anyone else could have done the same thing. After all, it was just a wild idea in the first place. Maybe you have one too. . . .

Appendix

Statement of Eric Hamburg
Hearing of the Assassination Records Review Board
Los Angeles, California
September 17, 1996

Thank you for the opportunity to testify here today. I am a film producer here in Los Angeles, working with Oliver Stone. I co-produced the film *Nixon,* and also edited the book of the film. In a prior incarnation, before coming to Hollywood, I worked for eight years on Capitol Hill in Washington, as an aide to Senator John Kerry of Massachusetts and Representative Lee Hamilton of Indiana.

While on Congressman Hamilton's staff, I worked extensively during 1991 and 1992 on the legislation which became the President John F. Kennedy Assassination Records Collection Act of 1992. It was this legislation, as you know, which created the Assassination Records Review Board, so it is very gratifying to appear before you today.

I can assure you, from personal experience, that this bill could never have been passed by Congress if not for Oliver Stone's film *JFK.* Following the release of that film in late 1991, the Congress was inundated with letters from the American public demanding the release of the secret government files on the assassination. Many prominent members of Congress, who had previously been indifferent to this issue or even had actively opposed release of the files, changed their positions shortly after the release of *JFK.* The American public have Oliver Stone and his film to thank for the legislation which created this Review Board and allowed the opening of the JFK files. I hope no one has any doubt about that.

It was obvious then, and is still clear today, that the American people want to know the truth about who killed President Kennedy, and why. That is why this law was passed, and this Board created. I hope that you will never lose sight of this fundamental fact as you pursue your work. The American people, overwhelmingly, believe that there was a conspiracy to kill President Kennedy. Polls over the years, starting long before Oliver Stone made *JFK*, have shown that 80% to 90% of the American public believe that there was a conspiracy, and that they have not been told the full truth. These figures remain the same today.

While we do not yet know the full story, it is gratifying to know that an estimated 2 million to 3 million pages of government documents related to the assassination have been released since the passage of the "JFK bill" (as I call it). The Review Board should be commended for the role that you have played in facilitating the release of these documents. I particularly commend you for fighting for the release of documents pertaining to the Garrison investigation which have been withheld by New Orleans District Attorney Harry Connick, and also for seeking the release of some documents which the FBI has sought to withhold. It is very important that all of these documents be released and made public.

It should be remembered that it was the intent of Congress to make all documents and files available in uncensored form to the maximum extent possible. Indeed, when this legislation was introduced, Senator David Boren, who was then Chairman of the Senate Intelligence Committee, stated that it was the intention of the bill's sponsors that "99.99999%" of all assassination-related material should be made public, and only in the rarest circumstances would a name or a word be blacked out from a document. Unfortunately, this standard has not been met.

The FBI, and also to some extent the CIA, seem to have a mindset dating back to the days of the Cold War. And Army intelligence, to my knowledge, has yet to release any documents at all. Frankly, it is ridiculous to think that, thirty-three years after the events in question, there are still "sources and methods" to be protected. And in any case, the public's right to know the facts about the assassination outweighs any such considerations after this length of time. In my view, all of the documents from these agencies should be released, unredacted, as soon as possible.

Any material that is withheld will simply serve to undermine public confidence in this entire process.

With this in mind, I would like to make a few suggestions as to areas which I think can and should be pursued in relation to additional documents. One area that has been of particular interest to me has been the question of Cuba, and the possible participation of Cuban exiles in the assassination plot. Most serious researchers who have studied the assassination have concluded that there were most likely elements of three groups involved in the plot—rogue elements of U.S. intelligence agencies, elements of organized crime or "the Mafia," and elements of the Cuban exile groups in the United States. The plot, if there was one, most likely evolved out of the assassination plots against Fidel Castro which involved these three groups.

I have long felt that for many reasons, including barriers of language and culture, we have had perhaps the least understanding of the "Cuban" element. For this reason, I was very interested when the Cuban government put forward a semi-official version of their view of the assassination events in late 1993. I myself made two trips to Cuba in 1994, and spent a total of two weeks there, holding extensive meetings with General Fabian Escalante, the Cuban official in charge of their investigation of the JFK assassination. I also had additional conversations with General Escalante and his colleague Arturo Rodriguez at a conference last year in Rio de Janeiro. I was very impressed by the depth and extent of the Cubans' knowledge about these events, and also the potential for useful exchanges of information and documents with the Cubans.

Needless to say, Cuba is a Communist country and is not a democracy, and any information emanating from Cuba must be treated with appropriate caution. Nevertheless, Cuba has a great volume of files and documents which are relevant to this case. They have many files dating back to the early 1960s on Cuban exile groups and specific individuals, as well as Mafia and CIA figures who were active in Cuba. Many of these would be very relevant to your work and would be of great interest.

As you may know, the House Select Committee on Assassinations did visit Cuba and met with Fidel Castro and other Cuban officials in pursuit of information relevant to their inquiry. I would strongly recommend that this Board do likewise. Notwithstanding the fact that the United States does not maintain diplomatic relations with Cuba, I believe that the Cuban government would be receptive to such an approach and would be willing to produce files and documents which have not yet been made public. This is a treasure trove of information which has not yet been tapped, and could be one of the most productive areas of inquiry left to be explored.

Specifically, General Escalante has stated, in interviews conducted for the book *ZR Rifle* by Claudia Furiati, that he believes two Cuban exiles, Eladio del Valle and Herminio Diaz Garcia, took part in the assassination in Dallas. He told me that this was based on informant reports by Cuban sources which are in their files. He also named three Chicago Mafia figures—Dave Yaras, Lenny Patrick, and Richard Cain—who he believes were in Dallas and also involved in the plot. Again this is based, he says, on their informant reports. It would be very important to obtain any documents which Cuba could provide to substantiate these claims.

I would like to mention a couple of other specific points which are examples of the kind of information which could be gained from the Cuban documents. These are specific points which I had followed up with General Escalante, and on which he provided new information to add to what we already know from American documents.

One is in the area of Lee Harvey Oswald's mysterious trip to Clinton, Louisiana, in August of 1963. It has never been clear why Oswald went to Clinton or what he was doing there. I was intrigued by the fact that, according to information obtained by Jim Garrison's investigators, Oswald had told people in the Clinton area that he was living or staying with a Cuban doctor at the local hospital named Frank Silva, or Francisco Silva. I asked General Escalante to check his files and see if he had any information on this individual.

He reported back that according to his sources, Silva's full name was Francisco Silva Clarens, and that he was related to a Frank Bartes, whose full name was Francisco Bartes Clarens. Bartes lived in New Orleans and was a close associate of Carlos Bringuier, the head of the Cuban group DRE in New Orleans who had a street brawl with Oswald. This incident took place shortly before Oswald's trip to Clinton. Bartes appeared at

Oswald's court hearing after the incident on August 12, 1963, as a "show of support" for Bringuier.

Bartes is discussed extensively in the book *Oswald and the CIA* by John Newman, where he is described as a CIA informant and operative. General Escalante even speculated that Frank Silva and Frank Bartes may have actually been the same person, since both shared the first and last names of Francisco Clarens. This information would appear to provide a "Cuban connection" to Oswald's trip to Clinton, which is very interesting. Obviously, this should be followed up with a request for documents to corroborate this information.

General Escalante also provided additional information on another mysterious Cuban exile named Carlos Roca, who is discussed in the book *Oswald Talked* by Ray and Mary LaFontaine. Roca was also a member of the Cuban exile group DRE, which was funded and run by the CIA under the code name of AMSPELL. The DRE issued a press release in Mexico City on December 8, 1963, stating that Carlos Roca and three other DRE members had been killed in a battle in Cuba's Escambray mountains in mid-September. The others were identified as Andre Tartabul, Julio Garcia, and Sergio Perez.

According to Escalante's information, only Tartabul was actually killed in this battle. Furthermore, he stated that Roca was seen in Miami a day or two after the assassination of President Kennedy in the company of Juan Manuel Salvat, another member of the DRE. According to Escalante, they were on their way to Nicaragua at that time.

Escalante said that Roca was also connected to Carlos Bringuier in New Orleans, who operated a business there called "Casa Roca" or Roca House. Roca had gone to religious school in Cuba with Jose Bringuier, the brother of Carlos Bringuier. After the Cuban revolution, Roca had sought asylum in a Latin American embassy in Havana along with Jose Bringuier, according to this information.

Escalante also stated that his files indicated that Roca was a qualified single engine pilot. He pointed out that in Jim Garrison's investigation, David Ferrie had told investigators that he traveled to Houston after the assassination and was supposed to pick up two of the assassins who were flying from Dallas in a single engine plane. One of them was a

Cuban named "Carlos" who would be flying the plane. Escalante speculated that this may have been Carlos Roca.

According to his files, Salvat was in Dallas during the week of November 22, went to Miami, and then on to Nicaragua with Roca. He also stated that Salvat was in Mexico City when the allegedly false story about Roca's death was published in early December. Escalante said that according to his information, Salvat was an agent of David Phillips of the CIA, as was Angel Gonzalez, the DRE representative in Mexico City who issued the press release. He told me that his source was a "human source for intelligence" and that he had files and documents on this.

Escalante speculated that Roca and the other DRE "captains" named in the press release, Julio Garcia and Sergio Perez, may have been involved in the assassination of President Kennedy. He thought that after the assassination, they were probably taken to a Cuban exile training camp at a place called Monkey Point in Nicaragua, near the border with Costa Rica. He thought that they had probably been killed there sometime between Nov. 24 and Dec. 8, and then a false press release was issued in Mexico City stating that they had been killed in a battle in Cuba in September.

While I have no way to know if this is true, and am not endorsing his views, this is obviously an area which should be followed up. If there are documents to corroborate any of this, they should be sought and made public. In Escalante's view, the Cuban exile groups DRE, Alpha 66, MRR and Commandos L were all linked to each other and to the assassination. All available information and documents on these groups and others should be sought from both U.S. and Cuban sources, in my opinion.

Escalante has also named another Cuban exile associate, Isidro Borja, as being the person who was handing out leaflets with Oswald in front of the International Trade Mart in New Orleans on August 16, 1963. Borja was also a member of the DRE. Borja is also discussed in John Newman's book. He was interviewed by the HSCA and told them that the DRE had relayed information to the CIA in August 1963 on Oswald's contacts with Bringuier in New Orleans. The DRE is discussed at length in both the Newman and LaFontaine books, and is likely to have been a key group in the assassination conspiracy.

In this connection, I would mention that it is my understanding that a large collection of files on the DRE have recently been donated to the University of Miami by Mr. Salvat. These should be sought by the Review Board and added to the collection at the National Archives. Since it will be recalled that the University of Miami was the home of the CIA's JM/WAVE station, it may not be the most suitable repository for these documents.

Escalante also told me that Cuba has numerous files on David Morales, formerly the second in command of the JM/WAVE station. Escalante believes that Morales may have been in Dallas on Nov. 22 and may have been in charge of the assassination operation. He speculated that Morales may have been the person driving the Nash Rambler which allegedly picked up Oswald outside the Book Depository. Morales is discussed extensively in the book *The Last Investigation* by Gaeton Fonzi. Escalante also told me that according to his sources, Morales had met with Rolando Cubela, alias AMLASH, in Paris in September or October of 1963 as part of the CIA's ongoing effort to assassinate Fidel Castro. He believes that this was related to the plot against President Kennedy as well.

There is much more, but this should be sufficient to illustrate why I feel it is important to seek any files and documents pertaining to the assassination from the government of Cuba. I hope that you will pursue this area. I also think the Review Board should seek any files on this matter held by other foreign governments, especially the governments of Russia, Belarus, France, Japan and Mexico. As you know, Oswald lived in both Russia and what is now Belarus, whose capital is Minsk.

We know that the KGB had an extensive file on Oswald. Parts of this have been made available to ABC News and to author Norman Mailer, among others. The French government reportedly assisted in the publication of a book called *Farewell America* about the Kennedy assassination, and would also have files pertaining to what has been called the "French connection" to the assassination. This is discussed in the book *Conspiracy* by Anthony Summers, among others. And of course, Oswald also allegedly made a mysterious trip to Mexico in 1963. Any files on this held by the Mexican government should also be sought. Oswald also spent time at the Atsugi Air Force Base in Japan, and the Japanese government may have files on his time there.

Another area which should be pursued is the question of Kennedy and Vietnam, and whether the assassination may have had any relationship to Kennedy's efforts to end U.S. involvement in the war. Government records on this issue should be sought by the Board. Specifically, a tape of a crucial National Security Council meeting of October 2, 1963, is held by the Kennedy Library in Boston. This should be made public. Also, all records of the Honolulu conference of November 20 and 21, 1963, which dealt with this issue should also be made public.

I would also suggest that the Review Board seek to obtain files and documents from the collections of private researchers and organizations. As I'm sure you are aware, many of the prominent private JFK researchers have extensive collections of documents, as do some of the leading private research organizations. All of these collections should be sought and copies of these documents made available to the public at the National Archives to the maximum extent possible.

I am also submitting a copy of a letter which has been sent to the Review Board by Marina Oswald Porter, the widow of Lee Harvey Oswald. Mrs. Porter's letter details a number of areas of documents which should be pursued. It is my understanding that many of the documents mentioned in her letter still have not been released.

Probably one year is not sufficient time for the Review Board to complete all of the work which needs to be done. It would probably be a good idea for the Board to seek an extension of its term by Congress, perhaps for another two years. But if the Board is to extend its life, it should also extend the scope of its work. One of the powers which has been granted to the Board by Congress is the power to subpoena witnesses and to take their depositions. I understand that this power has been used by the Board already in a few instances.

I think it would be a good idea for the Board to make much broader use of this power, to take sworn statements from many key individuals who could provide information pertaining to the assassination and to possible sources of additional documents. There are many people still living who could potentially provide useful information. A few such names might include Gerald Ford, George Bush, Richard Helms, Ted Shackley, Howard Hunt, Nestor Sanchez, Silvia Odio, Juan Manuel Salvat, Carlos Bringuier, Antonio Veciana, Francisco Silva, Lenny Patrick, Frank Ellsworth, James Hosty, John Elrod, and John Thomas Masen among others. While I am not suggesting that any of these people were involved with the assassination of President Kennedy, they could provide useful information to the Board and to the public.

The Review Board has been entrusted with a great responsibility by Congress and by the American people. I hope that you will bear this in your minds as you pursue your work over the next year. I don't think that you will want to be remembered by history as the Warren Commission, the House Select Committee and other official bodies have been remembered—leaving a legacy of doubt, distrust, and unanswered questions. The American people expect more from you.

I commend you for the work you have done so far. You have set an important precedent for the opening up of closed chapters in our history, one which should be followed in other areas as well. I hope that you will continue your work in the spirit of openness, accountability, and a search for the truth wherever it may lead.

Acknowledgments

I have received so much help from so many people during my dual careers in Washington and Hollywood that it would be impossible to thank them all, and hard to even know where to begin. My first thanks go to my parents, for more than I can express, and to my wife Jacqueline. Thanks also to my sister Peggy and her family, and to all my relatives in Los Angeles. And I also am eternally grateful to my late grandparents on both sides, who gave me moral support and more.

I owe special thanks to Peter Osnos, a visionary publisher who saw a book even before there was a book. At PublicAffairs, Lisa Kaufman's editorial wisdom helped this become a book, and a much better one than it would otherwise have been. And David Patterson's assistance was invaluable in many ways.

In Washington, my career was started on its way by two great men—the late Judge David Bazelon and the late Senator John Heinz. I was also privileged to work for two of the finest members of Congress—Senator John Kerry and Representative Lee Hamilton. My deepest thanks to both of them. I would also like to thank members of their staffs, including especially David McKean, Jonathan Winer, Dick McCall, Ron Rosenblith and Patricia Ferrone, among others. Thanks also to Jim Lesar for his help with the JFK bill and many other things.

In Hollywood, I was a stranger in a strange land. I am grateful to Oliver Stone for giving me a chance, and I wish him the best. I am also grateful to Azita Zendel for being a good friend, and also for introducing me to my wife! I was aided in my Hollywood education by everyone at Ixtlan, and also helped by others, including Craig Emanuel, Bob Lange, Larry Kopeikin and Rick Berg. Very special thanks go to John Dean, who helped make *Nixon* possible and became a friend and collaborator. I also am deeply grateful to Steve Rivele and Chris Wilkinson for being not just great writers, but great human beings. I thank everyone who worked on *Nixon,* including first and foremost the great Anthony Hopkins, along with James Woods, Joan Allen and many, many others. Special thanks also to Bob Palmer.

This book would probably never have happened if not for the initial encouragement of Michael Mandelbaum and Anne Mandelbaum, who told me I should keep a diary. They were right. Many other friends also helped in many ways, including Rick English, Bruce Foster, Maureen Foster, Mark DeAntonio, Polly Estabrook, Marsha Renwanz, Astrid Tuminez, Dan Drell, Sid Drell and too many others to name. Thanks also to the entire Arastouzadeh family for their support. At UCLA, thanks to Dick Rosecrance and Mike Intriligator for taking me in as a visiting scholar. In Cuba, thanks are due to David Deutschmann, Mirta Muñiz, Claudia Furiati, and Fabian Escalante. On *Any Given Sunday,* special thanks to Richard Weiner, for initiating the project with me and being there all the way. Thanks also to Jamie Williams for his contributions to the script and the film. I also want to thank the other writers I worked with on other projects, including especially Ray and Mary LaFontaine. And to all my good friends not listed here, my apologies and my thanks.

One special person has guided me along the way. Our son David gestated along with this book. He has been a source of continuing inspiration and always will be.

Index

poor decision making by, 105–106, 220
self-promotion of, 114, 132
stealing of projects by, 109–111, 176,
    186–187, 227–228, 230
Hamburg, Eric
academic pursuits by, 13–15, 25, 253,
    258
Any Given Sunday development by,
    184–187
background of, 1–2
"The Blood of Abraham," Carter and,
    250–251
burnout with Senate, 13
business affairs for Ixtlan by, 49–50,
    92–93, 128, 129, 132
Capitol Hill job search for, 4–5
CIA-Contra-drug story and, 68–70
as conscientious objector, 8
conspiracy theory stories and, 70–72
Cuba, Bay of Pigs, Kennedy (JFK) con-
    spiracy and, 265–278
Cuban missile crisis story and, 65–67
declassification, Stone and, 37–41
documentary King/RFK and, 222–228,
    230
foreign policy interests of, 13–15
Gorbachev, "Revolution" and, 226, 250
Harper's (Bay of Pigs) article by, 79–82
as House staffer, 25–26, 28, 30–32, 36,
    38–39, 58, 92
journal of, 88–89
law school/lawyering, 3–4
letter to Stone/*JFK* on Kennedy conspir-
    acy by, 33–35
Oscar attendance by, 212–213
parents of, 1, 25, 63, 152, 180, 202,
    225, 226, 250, 252, 253, 257–258,
    272
Pentagon Papers development by,
    248–249
(possible) political films by, 248–252
(co-) producer activity of, 129, 132,
    185–187, 191, 230, 254
reasons for working with Stone, 44–47,
    129
research in Cuba by, 82–87, 138
scene involvement in *Nixon* by, 162–163
script writing by, 170, 214, 249–251
as Senate assistant/speechwriter, 6–14,
    13, 33, 89, 268
Stone's diatribes/tantrums against,
    126–127, 171, 200–201
suspension at Ixtlan, 128–130, 211

termination by Stone of, 228–229
Washington people visit, *Nixon* and,
    149–158
written memos of, 109–110
Hamburg, Jacqueline, 212–213, 222, 253,
    259, 260, 266, 269, 271, 274, 275–
    276, 277
Hamilton, Lee, 43, 50, 58, 65, 121, 150
decency/respectability of, 25, 258
for declassifying Kennedy (JFK) docu-
    ments, 30–32, 36, 38–40, 42
House Foreign Affairs Committee and,
    25, 30, 44
House testimony by, 40
Stone meeting with, 37–39
Hammarskjöld, Dag, 252
Hamsher, Jane, 57, 59–61, 64, 93–95, 99,
    102, 103, 130, 188
Hanks, Tom, 117
Hare, Kristina, 37, 45
Harkin, Tom, 268
Harrelson, Charles, 137
Harrelson, Woody, 77
Harris, Ed, 149
Harrison, George, 71
HBO, 62, 230
Heaven and Earth, 62, 95, 117, 197, 210,
    246, 257
box office of, 263
Heinz, John, 7
Helms, Richard, 22, 24, 80–81, 146–147,
    174–175, 177, 178
Hemingway, Ernest, 246, 258, 278
Henson, Lisa, 77, 211
Hess, Stephen, 150, 154
Hippies, 2, 9, 33
Hiss, Alger, 162
Hitler, Adolph, 45, 133, 224
Ho, Alex, 52
Hoffa, Jimmy, 16
Hoffman, Dustin, 117
Holden, Stephen, 261
Hollywood. *See also* Television
adolescent/high school nature of,
    115
aggressive/dishonest types of, 106–116,
    224
bombing and, 208–210, 228
box office for, 210, 221, 263–264
credit problems in, 93–94, 132, 187
failure in, 112
insecurities in, 51–52, 53, 60, 61, 89–90,
    97, 127

PublicAffairs is a publishing house founded in 1997. It is a tribute to the standards, values, and flair of three persons who have served as mentors to countless reporters, writers, editors, and book people of all kinds, including me.

I. F. STONE, proprietor of *I. F. Stone's Weekly,* combined a commitment to the First Amendment with entrepreneurial zeal and reporting skill and became one of the great independent journalists in American history. At the age of eighty, Izzy published *The Trial of Socrates,* which was a national bestseller. He wrote the book after he taught himself ancient Greek.

BENJAMIN C. BRADLEE was for nearly thirty years the charismatic editorial leader of *The Washington Post.* It was Ben who gave the *Post* the range and courage to pursue such historic issues as Watergate. He supported his reporters with a tenacity that made them fearless and it is no accident that so many became authors of influential, best-selling books.

ROBERT L. BERNSTEIN, the chief executive of Random House for more than a quarter century, guided one of the nation's premier publishing houses. Bob was personally responsible for many books of political dissent and argument that challenged tyranny around the globe. He is also the founder and longtime chair of Human Rights Watch, one of the most respected human rights organizations in the world.

For fifty years, the banner of Public Affairs Press was carried by its owner, Morris B. Schnapper, who published Gandhi, Nasser, Toynbee, Truman, and about 1,500 other authors. In 1983, Schnapper was described by *The Washington Post* as "a redoubtable gadfly." His legacy will endure in the books to come.

Peter Osnos, *Publisher*